Hope, Utopia and Creativity in Higher Education

Also available from Bloomsbury

Critical Narrative as Pedagogy, Ivor Goodson and Scherto Gill
On Critical Pedagogy, Henry A. Giroux

Hope, Utopia and Creativity in Higher Education

Pedagogical Tactics for Alternative Futures

Craig A. Hammond

Bloomsbury Academic
An imprint of Bloomsbury Publishing Plc

B L O O M S B U R Y
LONDON · OXFORD · NEW YORK · NEW DELHI · SYDNEY

Bloomsbury Academic

An imprint of Bloomsbury Publishing Plc

50 Bedford Square	1385 Broadway
London	New York
WC1B 3DP	NY 10018
UK	USA

www.bloomsbury.com

BLOOMSBURY and the Diana logo are trademarks of Bloomsbury Publishing Plc

First published 2017

British Library Cataloging-in-Publication Data
A catalogue record for this book is available from the British Library.

ISBN: HB: 978-1-4742-6165-4
ePDF: 978-1-4742-6166-1
ePub: 978-1-4742-6167-8

Library of Congress Cataloging-in-Publication Data
A catalog record for this book is available from the Library of Congress.

Typeset by Newgen Knowledge Works (P) Ltd., Chennai, India.
Printed and bound in Great Britain

For Emma (my Anthelion), a light in the darkness . . .

Contents

Acknowledgements

First, I would like to thank Paul Trowler, Gary Heywood-Everett and Steve Whitehead, whose academic excellence and perseverance (back in the late 1990s) enabled me to start to venture beyond my anger and frustration and look towards engaging in a creative passion – using critical pedagogy. I would also like to thank my good friend David Hayes (a.k.a. Dajvid Haze), who first introduced me to the work and ideas of Ernst Bloch. Our meandering and inspirational conversations contributed significantly to my learning and hunger for knowledge. I would also like to make a special mention of one of my colleagues; way back in 1999, when I first stumbled in to the jumbled collective of my first communal staffroom at Blackburn College, my academic lead (and now friend) Mr Ashley Whalley mentored, coached and nurtured me – and built my confidence – in ways that I could never have imagined possible. I'd like to take this opportunity to recognize and thank him for all of the skills, knowledge and radical characteristics that he brought out in me.

Many thanks to my research assistant, Mr Nathaniel Joel Robert Bennison; his tireless and dedicated commitment to transcribing huge swathes of notes and quotations meant that the unwieldy workload in producing this book was an ultimately manageable and a much more enjoyable experience. Thanks and recognition also to Dr Gail Crowther; her support and expertise on all things creative and autobiographical meant that the collating and curating of the student artefacts, and responses to the questionnaire, was a meaningful and productive process. My students also found her passion for feminist research, and her input into the 'Utopian Visions' module (during the academic year 2014–2015), to be an exciting, valuable and ultimately life-changing experience. I'd also like to thank Alison Baker and Maria Giovanna Brauzzi at Bloomsbury Academic Press for their knowledge and support throughout the writing and production of this work.

Heartfelt thanks and recognition to all of my 'Alternative Education' and 'Utopian Visions and Everyday Culture' student cohorts from the academic years 2011–2015; without your life-affirming passion, bravery and willingness to engage in creative revelations through the utopian pedagogical experience, none of this could ever have been built or established. Continue to strive to change your worlds – and of those around you – for the better!

Of course, without the support and understanding of my family, this work could never have been conceived (let alone completed); so, love and thanks to Bob, Margaret, Big Nath, Liam, Zac, Eden and Little Nath, who have foregone my physical presence for too many evenings and weekends (and my mental absence for far longer periods). For Mum, Dad, Crista and Lauren, a week doesn't go by where your absence isn't felt; though our paths no longer cross, my love for you, as ever, remains.

Finally, my wife and best friend, Emma Hammond, as well as supporting me in my ever-continuing academic endeavours, has taught me so much about dedication, unconditional positive regard, love and spiritual growth; without her unique beauty and strength, embracing support and presence, I simply wouldn't be the person I am today.

1 Kings 19: 11–13; Isaiah 60: 1; 62: 2

Introduction: Critical Pedagogies – Horizons of Possibility

Notes for a book: A context

The foundations for this work stretch across a *fuzzy aggregate* of infused cultural remnants – non-linear bibliographic residues of life-potent mis en scenes. As embedded, scattered and *misshapen* legacies, they continue to refract and resonate. Rather than decaying in a memorial wasteland, the personal debris of cultural murmurs continue to echo as audacious dreams and aspirations. Like secret friends, their traces speak and continue to reveal audio-visceral nudges. As shifting palimpsests of possibility, filmic fragments conspire, and, as unlikely congregations, they whisper against consignments from the past. Beyond the heavily worn *word-tracks* of books, uncanny doppelgangers of hope fracture and meander towards beautiful stories of redemption. Swirling lyrical shards and musical rhythms reverberate and open up catalytic entrances, which peer beyond the fluid horizon of the future. This is not the typical, nor maybe the expected material for a mainstream pedagogy; but the poignant and bespoken cultural patterns hinted at here are indeed the foundations and interconnecting threads which recurrently emerge throughout the faceted development of this book. As such, the cumulative emergence of a utopian pedagogy – emanating from creative adaptations of principles and practices associated with critical pedagogy – collectively fuse with everyday occurrences and personal irruptions, as part of an open system of flexible hope.

Outsiders welcome

I should never have been *destined* for an academic career. The historical and economic mechanics of my working class childhood, and youth, invoked a series of structures and influences which formed a very different life journey to the one that I was to subsequently pursue as a young adult.[1] Born and nurtured in Blackburn, a post-industrial Cotton Town in the north-west of England, during the 1970s and 1980s, I witnessed the impact of the decomposing environment of abandoned cotton mills, alongside the Thatcherite-driven decline of local industry and widespread unemployment.[2] My social activities as a youth consisted of youth clubs, Working Men's Clubs, 2nd Division football,[3] and, eventually, peer groups associated with Manchester-based 'indie' music. I fared abysmally at secondary school, unceremoniously deemed by my teachers to lack the academic potential to be entered for GCE O-Level exams.[4] GCEs were the higher and more respected of school-based qualifications up until the late 1980s; good GCE passes were a statutory requirement to secure a coveted trade apprenticeship with one of the established local engineering companies. Disappointed with the prospect of leaving school at 16 with few qualifications, and either applying for production work in a factory or seeking work as an unskilled labourer in the building trade, I took the only other available escape route out of unemployment, and applied to join the army. After serving two years as a Trooper in the Life Guards in the Household Cavalry, it was clear that I was unsuited to the discipline, rules and conformity required to be a safe and successful soldier. As a result, two months after turning 18, I was discharged from Woolwich military hospital. Returning to Blackburn with a young family, I needed to earn regular money, and secured employment as a weaver, working on a three-shift basis at one of the last remaining textile companies. The work was arduous, physical and isolating; and reeling from the tumult of the years since leaving school, my energy for life and youthful arrogance quickly dissolved.

After several years of machinated, production-line existence, a deepening sense of agitation started to grow; something was missing, I felt an overwhelming ache, that I had more to do and more to give; that I had abandoned something between youth and adulthood. Gradually – by this time, age 24 – resuscitated culture shards of hope started to resurface; sporadically, through poignant and personal encounters with films, books and pieces of music, I felt that I was being signposted, guided almost, against overwhelming odds, to reach out towards something new. And so one afternoon, after finishing a 6.00 am–2.00 pm shift, I detoured to one of the Town Centre bookshops (before collecting my daughter from the Nursery) with the intention of becoming better read and, ultimately, educating myself. Not knowing what to look for when I arrived at the bookshop, the only book in the philosophy section that I vaguely recognized was Friedrich Nietzsche's *On the Genealogy of Morals* (of course I hadn't heard of – or was in any way aware of – the book, but I had heard, through wider cultural references, of Nietzsche's name). There and then, I was grabbed by the intriguing aphorisms on the first page of the preface, and attempted to make sense of the purpose and context of the book; I continued to read and grapple with it at home, trying desperately to dissect and understand it. I quickly realized that, while excited that I could understand and *glean* meaning from some areas and sections of the book (and in doing so, start to question my schoolteachers' labels and judgements about having low intelligence), I needed to return to study in order to learn *how to learn* and to expand my knowledge.

In February 1994, I enrolled with the Open University (OU) to study on the D103 *Introduction to the Social Sciences* foundation course. In the canteen during break times at work, I would read, study, make notes and sometimes write parts of my OU assignments; at home late at night and in the early hours, I would continue to study, and I loved the learning. But it was in a secret and interior world, *one* that I shared with *Educating Rita, Shirley Valentine*, the *Shawshank Redemption, Joy Division, New Order*, the *Stone Roses* and *Charles Bukowski*, that the drive, hope, and importantly the self-belief that I could, maybe, do something more, started to awaken. In the mirror, I would see an unhappy, introverted working-class man, with a legacy of missed chances and a limited future of restricted opportunities; but with *Andy Dufresne* and *Bye Bye Badman*, my hopes, daydreams and horizons of possibility started to open up, and I dared to start to dream again of new adventures.

Acquiring new knowledge with the OU and learning how to develop and, importantly, frame an academic argument started to increase my confidence. As I progressed with the course, an increasing political awareness started to emerge, and with this, a zeal for trade unionism and working-class interests; however, frustrated by the ways in which my life (and the lives of the members of my family) and opportunities had been structurally and politically influenced, my political turn was infused with an increasing sense of injustice and a *bubbling* anger. I recall posting handwritten quotes from Marx and Engels's *The Communist Manifesto* and Bakunin's *God and the State* on management and worker information noticeboards throughout the factory. Not only did this dismay the managers, but, for some reason, my colleagues and *comrades* also thought that this controversial approach to *class* agitation was too obtuse, aggressive and divisive.

After successfully completing D103, I was accepted on to a full-time combined honours degree course, and chose to specialize in *Education Studies with Sociology*. And so, at age 25, I moved away from Blackburn again, but this time it was a very different type of challenge and journey. Thankfully, two education studies lecturers were willing to look beyond the awkward defence mechanism of my arrogant and often abrasive working-class 'chip', and recognized a potential in me that I hadn't even started to suspect. As we covered, and discussed, Karl Marx, Paulo Freire, Henry Giroux, bell hooks and the Situationists, my raw polemic and unhelpful anger was gradually redirected, and it started to transform into an increasingly coherent and a capable array of academic articulations. During the second year of my studies, a chance conversation with a friend studying political philosophy introduced me to Ernst Bloch's *The Principle of Hope*. I immediately sought out the three-volume work in the university library; and with this, the constellations of my history and disappointments, my culture-hued hopes and impassioned pursuit of personal and political dignity started to align.

After graduating, I decided to pursue a career as a Further Education lecturer; and on completion of my Post Graduate Certificate in Education (PGCE), I secured some hourly paid work at Blackburn College, teaching GCSE resits, AS/A levels and Adult Higher Education Access courses. Despite struggling initially with my perception of the *middle-class-ness* of the professionalized environment (and my assumption that I just didn't fit in), I discovered that teaching and inspiring people of all ages and abilities, many from lower socio-economic backgrounds than mine and with similar compulsory schooling–inflicted experiences of isolation and disappointment, was an amazing and humbling privilege. Across the first five years of my teaching, I secured a permanent contract, completed my master's degree and, after a little hesitation, embarked on a PhD journey. This coincided with the politically motivated expansion of Higher Education (HE) through the validation and delivery of degrees at further education colleges. Quickly establishing itself with a large and dedicated HE Centre, Blackburn positioned itself on the crest of the wave of this transition. In the midst of these changes, I took the decision to professionally and physically move across to the HE Centre, and set about learning to write, validate and lecture on Lancaster University validated degree programmes.

The local and wider context for this book

It may seem that the University Centre Blackburn College (UCBC) is an unusual and unlikely place for the birth and development of a utopian pedagogy. While unorthodox, in the sense that UCBC provides HE in a Further Education context (often referred to as *HE in FE*, or College Based Higher Education, *CBHE*),

I have found it to be a wonderfully fertile environment – a phoenix-like estab-
lishment, prepared to embrace not only new but also maverick and innovative
academic practices, along with a willingness to nurture developments which
manifest the potential for wider adaptation. No doubt, this culture of vitality
and change is born out of an acute and conscious necessity; located in the centre
of a post-industrial and socio-economically deprived town, it has had to confront the need to adapt and survive, to birth new visions and ideas, in order
to navigate the decline of its traditional areas of provision.[5] While apparently
niche and unorthodox in some respects, UCBC is also a microcosm of wider
pressures and changes. The immanent economic and political (local and global)
challenges posed by neo-liberal markets, the individualisation of consumers and
the associated mechanisms to service and promote the process of educational
consumption are now a universal *Western* academic narrative. As such, the fact
that UCBC delivers HE in a CBHE context is a moot point; its HE provision is
subject to the same changes, research and scholarship expectations, structures,
governance, mechanisms of scrutiny and consumer-based pressures as any
university.

In my earlier and subsequent areas of academic research and educational practice, I have maintained an interest in working-class and lower socio-economic
entrants to HE. Furthermore, I have set out to extend my own biographical
experiences and academic connections in ways that usefully transgress the local
and merely subjective. Of course, the utopian pedagogy proposed as part of this
work maintains connections to, and in some areas is an extension of, the uncovering and unravelling of my own personal traces; however, through experimentation, collaboration, error and success – at least in some areas – I have sought
to navigate a range of curricular and pedagogical tactics in ways that shift the
material beyond the solipsistic tendencies of my own cultural moments. My
research and pedagogical practice has been and continues to be influenced by
the works of Paulo Freire, Henry Giroux, Peter McLaren, bell hooks, Roland
Barthes, Ernst Bloch, Gaston Bachelard and the Situationists. However, while
the Critical Pedagogical principles associated with Freire, Giroux, McLaren and
hooks whetted my academic appetite, their ideas did not, indeed could not,
offer the contextual specificities for a flexible and implementable pedagogical
framework; hence, my own efforts and contributions to this area through my
work here.[6]

Across the last four academic years, I have engaged with colleagues and
undergraduate collaborators in the development of the processes and democratic elements associated with this utopian pedagogy (as part of modules which

extend across the disciplinary boundaries of sociology and education studies).[7] Through exploring mixtures and amalgamations of key philosophical and conceptual principles and further developing constructive collaborations in pursuit of pedagogical tactics for engaging and enhancing learner democracy, this book brings together the culmination of these themes and experiments to state the case for a *mainstream* H E 'utopian pedagogy'. As such, I hope this book fulfils a necessary and timely need of encouraging HE practitioners and students within and across social science and education studies–related subjects – but certainly *not* restricted to them – to actively engage with new ways of thinking, new ways of learning and new possibilities of educating. Whether intent on formulating pedagogical alternatives within a politically localized context or with aspirations to target and proactively challenge wider political and economic torrents, the utopian tactics and counter strategies that emerge as part of this study present a pedagogical model that is ripe for wider and fluid adaptations. As part of the flexibility of the utopian pedagogy, the primary notion of *hope* – as part of the title of this work, and the book as a whole – is posed as a trans-human impulse, one which drives a shifting human hunger for creative ideas and transformatory change. In adopting such a position, the book makes a number of assumptions, but one in particular needs to be highlighted: that the impulse and process of *hope* and the personal harbouring of threads and private traces of all kinds of culture-imbued nostalgia contain a utopian potential. The book and the pedagogy therefore operate around the assumption that, as shared facets of human interiorities (albeit in very different and subjective ways), culture-threads register and lie dormant as creative seeds, which can reappear when catalysed and emerge as utopian, meaningful visions or daydreams of possibility.[8]

A nexus of theoretical sympathies

Related to the proposed curricular material and wider ambitions of the work, the following historical coherences and theoretical affinities, between Gaston Bachelard (1884–1962), Roland Barthes (1915–1980), Guy Debord (1931–1994), Henri Lefebvre (1901–1991) and Ernst Bloch (1885–1977), warrant recognition and elaboration. While the frameworks and concepts associated with these theorists consist of obvious unique differences and divergences, they also contain an array of philosophical sympathies and similarities. This is further supported by the fact that the majority of the theorists were Marxists – albeit of unorthodox nature.[9] Symbiotic aspects cut across the frameworks of the respective theorists as, generally, they strive to relocate and reinvigorate subjective empowerment, so that proliferations of non-linear creativities and liberated personal voices of alternative possibilities manifest and develop. The similarities of many of their ideas and concepts mean that sympathetic meldings and infusions can be aligned to articulate a radical everyday praxis; and with this, as is argued throughout the context of this study, productive utopian/Critical Pedagogical collaborations can be had with Paulo Freire, Henry Giroux, Peter McLaren and bell hooks.

Game (1995), in 'Time, Space, Memory, with Reference to Bachelard', notes that clear convergences are apparent between the works of Roland Barthes and the later *poetics* work of Gaston Bachelard; a nexus of conceptual sympathies operate across the two theorists' ideas, which seek to uncover the active role of the subject in personal and particularistic experiences of culture. Corroborating this, Jonathan Culler (2002) notes that while Barthes claimed not to have read Bachelard, core ideas cut across their respective works, to the point that they are not only sympathetic but distinctively similar.[10] Generally, for both Barthes and Bachelard, cultural works are not to be treated as purely external, objective artefacts; but instead, they should be approached and appreciated as gateways, as creative catalysts that liberate subjective readers to actively participate in bespoken and mutating interpretations.

The coherence of these theoretical threads continues with the coupling of Roland Barthes with Guy Debord; Debord's work *Society of the Spectacle* is very much related to the essayistic style and themes contained in Roland Barthes's *Mythologies* on wrestling, cinema, toys, and so on (for example, see Kibbey, 2005; and Meek, 2010); the influence and collaboration of Barthesean ideas with Debordean political/liberatory tactics is well recognized and documented (see Boscagli, 2014; and Hetherington, 2007). With these influences, Debord coined and developed a series of concepts as tactics and counter-strategies, which included the disconcerting and irreverent notions of the *dérive* and *détournement*; the fluidity of these ideas and cultural methods were aimed at inciting fractured and personalized actions geared towards unleashing wider creative and political struggles. In conjunction with the philosophical accord afforded by Barthes (and also Henri Lefebvre – described later), Guy Debord and the *International Situationists* (or the SI) played a not insignificant contributory role in the incitement of the 1968 student uprisings in Paris.[11] Conceiving and distributing slogans and pamphlets, their efforts centred upon tactics for subjective revival within a system of wider political control and technological tyranny. Reclaiming individual autonomies from the psychological grip peddled by the consumerist spectacle served – and continues to serve – as a reminder that micro scale changes in relation to thought and behaviour harbour a potential influence, and reach, that can extend well beyond the relative scale of the subject.[12]

A related and key influence within the SI movement was Henri Lefebvre's *The Critique of Everyday Life*. While never actually becoming a full-fledged member of the SI, Lefebvre collaborated with Debord for a period of time; however, theoretical antagonisms led to irredeemable differences between them.[13] With Lefebvre, we also have an additional connection and corroboration with Gaston Bachelard: Lefebvre's work on *space* and *rhythm* is closely related to Bachelard's work on poetics and creativity, as evidenced by Lefebvre's *The Production of Space*, and of course the equally Bachelardean *Rhythmanalysis* (the term is actually taken from Bachelard's *The Poetics of Space*). Adding further emphasis to the multiple points of connection, Poster (1977) and Kelly (2000) tease out theoretical and conceptual affinities between Barthes and Lefebvre, which identify wider professional and social encounters between the two theorists.

Moving on to the schismatic role of an unorthodox German philosopher, within a profile of otherwise French cultural theorists, Wayne Hudson (1982) makes reference to Ernst Bloch's philosophical influence and theological impact on the 1968 German student uprising and other anti-capitalist movements across Europe during the mid-1960s to late-1960s (Hudson, 1982: 17). Not that this is the only *tenuous* connection between the French theorists and Ernst Bloch. There are a number of other complementary aspects in relation to the philosophical frameworks of Gaston Bachelard and Ernst Bloch. For example, within Bachelard's work, a transition point – a rupture even – occurs between his earlier *philosophy of science* works and ideas, and what became his later writings on *Poetics*; an engagement with Einsteinian and Bergsonian relativity alongside a developmental interest in psychoanalysis and poetry created a notable departure within Bachelard's work and thought. There are similar areas of theoretical connection in relation to Bloch's work on utopia, aspects of which are also steeped in re-worked psychoanalytical theory, and Einsteinian/Bergsonian relativity – especially in relation to the chaotic reception of culture. Furthermore, both Bloch and Bachelard incorporate and rework aspects of Riemannian differential geometry and the Copenhagen interpretation of quantum mechanics (for more detailed expositions on these areas and connections, see Hammond, 2012; and Hammond, 2015).[14] The impact and influence of relativity on their respective frameworks and ideas serve to emphasize, again, the role of subjective engagement with myriad cultural sources (poetry, fairy tales, space), and the unpredictable irruption of bespoke and creative manifestations.

A note on the notion of pedagogical tactics

It should be clear at this point that rather than invoking and operating the concepts of hope, utopia and creativity as rigid and stringently articulated definitions, or static technical blueprints, the work will be utilising them as flexible and fluid pedagogical *tactics* and *counter*-strategies. Throughout the study, Michel de Certeau's work *The Practice of Everyday Life* (1984) should be referred to as the basis for defining and framing the use and meaning of the terms *tactic* and *strategy*. In *The Practice of Everyday Life* de Certeau aligns the notion of 'strategy' with political, institutional and structural power. As such, strategy for de Certeau consists of a set of processes and activities associated with those who *rule* and administer the parameters of a particular space; through mechanisms of governance, an identified and legally named area establishes the types of expected behaviour within that space. As de Certeau notes:

> I call a strategy the calculation (or manipulation) of power relationships that becomes possible as soon as a subject with will and power (a business, an army, a city, a scientific institution) can be isolated. It postulates a place that can be delimited as its own and serve as the base from which relations with an exteriority composed of targets or threats (customers or competitors, enemies, the country surrounding the city, objectives and objects of research, etc.) can be managed. As in management, every 'strategic' rationalization seeks first of all to distinguish its 'own' place, that is, the place of its own power and will, from an 'environment'. (de Certeau, 1984: 35–6)

In contrast, for de Certeau, the connotations and actions associated with the very different practice of the 'tactic' is more liberating, as it can pose a direct and political contradiction to the strategy (or the powerful strategist). As de Certeau notes, a tactic is a

> calculated action determined by the absence of a proper locus. No delimitation of an exteriority, then, provides it with the condition necessary for autonomy. The space of a tactic is the space of the other. Thus it must play on and with a terrain imposed on it and organized by the law of a foreign power. It does not have the means to keep to itself, at a distance, in a position of withdrawal, foresight, and self-collection: it is a manoeuvre "within the enemy's field of vision," . . . It operates in isolated actions, blow by blow. It takes advantage of "opportunities" and depends on them . . . In short, a tactic is an art of the weak. (ibid.: 37)

In sum, individuals who are expected to conform to strategic prescriptions within the identified parameters of a bureaucratized space, with its roles and behaviour, rarely adhere to the structural compulsions in their entirety. At the level of the individual, *anti-conformist* tactics can be coined and invoked, which mean that the bureaucratic expectations, determined by the plans and policies of the organisation or ruling body, are never fully or purely implemented. As such, everyday life within the regulated space of an organisation produces a littering of tactical practices, which can challenge and even short-circuit the generality of the rules of the wider social body by poaching the territory of the regulators. Using organisational rules, policies and other strategically cascaded materials, subjective tactics can set out to alter and subvert the pressures brought to bear by institutional rules, with a view to reinhabiting them and making them *their* own. Rescuing individual autonomy from within any type of strategic and powerful system thus becomes a micro-political problem; tactics offer ripe and fertile conditions for the creative manipulation of everyday contexts and activities. Tactics (and individual tacticians) must therefore be vigilant and seek ways of utilising the cracks, fissures and inconsistencies that open up amidst the mechanics of regulation and control, wielded by the strategic might of the organising power. As de Certeau clarifies, a tactic

> takes an order by surprise. The art of 'pulling tricks' involves a sense of the opportunities afforded by a particular occasion . . . a tactic boldly juxtaposes diverse elements in order suddenly to produce a flash, shedding a different light on the language of a place and to strike . . . fragments, cracks and lucky hits in the framework of a system . . . [and] change the organization of a space, to the relations among successive moments in an action, to the possible intersections of durations and heterogeneous rhythms, etc. (Ibid.: 37–38)

This useful distinction between strategy and tactic provides a flexible and important schema, one which can be usefully adapted and applied to the context of HE and the university. The bureaucratic architecture and environment of the university (and University Centre) are structurally appropriated; it is a politically and economically motivated place that strategically and panoptically wields behavioural power over its inhabitants. As such, it has become 'a triumph of place over time' (ibid.: 36), in that the university structure serves to regulate and control its academic subjectivities into pre-specified roles and parameters engineered through systems of regulation and proto-conformity. The division of academic space into sub-areas and parts, such as schools, disciplines and so on, is tendrilously connected to a reciprocal *Leviathan* of governance, which infiltrates and extends far beyond the local borders of specific organisations. The immediacy of university strategies is incrementally connected to government strategies and other external interferences from regulatory agents of state-invested focus. This social systemic and concentric *strategy* for higher education means that every attempt is made to herd meandering and geographically disparate subjectivities into spaces and practices 'that can be observed and measured', and thus controlled (ibid.: 36). De Certeau cautions that the *innards* of such strategies beat with the rhythm of a particular type of knowledge, one that is determined and sustained by epistemological interests and resource measurement, that is, arrested knowledge, packaged, bureaucratically sanctioned and contained within empiricized and sanitized systems. This conductivity celebrates the authority and control of its organising body. In this sense, 'power is the precondition of this knowledge and not merely its effect or its attribute. It makes this knowledge possible and at the same time determines its characteristics' (ibid.: 36); organisations produce themselves in and through this type of legalistic and controllable knowledge.

However, for de Certeau there are always shards of light that rip and glimmer through the sutured seams of organisational strategies. Where strategic power is bound and perpetuated by its enshrinement and visibility, the invisibility and flexibility emergent from subjective tactics can be invoked and nurtured in the gaps and spaces of the policies and rules of the wider structure. Tactical fluidity operating within the fissures of the invisible is always and unpredictably possible. Furthermore, the notion and practice of strategy is not only restricted to the wider domain of the powerful. Invoking dynamic tactics, and re-purposing the pre-specified arrangements of space and academic behaviour in alternative ways, counter-strategies can be developed, which challenge organisational expectations. Using the typology as set out by de Certeau, the utopian pedagogy proposed as part of this wider and unfolding work contains, and offers, a potent array of tactics. The theoretical material and concepts associated with Ernst Bloch, Roland Barthes, Gaston Bachelard and Henri Lefebvre are explored with a view to being presented as tactical possibilities: mechanisms for the recruitment of participatory engagements between pro-dynamic practitioners and learner collaborators.[15] The aim is to equip and empower learner collaborators with ideas and conceptual tools to facilitate creative and democratic academic engagement. Instead of engineering the production and reproduction of a staid and uniform type of regurgitated knowledge, as legislated and required by the formal bureaucracies and strategies of the regulating institution, a lively, bespoke and *almost* dangerously democratic type of hopeful knowledge can emerge.

Admittedly, as a singular lecturer with an apparent array of conformity-challenging ideas and tactics, there are some unavoidable contradictions and *weaknesses* attached to these counter-strategic proposals. Aligned with the situationist practices of the *dérive* and *détournement* (explained later, and also covered as part of Chapter 4), the practices of Creative Autobiography, bespoke presentation, and Peer Assessment – while admittedly imperfect – offer an array of opportunities aimed at facilitating the authentic emergence of creative and collaborative eclecticities. In conjunction with Barthes, Debord and the Situationists and the Critical Pedagogues (Freire, Giroux, McLaren & hooks, covered as part of Chapter 6), there is a fundamental questioning of the purpose of the rigid and epistemic role of learning outcomes and assessed learner performances. But, within this, limitations and contradictions are also inevitable: there are practicalities and other aspects of the proposed mainstream utopian pedagogy that have to engage with – or, at the very least, recognize – existing strategies and mechanisms controlled and maintained by powerful and regulating academic institutions. This results in a stark choice, either that the utopian pedagogy be posed and developed as a mainstream option and real world possibility within established local and wider HE frameworks and contexts, or it be posed *only* as a distant and potentially workable possibility (should strategic pressures and constraints ever shift or dilute). Hopefully, readers will appreciate, and support, my decision to subscribe to and promote the former option. This in no way negates the issues and constraints confronting the options and counter-strategic suggestions on offer, which must operate inevitably from within a position of tactical weakness. Indeed, de Certeau would suggest that this is unavoidable; I would corroborate, and suggest that this maybe one of the only remaining forms of potential insider resistance as a response to the new globalising system of neo-liberal and consumer ideology.

The structure and content of this book

Beyond this introduction (Chapter 1), the subsequent ten chapters of the book (inclusive of the conclusion) are constructed around, and respond to, the following three cumulative themes and parts. Part I is entitled *Tactics: Conceptualising Hope, Utopia and Creativity*, and sketches out and develops the key theoretical, conceptual and, ultimately, tactical foundations for the wider work. Part II, entitled *Pedagogical Strategies for Creative Possibilities*, develops the practical, logistical and counter-strategic framing of the tactics established as part of the first part. Part III, *Learner Stories, Reflections and Projections*, is introduced by way of the everyday heterogeneous principles of Henri Lefebvre; beyond this, space is afforded for commentary and dialogue with students who have previously engaged with the utopian pedagogical principles. The content for the three successive parts is elaborated in more detail below.

Part I, *Tactics: Conceptualising Hope, Utopia and Creativity* addresses the principles of hope, utopia and creativity, and articulates an array of curricular tactics designed to empower and engage creative learners. Readers are introduced to the works of Ernst Bloch (1885–1977), Roland Barthes (1915–1980) and Gaston Bachelard (1884–1962). Each of the three initial chapters provides a very brief introduction to the biography and theoretical contributions to each theorist; they then 'flesh out' an array of conceptual terms and flexible thinking tools. The diversity of each theoretical framework is accessibly explored and presented as material that can be tailored and bespokenly adapted in a number of curricular and pedagogical contexts, so as to incite and facilitate learner engagement. The remit and scope of this initial collection of chapters set out the following arsenal of thinking-based themes and pedagogical *tactics*: first, with Ernst Bloch, the main concepts to be covered are utopia, hope, the *Trace*, the Not-Yet, *Expressionism*, empty-space, and the future. Continuing from this, the chapter on Roland Barthes covers *The Death of the Author*, the *rustle of language*, punctum & studium, and the 3rd meaning; and, finally with Gaston Bachelard, the final chapter of Part I explores reverie, space, the 'house' of imagination, geometries of echoes, fairytales, and reveries on childhood. Cumulatively, the philosophical and conceptual tactics offered here should be received as sources for interpretative freedom, as springboards to facilitate personal learner connections and associations within multifaceted thought-spaces. As such, it is argued that in offering the themes and concepts identified above, as 'empty spaces', personal futures can open up and progress towards developing dialogic narratives and creative, bespoke and reflective encounters.

Part II: *Pedagogical Strategies for Creative Possibilities* establishes a metaphorical 'passing of the baton'. As part of Chapter 5 *Dérive and Détournement: Pedagogical Strategies for Creative Engagement*, the previously established concepts, ideas and tactics become implicitly framed as part of an array of practical themes and pedagogical counter-strategies aimed at democratically cascading to each eclectic learner-collaborator and diverse student group academically malleable *Expressionistic* portals. Chapter 6 *Bye Bye Badman: The Redemption of Hope through Popular Culture* presents an author/tutor-led example of *Creative Autobiography*. The purpose is to illustrate, through the vehicle of popular culture, ways in which learners can be invited to creatively invoke the array of conceptual tactics and, in doing so, uncover and explore traces of subjective encounters associated with daydreams, astonishment, hope, escape, and so on. Facilitating alternative and multifaceted learning dialogues, learners can develop – and assume increasing responsibility for – the conceptualisation and articulation of key personal memories, popular cultural attachments and, ultimately, latent possibilities. A multifaceted chorus of hope, critical dialogues with power and exclusion, and creative visions of possibility and transformation can start to emerge.

As the core chapter on pedagogy within the book, Chapter 7 *The Wisdom of the Crowd: Liberating Creativity* introduces Surowiecki's notion of 'the wisdom of the crowd' (Surowiecki, 2013) as a key democratic mechanism to facilitate and safeguard student creativity. Key ideas associated with Paulo Freire, Henry Giroux, Peter McLaren and bell hooks are aligned with a peer-assessment framework to enable maximum personal creative freedom, and to ensure a multi-modal and multi-cultural Expressionistic-space for all learners. Moving away from a model of personal risk, associated with the awarding of a singular grade by an 'expert' lecturer, it is argued that collaborative peer-assessment protects the highly bespoken style and creative connections associated with each learner story.

Embracing alternative academic tactics and democratic virtues through a composted fertility of latent ideas (and refracted interpretations through the works of Bloch, Barthes and Bachelard), it is also important, in a Freirean sense, to offer real world, practical and pedagogical options. As such, Chapter 7 of this book concludes with the offering of a draft 'Hope, Utopia and Creativity' module handbook. The purpose of this module is to offer a framework that not only presents the possibility of structuring and implementing the conceptual tactics as part of a HE curricular framework, but also proposes the notion that the curricular material can be 'learner assessed' in alternative ways. Armed with Blochian, Barthesean and Bachelardean tactics for creative empowerment, (established as part of Chapters 2, 3 and 4 of this book), an array of supporting pedagogical strategies or *counter* strategies are brought together as part of Chapters 5, 6 and 7 of this book. These suggest that alternative strategies can be established and implemented.

The final Part III: *Learner Stories, Reflections and Projections* affords space for a collection of commentaries, thoughts and examples of works produced by learners who have participated in the utopian pedagogy-based collaborative learning experience. Situated within a Lefebvrean notion of *rhythmanalysis*,

Chapter 8 *A Garland of Rhythms* presents a snapshot of artefacts produced by students from across the last four academic years. Chapter 9 *Encounter, Stories, Connections*, offers an array of commentaries and narratives that emerged from semi-structured questionnaires conducted with cohorts of previous learners.[16] Chapter 10, *Beyond the Trace: Reflections from Past Learners*, too provides narratives and commentaries from previous learners.

Finally, the conclusion to the book, Chapter 11, *Conclusion Elpis/Eidos – Elpetidetics: Hopeful Visions*, offers a further *Expressionistic* genesis in the form of an invitational starting point for other student and academic collaborators. This final chapter poses a Blochian-influenced philosophical argument for the possibility and further development of utopian pedagogical practices, based on an overarching concept of Elpeidetics (Elpis: hope; and Eidos: to see, or reveal). As a pedagogical framework, Elpeidetics encapsulates the malleability of the theoretical and curricular/pedagogical frameworks offered throughout this book and argues that through liberating relative Expressionistic traces, a creative continuum of unmade futures is ripe for permutations of new visions and practices to emerge. Elpeidetics thus suggests the potential for a growth of these democratic and creative principles within and across existing and other HE programmes and disciplines. Building on the theoretical and conceptual material set out during the earlier chapters, the scope and remit of Elpeidetics further explores the working-through of the future-based, chaotic and also utopian characteristic of Blochian philosophy.

Below is a grid-based visual representation of the key sections, chapters and themes explored throughout the book, highlighting the key areas of the de Certeau-esque notions of strategy, tactic and counter-strategy. The grid also emphasizes the phased transition from theory and concept (as part of Section 1), to the array of draft proposals for practical pedagogical techniques and counter-strategies (as part of Section 2), and then Section 3, which brings out learner voices, reflecting on their experiences of engaging with the utopian pedagogical experience.

Book Section	Book Chapter	Theorists, Concepts and Book Themes
Introduction	1. Critical Pedagogies – Horizons of Possibility	Authorial biographical context
		Michel de Certeau: The principles of Strategy & Tactic
		Connections: Gaston Bachelard, Roland Barthes, Ernst Bloch, Guy Debord & Henri Lefebvre

Book Section	Book Chapter	Theorists, Concepts and Book Themes
PART I **Tactics:** **Conceptualizing** **Hope, Utopia and** **Creativity**	2. Ernst Bloch, Hope and Utopia: The Stuff of Possibility	Blochian concepts / pedagogical tactics: Utopia & Hope; The Trace; The Not-Yet; Expressionism; astonishment
	3. Roland Barthes: Punctum! Death of the Author	Barthesean concepts / pedagogical tactics: The Scriptor; interpretive skids; punctum; 3rd Meaning; pro-dynamic practitioner
	4. Gaston Bachelard: Poetics, Space and Daydreaming	Bachelardean concepts / pedagogical tactics: Reverie; imagination; fairytale; forest; childhood
PART II **Pedagogical** **Strategies** **for Creative** **Possibilities**	5. Dérive and Détournement: Pedagogical Strategies for Creative Engagement	Situationist counter-strategy: Reinhabiting the educational terrain; creative 'wandering'; hijacking knowledge; challenging educational consumption
	6. Bye Bye Badman:The Redemption of Hope through Popular Culture	Creative Autobiography as counter-strategy: Creative autobiographical example provided by the author; anti-ideology; combination of previously established *tactics* and *strategies*
	7. The Wisdom of the Crowd: Liberating Creativity	A Utopian Pedagogy as counter-strategy: The Critical Pedagogues: Freire, Giroux, McLaren & hooks; proposal for a 'practical' pedagogical framework; draft module handbook
PART III **Learner Stories,** **Reflections and** **Projections**	8. A Garland of Rhythms	Everyday Life as counter-strategy: Complexity and Everyday culture; Marcel Proust, Walter Benjamin & memory; introduction to the multifaceted student work examples (as part of next chapter)
	9. Encounters, Stories, Connections	An array of snapshots and examples of student works produced (as part of the utopian pedagogy)

Book Section	Book Chapter	Theorists, Concepts and Book Themes
	10. Beyond the Trace: Reflections from Past Learners	Collation of findings from qualitative reflections, (from past students):
		Reflections on student 'utopian pedagogical' tactical and counter-strategic encounters
Conclusion	11. Elpis/Eidos: Hopeful Visions?	Ernst Bloch; Edmund Husserl; and Ivan Illich: a proposal for further possibilities and adaptations of creative, expectant hope and education.

Notes

1 My father was an unskilled engineer/pipe-fitter by day and a successful 'Working Men's Club' singer on Friday, Saturday and Sunday evenings; my mother progressed from factory work to become a secretary.

2 Blackburn became a unitary authority in 1998 and was renamed the Borough of Blackburn with Darwen.

3 In the Football League era prior to the introduction of the Premier League in 1992.

4 The hierarchical and tiered ordinary level General Certificate of Education (GCE) and lower status Certificate of Secondary Education (CSE) were replaced by the GCSE curriculum and examination framework as part of the 1988 education reform Act.

5 University Centre Blackburn College is now one of the larger providers of higher education within the further education sector, with a higher education student population of approximately 3,000 students, amounting to approximately 2,500 full-time equivalents. These numbers place it in the top three higher education providers in the English further education sector and mean that it has a higher education student body that is larger than the thirty smallest institutions in the UK higher education sector, including the six smallest universities.

6 Inevitably, there remains a *personal* bias to the choice of pedagogical theorists and philosophers as part of this work and resultant pedagogy; however, these are not stipulations but suggestions. Alternative theorists and pedagogical options based on practitioner parameters of experience and theoretical preference should be regarded as equally possible and acceptable.

7 The main academic vehicles that have operated as arenas for the experimentation and development of the pedagogical work that now forms the basis for this book

are the following UCBC/Lancaster University undergraduate (level 6) modules: 'Utopian Visions & Everyday Culture' and 'Alternative Education'. I have written, validated and delivered these modules as part of the Lancaster University validated BA (Hons) Social Science and BA (Hons) Education Studies programmes respectively.

8 The key areas of hope and utopia, in the context of this book and wider *flexible* pedagogy, are explored and developed as part of Chapter 2, 'Ernst Bloch, Hope and Utopia: The *Stuff* of Possibility'.

9 The following brief excerpt/example provides a brief insight to Barthes sympathies for critical Marxist tendencies: 'M. Jean Guerin enjoins me to say whether I am a Marxist or not . . . These kinds of questions are normally of interest only to McCarthyites. Others still prefer to judge by the evidence. M. Jean Guerin would be better advised to do as they do. Let him read Marx, for example. There he will discover – at least I hope he will – that you don't become a Marxist by immersion, initiation or self-proclamation . . . that Marx isn't a religion but a method of explanation and action; that that method demands a great deal of those who claim to practice it; and that, as a result, calling oneself a Marxist is more about self-importance than simplicity' (Barthes, 2015b: 46–48). Stuart Eldon, as part of the preface to Lefebvre's *Rhythmanalysis*, notes that 'Lefebvre was concerned with correcting what he saw as Marxism's over-emphasis of the temporal – and concomitant under-emphasis of the spatial – he was also involved in a lifelong struggle both within and without orthodox Marxism to pluralise its understanding of time and history' (Lefebvre, 2010: ix). And Jack Zipes points out that Bloch tried 'to locate the basic needs of oppressed groups . . . elaborating a Marxist critique of alienation and exploitation. In the process he maintained his optimistic belief in the potential of art to provide not only hope for a better future but also illumination toward the realization of this goal (Bloch, 1993: xi).

10 Johnathan Culler makes reference in Section 4 of his book, 'Barthes: A very short Introduction', to this point; while Culler implicitly references Barthes first major publication *Writing Degree Zero*, this does appear to be contradicted by Barthes own work, who makes clear reference to Bachelard and Bachelardean poetics, on page 37 of *The Pleasure of the Text* (1975).

11 Debord and the SI are explored and discussed in detail as part of Chapter 4 of this book.

12 A brief additional point here, the creative adaptation and development of Debord's détournement across cultural developments during the 1960s and 1970s contributed towards the formulation of Punk and the wider DIY punk ethos. This, in turn, influenced Tony Wilson's Factory records and Factory's bands: *The Joy Division*, *New Order*, *The Happy Mondays* and Manchester's *Hacienda*. My youthful involvement and continuing fascination with these Manchester-based movements

also lend a personal biographical connection to the theoretical formula (see James Nice [2011], *Shadowplayers: The Rise and Fall of Factory Records*, for a detailed discussion and exposition of the influence of Debord and the Situationists).

13 Lefebvre in an interview with Ross (2004) notes on this point that, 'The Situationists . . . It's a delicate subject, one I care deeply about. It touches me in some ways very intimately because I knew them very well. I was close friends with them. The friendship lasted from 1957 to 1961 or '62, which is to say about five years. And then we had a quarrel that got worse and worse in conditions I don't understand too well myself but which I could describe to you. In the end it was a love story that ended badly, very badly. There are love stories that begin well and end badly. And this was one of them' (Ross, 2004: 267–268).

14 See the latter chapters of Ernst Bloch's *A Philosophy of the Future*; and Gaston Bachelard's *Dialectic of Duration*.

15 The counter-strategies are offered by the Critical Pedagogical principles and practical options as set out in Chapter 6; these are further clarified and bolstered by the Situationist practices of the dérive and détournement.

16 See Appendices 1 and 2 at the end of the book for more detailed information on the organisation of the research process (including *permissions*), the organisation of responses and the curating of student work examples.

Part I

Tactics: Conceptualizing Hope, Utopia and Creativity

2

Ernst Bloch, Hope and Utopia:
The *Stuff* of Possibility

Ernst Bloch

Ernst Simon Bloch was born on 8 July 1885 to a working-class Jewish family in the German industrial city of Ludwigshafen. After a long and varied life and eventual academic career (Bloch didn't gain his first formal academic position until he was in his 60s), he died in 1977 in Tübingen. Commentators tell us that Bloch developed an interest in and keen understanding of philosophy at an early age; at age 13, he was regularly corresponding with a number of key German philosophers (Roberts, 1990: 3). Furthermore, Dennis J. Schmidt, the translator of Bloch's *Natural Law and Human Dignity*, notes that Bloch's adolescence consisted of a double existence; in one sense, we have the constrained Bloch living amid the workers of industrialized Ludwigshafen, but this Bloch was to become increasingly contrasted against the incarnation of a hopeful and longing Bloch frequenting the cultural experiences of Mannheim – the haven across the river – with its castle, library and theatres.[1] The contrast is an important one and contains a key and central theme which was to resurface throughout Bloch's life and work. Living on the *wrong side* of the bridge provided Bloch's childhood and adolescence with an important horizon, a target to focus his powerful imagination; his creative imaginings in turn prompted hopeful daydreams of adventure and escape.

In 1905 Bloch left Ludwigshafen to study philosophy and German literature at the University of Munich; from here, he was to move on to the University of Wurzburg to study experimental psychology, physics and music; during this period Bloch also developed an interest in Kabbala and Jewish mysticism. During this time at Wurzburg, Bloch wrote a text which identified a key concept: *Über die Kategorie Noch-Nicht* (On the Category of the Not-Yet), a concept which was to recur and significantly influence his life's work. The 22-year-old Bloch had conceived of the foundation for a philosophical system that would continue to be refined, refunctioned and developed across the remaining (and prolific) seventy years of his life (Roberts, 1990: 5).

Bloch's ideas, publications and larger-than-life persona began to establish him as an influential yet unorthodox Marxist thinker. Between 1938 and 1949 Bloch lived in exile in the United States; here he wrote the major part of his wide-ranging and comprehensive work – *Das Prinzip Hoffnung* (The Principle of Hope). Across three volumes Bloch meticulously catalogues and argues that hope always has, and inevitably always will, permeated the spirit of the times. As an eternal hunger, hope re-emerges through subjective consciousness and is continuously rearticulated through utopian ideas, dreams and expressions. In 1949 Bloch accepted the offer of a philosophy professorship at East Germany's Leipzig University and thus, at the age of 64, took up his first academic position; however, his time here was far from smooth running as he set about re-establishing his creative style of philosophical Marxism. Hudson (1982) points out that there was little 'doubt that Bloch's reassertion of philosophical Marxism was heretical by East German standards. He was ruthless in his attacks on 'narrow-gauge' Marxism, and in his rejection of 'objectivism', 'schematicism' and 'mechanical materialism" (Hudson, 1982: 15). In 1961, as Bloch was visiting Tubingen and Bayreuth in the West, the East German regime commenced the construction of the Berlin Wall; with this, Bloch took the decision to remain in the western sector and to file for political asylum, thus effectively defecting to West Germany (Bloch, 1986: xxvii). Bloch's disillusionment with the socialist East was now complete. Securing an academic position at West Germany's Tübingen University on 17 November 1961, a 76-year-old Bloch delivered his inaugural lecture: Can Hope Be Disappointed? (Bloch, 1998: 339–345).[2] Ever the militant optimist, Bloch refused to go away quietly, and with this lecture he reasserted the value, indeed the necessity, of incomplete and radical hope.

The *stuff* of possibility

Reappraising the utopian philosophy of Ernst Bloch in relation to pedagogy, creative learning and alternative educational practice is inherently difficult in several ways; Bloch's sprawling philosophical system contains many vagaries and significant assumptions which require appropriate recognition. As a *process-philosophy* of 'becoming', Bloch's system makes assumptions to predict and uncover a trans-historical and redemptive unfolding of a future utopian destination articulated through his flexible category of the Not-Yet (Hudson, 1982: 20).[3] As such, for Bloch, a potential utopian destination for humanity gradually and chaotically reveals latent secrets through personalized manifolds of daydreams, irruptive occurrences of hope and momentary recognitions that 'something's missing'. Within Bloch's schema, all kinds of culture-works can act as utopian conduits, hieroglyphic prompts which emanate and recur throughout all facets of individual life-courses, generations and societies. Hence, for Bloch, popular film, popular fiction, fairytales and music (along with the headier realms of theology, philosophy, Beethoven and Mozart, for example) are of pivotal importance. Within private, subjective worlds, personal catalogues or traces of cultural fragments of hope become embedded in the incompleteness of atomized pasts; these echoes linger and, when triggered and remembered, awaken anticipatory pangs for redemptive solutions. Culture-refracted traces in moments of reflection and daydream can set thought-threads wandering into labyrinthine hope-puzzles and elicit refracted murmurs of potential utopian unveilings of alternative and transformed futures.[4]

The way Bloch's philosophical style tenuously sutures the wide-ranging and pivotal extremes of the unfolding dignity and utopia of humanity, on one hand, and the chaos of subjective hungers, hopes and daydreams, on the other, leaves a difficult space to traverse. Of course, this is not an error or omission on Bloch's part; rather, the reciprocal space between a personal trace of hope and the unfolding transhuman utopian future is a purposeful gap, an Expressionistic-space into which we each divine our own creative, incremental paths, towards the potential for a future *utopia*. Through self-encounters or momentary flashes of astonished possibility *We* can start to actively daydream beyond the historical and ideological contexts of our given constraints and disappointments (Bloch, 2000). Thus, by detecting and responding to refracted utopian irruptions, we all become nudged or prompted to play our part in the unfolding, *ultimate* move towards a fuzzy apparition of collective hope and possibility.

Undoubtedly, Bloch's work is audacious; to suggest that beyond the chaotic quanta of subjective time-worlds an overarching and guiding utopian plan is to be *divined* is certainly challenging.[5] However, Bloch's work also serves as a powerful reminder that the future is Not-Yet made or indeed guaranteed and, as such, alternative 'futures' must inevitably emerge. As a category for contemplation and potential sculpting, the *future* can be purposefully influenced in new and transformed ways. The fact that the future is not guaranteed means that it can either progress towards 'perdition or redemption' (Bloch, 1998: 345); this is why for Bloch hope is singled out as the most essential of human principles and experiences. Hope, the *hunger* for hope, and the emanation of chaotic subjective encounters from within the trace of a memory, or dream reflection, contain undisclosed codes of potential utopia; each personal life is therefore littered with culture-infused reminders that we always have the capability to reach out towards the possibility of progressive and creative transformations (Bloch, 1986).

Hope and utopia

It is important at this point to provide clarification and further detail on the notion of a Blochian utopia. After all, this is one of the key foundations and conceptual keystones of this wider work. Bloch repurposes or refunctions utopia and adapts it to such an extent that it ceases to resemble more typical or traditional applications. As a result, the Blochian category of utopia is quite unlike other ideology-based definitions of utopia. Blochian utopia is not a rigid schema or blueprint for an alternative way of living; it is an idea, an Aristotelian *Form*, a powerful impulse constituted of human hunger and future-facing potential.[6] Jürgen Habermas usefully notes that Bloch's analysis and treatment of utopia 'operates not only with a mere approximation to totalities but out of an anticipatory grasp of these [which] cannot meaningfully be reduced . . . to the content of regulative ideas' (Habermas, 1983: 75–76).[7] Furthermore, Ruth Levitas points out that Bloch's approach to utopia poses a multitude of problems, with its flexibility and multi-dimensionality, in that 'the field of utopian strivings is virtually limitless' (Levitas, 2011: 117). Elaborating on this, Levitas clarifies that despite its apparent unwieldiness Blochian utopia does contain a key distinction: for Bloch, utopia can be grouped into two vague though quite different categories, those of *abstract* and *concrete* utopia. The category of *abstract* utopia refers to personal, utopic experiences elicited by everyday cultural material and trace-murmurs; even the most banal, populist and mass-produced of cultural material can contain the potential to nudge personal flashes of hope and aches for escape. This 'stuff' is not necessarily the primary material or constituent building block of wider utopian possibility, but it is nevertheless important, as it operates, in a sense, as a binding agent for the more fundamental concrete utopian ingredients to cohere and manifest. The second category, that of *concrete utopia*, refers to the wider, collective manifestation of social, political and transformative possibilities. This is the more elusive of the two categories and refers to the possibility of future developments emerging out from and growing beyond the utopic chaos associated with abstract utopian connections. The purpose of the ultimate, future-laden and collective aspect of concrete utopia 'is to reveal and recover the anticipatory essence from the dross of contingent and compensatory elements in which utopia is [subjectively] dressed up' (Levitas, 2011: 103).

Hope, utopias reciprocal and experience-laden counterpart, is also a transitory essence and as such is subject to the constant threat of disappointment, apathy and inaction. However, for Bloch, this doesn't mean that we should accept (or expect) the finality of such a negative position; on the contrary, hope, disappointed within Bloch's framework, shifts towards a positive and affirmative axis. As a dynamic essence yet to be appointed, disappointed hope ceases to be discarded as a foolhardy attempt, a relic to be biographically recorded and filed away. Instead, through revival, *thwarted hope* becomes recapitulated as an open process, a beacon on the horizon, a contagious mirage of a place at which we have yet to arrive (Moylan, 2000: 275). A cipher of open opportunity, hope signposts daydreams and imaginations towards futures and destinies that have not yet been decided. Latent hope is a reminder that the potential to redeem ourselves and the world from stasis and passivity always remains. As Bloch tells us:

> Nothing is more human than venturing beyond what is . . . Hope knows, too, that defeat pervades the world as a function of nothingness; and that . . . The world-process has not yet achieved victory anywhere; but it just as surely has not been defeated anywhere. And humans on earth can alter course toward a destination that has not yet been decided – toward redemption or perdition. (Bloch, 1998: 345)[8]

In this sense, hope is a concentric, fundamental and powerful principle, which generates a hunger for something different, something new, but is no guarantee of a good or certain future (West, 1991: 107).[9] Hope's swirling traces remind the inner subjective realm of a hunger, or ache, to venture somehow towards better, transformed tomorrows. As a fundamental source of human ideals and transition, hope induces all kinds of human articulations aimed at visualizing and establishing human dignity and better ways of living (Bloch, 1971). In its most sublime or cosmically purest Form, hope (as a catalyst) and the wider ether of utopia cannot be definitively communicated. And yet, creative and culture-loaded expressions continually emerge from the hopeful source of this *deep impulse* (Hammond, 2015). The individual experience of the ubiquitous utopian impulse provokes *wonder* and imaginations to daydream beyond the constraints of contemporary situations. From the residue of incomplete hopes and utopian ideas, new personal and rhythmically creative moments of astonishment become reawakened and, in so doing, reignite a hunger for change.

Traces of Expressionistic hope

Rather than merely commentating on the possibility of theoretical permutations and patterns, Bloch offers his work as a hieroglyphic cipher (Jameson, 1971); a complex work of gravitational wonder. If we follow the personal invitation towards Bloch's open thinking territories, we begin to awaken our own subjective, relative threads and stories of unfinished nostalgias and aches for redemption. Weissberg (1992) informs us that Bloch's book *Traces* (2006) perfectly embodies his provocative and often challenging approach to writing and thinking; Bloch, in presenting readers with his own trove of cultural connections, memories and thwarted experiences, entices subsequent readers to embark upon similar archaeological ways of thinking and so kick-start journeys of decipherment and recoveries of their own fragments or *traces* of latent hopes. The unusual writing style of the book, for Bloch, is an Expressionist art form, one that makes visible thoughts, connections and memories that may otherwise remain hidden from more routinized ways of thinking. The personally creative and Expressionistic process of recounting and piecing together stories and wider fragments of hope enables the empty space of Not-Yet utopian material to resurface and appear (Weissberg, 1992: 29–31). Leading towards the uncovering of our own traces, this Expressionistic process of cultural montage directs thoughts and daydreams towards an open future of possibility.[10]

Despite the mass produced and reproduced availability of popular and other cultural material, the recounting and re-articulation of personally beautiful traces maintain a creative and *Expressive* potency, enough to emanate the hieroglyphically mysterious and beautiful *chords* of hope. Hope, with its Velcro-like and manifold trace-hooks, attracts and draws out utopian trace awakenings. A deeply personal trace revelation stemming from the retelling of a fairytale (or redemptive love story, or prison-break, for example) is chaotically dependent upon the particularistic aspects of subjective *memory*, *experience* and cultural taste. Relative trace-synchronicity connects within particular, and what are ultimately, totally unpredictable, multi-points of personal time and cultural biography.[11] Therefore, each successive and relative trace-genesis, prompted by the essence of the mystery of utopian hope, establishes connections in non-linear and poly-dimensional ways. In corroboration, Bloch suggests that the *brooding* material provided by Expressionism guides us towards 'the soft or roaring silence of creation, into the untranslated testimony of the primitive, of child-, captive- and lunatic-art . . . in which we glimpse our future, like the disguised ornaments of our innermost form' (Bloch, 1991: 238–240).[12] For Bloch, the metamorphosed images and archetypes associated with creative formation and the pursuit of redemption have a phenomenal potency to prompt further Expressionistic self-encounters and trace awakenings, along with astonishing reminders of Not-Yet utopian possibilities. As one of the main Expressionistic characteristics of Bloch's philosophical formula, the utopian tactic or strategy of Expressionist trace-montage, throws us back upon ourselves. Self-encounters and trace awakenings serve as reminders that incomplete material from the past posits *thought-images* of undisclosed material; cultural *stuff* that, once remembered, wisps future-bound to somewhere beyond the specificity of a particular cultural context.[13]

In his short essay *Motifs of Concealment* contained in *Traces* Bloch (2006) suggests that it is within moments of cultural recognition that we occasionally find our latent and embedded pasts calling out to us for revival; nostalgic sonar-pings echo and extend forward into the space of the future, where our *incognito* possibilities dwell 'in this and as this dispersed Now lives the still dispersed person . . . no eyes are yet ready for it, in part because the depths have too few inhabitants to be other than individual and lonely. That is the true, fruitful incognito' (Bloch, 2006, p. 91). This further links with Bloch's notion that the core, or kernel, of human existence is still *unbecome*; the future is Not-Yet and the shadow of its secret possibilities persistently and beautifully haunt us. Open enough to chaotically invoke the mirage of a territory that is beyond any grounded conception or familiar formula, the pollen-laden breeze of memory gently exhales towards a childhood of the future. Gentle debris of whispered memories strike gossamer trails which shimmer and fascinate in the darkness; with these fleeting and psychically aromatic moments, we are reminded of the mystery of latent possibility. Expressionistic trace moments emit a peculiar ability to re-connect the inner realm and to re-invoke subjective recollections of abandoned aspirations. Refracted shards of bespoken cultural materials provide enchanted entrances or extra-ideological openings, which fuse the threads of chaotic *disappointments* (or, Not-Yet-appointments) with the complexity of a forward-reaching and *hopeful* horizon of the open future (McManus, 2003). Within this framework of culture, memory and possibility, personal stories are afforded space to emerge, *pregnant* with the recognition of the need to remember; this is not a resigned reminiscence, but a powerful future-oriented remembering, with the purpose of 'thinking forward and beyond' the stasis of the past and constraints of the present.[14]

Furthermore, Bloch's essay *The Motif of the Door* in *Traces* (2006), notes that there is a tendency for Expressionistic fracturing's to crack and irrupt into the spaces of beautiful stories (fiction, poetry and fairytales) hued with the fleeting acknowledgement of a nostalgia for a utopian homeland that has Not-Yet been seen.[15] It thus becomes possible to re-conceive of new meanings and new directions towards personally refracted escapes and redemptions. For Bloch, stories that reawaken mysterious traces and incognito possibilities are not just recounted for the routine of the telling; quite the opposite, they become beloved and intimate *favourites*. To think and meditate upon the trace-impacts of such stories, and the ways in which they become beautifully harboured, suggest that there are deep and embedded reasons as to why they nudge, shock and cajole the awakening of astonished secrets. Relative and embryonic utopian gestations pang beyond the teller's narrative to reveal creative morphogeneses of hope. As Bloch notes, 'to hear stories, good ones, poor ones, stories in different tones, from different years, remarkable ones that, when they come to an end, only really come to an end in the stirring [is] a reading of traces every which way' (Bloch, 2006: 6). Beyond the text or thought-image of a story, strange and relative traces become untethered as dynamic point-tracks striating towards as yet chaotically uncharted stories and territories. Beyond the story, in the spaces of incompleteness and homelessness, subjective now-time(s) dynamically recognize the shadows of a 'trace-Mark!' The sputterance of an incognito *something* which can strike and register from little, and sometimes from seemingly insignificant, incidents reveals the empty space that harbours dormant trace-marks and the 'hole' on the future-cusping horizon; as Bloch notes, the 'hole is the Now where we all are, and which the story does not narrate away from . . . the little trap door thus needs to be built on' (ibid.: 72). Personally poignant revelations contain latent utopian promises of something more: aspects of possible future scenarios which have not yet come into being. Amid the unfolding chaos of thwarted opportunities, the mark of the empty space disturbs us, as it 'not only frightens us but stabs and lames us' (ibid.: 97), but it also whispers the jubilee, or restoration for the renegade amnesiacs of youth.

Blochian tactics for a pedagogy of the Not-Yet

Utilizing cultural material of the Blochian framework, irrespective of origin or previous historical readings, can permeate and intertwine with the empty space of contemporary inner worlds; and in so doing it can awaken the trace-promise of a beautiful, deep and distant 'something else'. The awakening of subjective utopian possibilities through moments of astonishment, memory, trace and longing offers fresh pedagogical opportunities: within a Blochian context fairytale stories, films and contemporary reinterpretations of fairytale themes are *vignettes* and operate as murmurs which can nudge and uncover a beautiful unravelling of utopian traces. As part of a Blochian utopian pedagogical tactic, learner collaborators can work with an initial encounter with a piece of culture or cherished story; when presented with space to open up the inception and development of their own subjective *Not-Yet-conscious* and *Not-Yet-become* awakenings and journeys, creative meanderings can be invoked. As part of this open pedagogical approach, learners can move towards independently locating a point (i.e. a theme, event or 'scene') of fascination, a mark, a *trace* of mysterious wonder, from a piece of cultural material that they have personally chosen.

For example, a key and characteristic facet of Ernst Bloch's work is the suggestion that the function and purpose of the fairytale is to refer to a more *colourful*, easier or liberated somewhere else (Bloch, 1993: 168). Within fairytales and other poignant or fantastic stories, a remote realm appears and approaches, one that suggests that circumstances can be better.[16] The enchanted elsewhereness of the fairytale territory means that they can never be thwarted by the practical constraints of the present; as Bloch notes, 'the fairytale narrates a wish-fulfilment that is not bound by its own time and the apparel of its contents' (ibid.: 198). Anything is possible, imprisoned heroines and heroes can climb beanstalks to heaven, spin pure gold thread and mysteriously find their way back home through vast enchanted forests. Even though events never run smoothly, due to troublesome *giants, trolls* and *witches*, there is always a secret trail towards redemption, escape or overcoming.[17] Thus, for Bloch, the hieroglyphic essence of fairytale and even fairytale-esque stories contain potent *utopian* symbolisms which are able to move and inspire people in powerful ways. In realms where captives are made and innocents led astray, courageous and clever heroes set out to save the lost and find their happiness; here, Bloch notes that the fantastic fairytale is 'always clever at overcoming difficulties' (Bloch, 1986: 354). The genuine utopian maxims of fairytale destinations are never only restricted to the past, they re-emerge through myriad contemporary cultural expressions (Bloch, 1993: 200–201).[18] Stemming from the redemption of the lost, lonely, and homeless, these tales emanate traces of revival, of personal release, escape and hope. Bloch suggests that this kind of dawning of magical experience:

[Is] not only fed from the inside, but, appears in intriguing fragments and traces from the outside, 'Long before the inward dimension streams with wishful images, they are stimulated by the fairytale features of nature, particularly by clouds. In them the lofty distance appears for the first time, a wonderful tower-topped foreign land, above our heads. Children think of white cumulus clouds as icy mountains, a Switzerland in the sky; there are castles there too, taller than those on the ground, as tall as castles should be . . . Thus all fairytales in which heavenly blue appears plunge it into vast waters above, and the voyage continues unimpeded to the coast which especially reaches into this imagination: to the morning star. (Bloch, 1986: 360–361)

The pedagogic function of the Blochian fairytale – or other *loose* source of cultural material which can serve as a trace catalyst – can therefore serve as an initial point of hieroglyphic contact from which a subjective trace-awakening and learner collaborator memory project can be contemplated and developed – separately, and uniquely, by each participant. Emergent themes and related connections can then be traced out as part of an Expressionistic cultural montage to open out towards other cultural artefacts. Moving beyond the mark established by the initial story, learners can begin to incorporate (for example) photographs, key scenes from favourite films, poems, pieces of music and songs in order to progress towards more acute utopian expressions. Influenced by the Blochian approach, the trace marks and connections which are uncovered and established during the accumulation of revelations gestate a dawning awareness of thwarted hopes, disappointments, isolation and socio-political dissatisfaction. Creative trace-memory projects, in their openness, can build a momentum towards revelations of previously hidden or latent aches for belonging, hope, victory, utopia and, ultimately, a new future.

A Blochian pedagogy of Expressionistic freedom means that learners can *reach-in* and *reach-out* towards free associations and experience a new-found, personal creativity to begin to express their own connections to the startling irruptions that emerge from within the mysteries of fairytale or other culture-infused stories and material. Unravelling the threads of their trace-awakenings, collaborators can creatively consider what they find there and contemplate the nature of their moments of wonder-arousing astonishment. With the Blochian tactic of Expressionistic recovery, *conceptual* space is created for refracted stories of non-linear Not-Yets to emerge from within remnant traces of memories. Importantly, the parameters of any revelations and articulations of hope and aspirant transformation should be left almost entirely to each collaborator's creative imagination; unnecessary interference from the teacher or lecturer, or other academic authority, should be kept, as much as practicably possible, to an absolute minimum. As Bloch informs us, moments of wonder should not be 'ultimately directed to that which has developed but to a question itself, passing through the world, undeveloped and unanswered' (Bloch, 1970: 7). The Blochian facet of tactics for a utopian pedagogy thus opens up a challenge to move away from traditional (or empirical) forms of academic questioning and the associated technical assessment and expert-driven quantification of student performance. Traditional preformed and rigid questioning in the pursuit of standardized and rigorous assessment, geared towards establishing a calculated measurement, departs from and misses the profundity of the puncture of the moment. Specific, particular and empirical questions are irrelevant where the personal impact of a momentary trace awakening is concerned. For Bloch, empirical questions

> become definite and, finally concrete, their shape is adjusted to suit what is presently available and accessible; therefore it is as if . . . wonder at the rain were really only an interest in the water cycle and nothing else . . . Thus the initial question, a veritable neophyte among questions which still has no idea at all what it really wants to know, can soon forget its own asking, and allow itself to be superseded by the offer of readily available thoughts and answers in the supermarket of things which have become what they are. (Bloch, 1970: 7)

Subjected to the strategies of institutional and bureaucratic control, the creative human spirit becomes hidden and maybe lost or forgotten, but never fully obliterated; its attractant shards, no matter how dim, will continue to glimmer and murmur. As hope-detectives, we can continue to collect and piece together cultural-utopian traces and clues in pursuit of 'that' which has become lost.[19] Peter Thompson summarizes (in the introduction to Bloch's *Atheism in Christianity*) that '[u]sing our own detective skills . . . we must move out of ourselves by throwing off the muzzles that are placed upon us . . . and combine with others to challenge the muzzlers' (Thompson, 2009: xii). Creative explosions of hope bear no resemblance to the dry bones of the architectural encasement of the formulaic and routinized university; bureaucratically stifled, its revolutionary potential is easily hijacked and channelled into safe, enclosed and measurable outcomes. Repeated echoes of past and regurgitated knowledge render the university a spiritless doppelganger, a mediatory temple of stone, enshrining principles of exclusion, surveillance, and regimentation through the complicit expertise of gatekeepers controlling the borders of knowledge. Bloch's part-formed or Not-Yet approach to knowledge recognizes the need for the important legacy or *heritage* of the past, but also, as a dialectic, that the immediacy of Now must also be future-potent. As a possible existence *in-formation*, humanity is *homo absconditus*; Bloch explains that this suggests and articulates an open and creative process whereby 'man has never seen himself face to face' (Bloch, 2009: 195). For Bloch, 'no secret is at the same time so remote and so near as that of *homo absconditus* in the midst of this world which has its own mystery and . . . at [its] deepest level [remains] unsolved, waiting for the answer that will bring identity' (ibid.: 250). Homo absconditus – or the absence, or hollowness of humanity – is the inevitable and creative condition of humanity. As a rebus of incompleteness, the challenge of the future is to revive and refocus an archaeological recovery of hope-traces, so that the now-time of *today* can become re-enthused and re-invigorated with visions and creative, anticipatory stories for a better and transformed tomorrow. The lingering traces and reinterpreted legacy of subjective utopian stories continue to lie 'before us [as] the beginning of that which cannot be outdated – the beginning of the way to the actual, the concrete utopia' (Bloch, 1971: 168). Unsettled debts, latent and incognito possibilities wait 'for us in the future rather than bind us to the past' (Bloch, 2009: 221).

Through personalized and creative processes of exploration, wonder-arousing questions arising from culture-related trace-awakenings have the potential to open out towards unseen or forgotten directions. As such, the freedom of a Blochian-infused Expressionistic tactic, as part of a wider utopian-pedagogy, can prove to be an empowering experience for students. By following the chaotic personal shock-threads of nostalgic trace paths, connections can be re-established between past memories and the unfulfilled or incomplete aspirations embedded within them. Imaginary and metaphoric worlds, intimate spaces of memories of thwarted dreams and unfinished journeys re-manifest as encounters of wishful hopes and possibilities.[20] Within a context of learner collaborator complexity and glimpses of possibility, renewal and redemption can give rise to *a* spirit of adventure. Creative nostalgias evoking astonishments and hope-clues from the past come into contemporary recognition; here the empty space of incomplete futures contain the potential to kick start Not-Yet attained journeys. For Bloch, we all latently gravitate towards the complexion and openness of hope and the incompleteness of the future, with its unfinished and unlimited possibilities. Through the unrevealed mystery of the future, we can gaze beyond the demarcated terrain of established knowledge and the ideologies of the present, learn how to 'sing new songs' and evoke renewed visions of different possibilities. Amid creative narratives and 'stories for tomorrow', collaborators can begin to write themselves into a utopian content that is Not-Yet. A Blochian Expressionistic pedagogical tactic establishes a fluidity, a theoretical transitoriness which affords infinite and multidirectional spaces, opening up the closed empirical mechanics of established knowledge, allowing creative space to mutate outwards and break free from institutional structures that have ossified around familiarity and academic routine. From unexplored, unarticulated reaches, it becomes possible for the proliferation of previously unknown and creative possibilities to emerge.

Notes

1 For specific reference to this point, see Bloch, E. (1988) *Natural Law & Human Dignity* (Trans. Dennis J. Schmidt, the translators notes on page viii); see also Bloch, E. (1991), *Heritage of Our Times* (Cambridge: Polity), especially the chapter on page 191: 'Ludwigshafen – Mannheim'.

2 Ernst Bloch (1998) *Literary Essays*: 339–345, in this text, Bloch's lecture *Kann Hoffnung enttäuscht werden* is translated as 'Can Hope be Disappointed?' whereas Richard R. Roberts (1990) *Hope and its Hieroglyph* translates it both as 'disappointed' and 'frustrated', p. 24; and in Ernst Bloch (1993) *The Utopian Function of Art & Literature*, Zipes and Mecklenburg translate it as 'Can Hope be Disappointed?' p. xxv.

3 Wayne Hudson provides a particularly useful definition of Bloch's notion of the Not-Yet here: "not yet' may mean 'not so far', in which case it refers to the past as well as to the present. Then 'not yet' may mean 'still not', implying that something expected or envisaged in the past has failed to eventuate. Here the stress falls on the past non-occurrence, and in some cases this failure to eventuate in the past increases the likelihood of a future realization. This ambiguity is even stronger in German since *noch-nicht* means both 'still not' and 'not yet'. Or 'not yet' may mean not so far, but 'expected in the future' . . . the utopian 'not yet' . . . implies that something is 'conceivable now but not yet possible' . . . which implies that the end is 'present now in a problematic manner, but still to come in its actual realisation'. Bloch uses all of these senses of 'not yet'" (Hudson, 1982: 20)

4 Ruth Levitas notes the inherent philosophical difficulties in sketching a Blochian utopian analysis of any aspect of culture; however, she also suggests that this difficulty is created more by Bloch's generalized treatment of culture and utopia, rather than the unworkability of his philosophical approach in itself: 'there is very little discussion of the significance of utopia's appearance in particular cultural forms . . . In theory, it would be possible to incorporate much greater consideration of the way in which particular forms provide the vehicle for the utopian function

in different historical circumstances. Although the task is more than daunting, the theoretical possibility of such explorations is one of the strengths of Bloch's approach' (Levitas, 2011: 117).

5 Of course, such an audacious claim has to be, and has been, criticized. Jack Zipes poses an articulate challenge to Bloch's problematic avoidance of taxonomic detail and equal lack of historical justification as part of his treatment of utopia (Zipes, 2002: 154–155). Despite this, Zipes proposes that Bloch's creative and shifting concepts, while problematic, should not be rejected, as they contain many unworked-through possibilities. Therefore, thinking and writing in a *Blochian* way, not only in relation to utopia and culture but also in relation to hopeful, creative learning, opens up a liberating and potentially productive terrain.

6 The concluding chapter to this work *Elpeidetics: Hopeful Visions?* establishes and develops these concepts and Blochian ideas in more detail.

7 Bloch's fluid, non-specific usage of the category of 'utopia' (as a form, and therefore Not-Yet materialized 'matter') has an affinity with the Aristotelian approach to matter, form and possibility. As Werner Heisenberg notes in *Physics and Philosophy*, within the Aristotelian approach: 'Matter is in itself not a reality but only a possibility, a 'potentia'; it exists only by means of the form. In the natural process the 'essence', as Aristotle calls it, passes over from mere possibility through form into actuality. The matter of Aristotle is certainly not like a specific matter like water or air, nor is it simple empty space; it is a kind of indefinite corporeal substratum, embodying the possibility of passing over into actuality by means of the form' (Heisenberg, 2000: 97). Blochian utopia is therefore best understood as a creative fusion of the Aristotelian approach to the potential (or potentia) associated with form and matter and Thomas More's definition of 'utopia' (no-placia). With Bloch, utopia is a Not-Yet-place, a future place whose creative building blocks of 'matter' is in a permanent state of unfulfilled potential.

8 Ernst Bloch (1977) 'Nonsynchronism and the Obligation to Its Dialectics', *New German Critique*, Spring 1977, issue 11, p. 31; Ernst Bloch (1976) 'Dialectics and Hope', *New German Critique*, Fall 1976, issue 9, pp. 6–8; Douglas Kellner and Harry O'Hara (1976) 'Utopia and Marxism in Ernst Bloch', *New German Critique*, Fall 1976, issue 9, pp. 21–25.

9 See also Levitas, R. and Sargisson, L. (2003) *Utopia in Dark Times*. In R. Baccolini and T. Moylan (Eds), *Dark Horizons: Science Fiction & the Dystopian Imagination* (Routledge). Collectively, Bloch's work considers that more exists in sentimental cultural works embraced by proletarian masses than mere ideological control. This was something that the mainstream Left, against Bloch's warnings, were far too ready to ignore (Bloch, 1993: xiii). For Bloch, there was a *deep* underlying utopian principle that gave rise to the intensively nostalgic needs of (in particular) the lower classes; a need or longing that contained traces of hope for something more

than Marxian-tinged and crude ideologico-political explanations could ever hope to account for (Rabinbach, 1977: 11). Bloch also warned the wider Left about the power of dark and right-wing forces (i.e. Nazism) inhabiting and hijacking the emotive spaces of culture, heritage and alternative futures.

10 Bloch would refer to this particular fleeting appearance of personal utopian material as *Vor-Schein*: Pre-appearance or anticipatory illumination. See Berghahn, K. L. (1997) 'A View through the Red Window: Ernst Bloch's *Spuren*', in J. O. Daniel and T. Moylan (Eds), *Not Yet: Reconsidering Ernst Bloch* (London: Verso), p. 212.

11 Synchronism, non-synchronism and the multi-dimensionality of the Blochian dialectic (in relation to the elasticity of space-time) is discussed by Bloch in his *Heritage of Our Times* (Bloch, 1991); and also Rainer E. Zimmermann (Zimmermann, 2009).

12 Taken from Bloch's essay 'Expressionism, Seen Now (1937)' in *Heritage of Our Times* (pp. 234–240).

13 See Jack Zipes comments in the introductory section of *The Utopian Function of Art & Literature*.

14 Vincent Geoghegan (1997) 'Remembering the Future', in Jamie Daniel Owen and Tom Moylan (Eds), *Not Yet: Reconsidering Ernst Bloch* (Verso); see also Bloch, E. (1998) *Literary Essays*, trans. A. Joron et al. (Stanford University Press). Section entitled 'Images of Déjà vu', pp. 200–206; see also Landman, M. (1975) 'Talking with Ernst Bloch: Korcula 1968', *Telos*, No. 25.

15 Bloch, E. (1986) *The Principle of Hope*, Vol. III (Blackwell), p. 1376.

16 Bloch notes in relation to *Disney* reinterpretations of traditional fairytale stories and themes: 'Walt Disney's fairytale films revive elements of the old fairytale without making them incomprehensible to the viewers. Quite the contrary. The favourably disposed viewers think about a great deal. They think about almost everything in their lives. They, too, want to fly. They, too, want to escape the ogre. They, too, want to transcend the clouds and have a place in the sun' (Bloch, 1993: 163–164).

17 In relation to this, Bloch suggests that the evocative metaphors associated with fantastic fairytale imagery sends 'us off on a voyage' (Bloch, 1986: 362).

18 Bloch refers to the 'modernisation' of the fairytale in relation to novels, stories and plays associated with Cocteau (Orpheus and Eurydice), Molnar (The Guardsman, and The Wolf) and Verne's (The Journey to the Middle of the Earth and The Journey to the Moon) (Bloch, 1993:200).

19 Ernst Bloch *Atheism in Christianity: The Religion of the Exodus and the Kingdom* (London: Verso, 2009), p. 62. See also Ernst Bloch 'A Philosophical View of the Detective Novel'. In *The Utopian Function of Art & Literature*(Boston: MIT Press, 1998), 245–264.

20 Vince Geoghegan's comments are pertinent here, as he notes that 'the term 'remembering the future' becomes immediately appropriate. My past memories

will have a constitutive role in the forging of my present and future perceptions . . . I enter the future with a body of assumptions and preoccupations located in memory. The infinite range of possible futures is winnowed down to my possible futures through this interactive process. In this sense I can be said to be 'remembering the future" (Geoghegan, 1997:17–18).

3

Roland Barthes: Punctum! The Death of the Author

Roland Barthes

Roland Barthes was born in Cherbourg, Normandy, on 12 November 1915 and died aged 65 on 25 March 1980 (exactly one month after being accidentally struck by a laundry truck while walking home through the streets of Paris). During the late 1930s to the late 1940s Barthes studied at the University of Paris, and over the next two decades he moved on to a number of academic positions at French institutions. Throughout the ascendency of his academic career, he established himself as a high-profile literary critic and a conceptually innovative social theorist; the influence and scope of his work attained a particular prominence during and beyond the 1960s. Barthes reached the zenith of his career in 1977 when he was elected to the position of *chair of Sémiologie Littéraire* at the Collège de France.

In his first book *Le degré zéro de l'écriture* (1953), an essay-based literary manifesto – translated into English in 1970 as *Writing Degree Zero* by Annette Lavers and Colin Smith – Barthes started to examine the fluidity and instability of language. With this work, Barthes laid out a number of ideas and conceptual foundations which were to continue to emerge and morph as part of his later essays and explorations: themes such as the *productive* misinterpretation of text, the arbitrariness of meaning, and the unpredictable chaos of personal association (especially in relation to culture).[1] His later books: *Mythologies* (1957), *Critical Essays* (1964), and *The Eiffel Tower and Other Mythologies* (1964), started to focus and develop the meandering diversification of these themes in relation to everyday life. With snappy and accessible little essays, Barthes's analyses ranged across the minutiae of everyday activities and routines as diverse as advertising, fashion, plastic, toys, and wrestling. And yet, across the eclectic oeuvre of his work, a potent and radical thread was to remain: the continuous challenge (and threat) to academic orthodoxies, traditions, and disciplinary constraints.

By the late 1960s, Barthes influence and reputation was effectively established; it was during this period that he was to write one of his most provocative and celebrated essay's *The Death of the Author* (*La mort de l'auteur*, 1967). With this influential and transitional piece, Barthes asserted that text, meaning and inter-pretation, and the fluidity of language need to be liberated totally from the con-strictive confines and singularity of 'the' *author*. Ten years later (the same year of his appointment as chair of *Sémiologie Littéraire*), Barthes's mother, aged 85, died; they had stayed and lived together for sixty years. The impact and intensity of this loss prompted him to write what was to become his last major work, an accessible little book entitled *Camera Lucida* (*La Chambre claire*, 1980). Partly an extended essay on the nature of photography, this work was also an elegiac and personal exploration of the legacy and personal impact of the collected fam-ily photographs of his mother.

The Death of the Author

The liberating power of Barthes's essay *The Death of the Author* (1989d) lies in the focus of his argument that perceptions and assumptions surrounding the affiliations and power of the modern author are not only fallacious but, where knowledge is concerned, exclusive and problematic. For Barthes, in the midst of the array of such associations, the meaning of *the text* 'in contemporary culture is tyrannically centred on . . . [the author's] person, his history, his tastes, his passions' (Barthes, 1989d: 50). For Barthes, the idea that the author is capable of somehow inseminating a universal meaning into a Gordian knot of criss-crossing letters, words, and ideas is vacuous, and perpetuates a reified and mythic construction of a 'false god'. He probes and explodes the simplistic notion that the brooding shell of a text (and the permeative legacy of *the* authored work) somehow incubates and promulgates an internal coherence; for Barthes, divin-ing the ubiquitous power and presence of the author through an ordered and typeset sequence of hieroglyphic shapes is fetishistic and empty. With this, the whole notion of stability and textual *definity* is brought skilfully and persuasively into question.

Through surreptitious and historical default, the author has become the entity who not only contains but also dominates the associative domain of the formulated work. In tandem with this, the intricate architecture of institutional ownership, and its associated sanctification of knowledge through publishing mechanisms, generates a seamed and stratified separation; the corroborative impact of such distanciation perpetuates the flow and momentum of a mono-directional vehicle, funnelling and filtering the shape and flow of words and images. Infiltrated and incarcerated, the work becomes owned, bound, copy-righted, and stifled. Such corpocracy further consolidates the assumption that the published and packaged text expresses 'the voice of one and the same person, the author' confiding in us (ibid.: 50). In *Death of the Author* Barthes starts to challenge and deconstruct these assumptions; he asserts that such an artificial and withering scaffold cannot support or contain the internal coherence of *a* singular and unified textual meaning in this way. For Barthes the principal, or more appropriately the 'initial', author assembles a preliminary sequence of tex-tual characters whose amniotic utterances can never be universally known. The site of a stationary text does not therefore reveal the author but instead opens up a gateway to the chaotic and dynamic realm of associations harboured within the *reader*; for Barthes, the reader (or the receptor) is the space where we find the inscriptions of 'all the citations out of which a writing is made; the unity of a text is not in its origin but in its destination' (ibid.: 54). The primordial function of the author then is to act as, or *perform* the function of, a catalytic agitator whose accidental source of creative serendipity ferments instigative activities and mul-tilinear torrents of fluidity.

As a site of abstracted textual arrest, a literary source becomes resituated as an *ante rem* of an unknown *language*; it consists of a multitude of different times, multiple traces, and signs. In the latency of its potential, it is a polyrhyth-mic pulse of unknown and unscripted futures, as opposed to the hiding place of a secret and concealed author (ibid.: 50). Ripe for the freedom of subjective traces to emerge, the text becomes a space of expressive fecundity and opens up a swirling non-reductive gap of moments between the author and the reader. With the Barthesean destabilization of the author, the ground and stasis of the modern text disaggregates; through the shifting prism of multimodal readings 'the author absents himself from [the text] at every level' (ibid.: 51–52); here 'the author enters into his own death' (ibid.: 49). The text ceases to release a single authoritative meaning and instead proliferates a multi-dimensional aura, a constellation of contested meanings, 'a fabric of quotations, resulting from a thousand sources of culture' (ibid.: 52–53). With the rupture and separation of the text between the author and the reader, an apparition of a spectral, or expres-sive, space reveals the space of the receptor or, as Barthes terms, the *Scriptor*. For Barthes, the Scriptor's voice and embryonic writing is 'borne by a pure gesture of inscription . . . a field without origin' (ibid.: 52). Released from the closed down and delimiting ground of the Author-*itarian* and predestined work, the artefact of the text is liberated for the Scriptor to inhabit afresh. Each time that a text is encountered, a new and uncharted *Scriptor* emerges, as for Barthes 'there is no time other than that of the speech-act and every text is written eternally *here* and *now*' (ibid.: 52).

Warding the anarchistic tendencies of knowledge

Taking the argument to a *logical* extreme, in his essay *Writers, Intellectuals, Teachers*, Barthes asks the following questions, 'Once the text [is] opened to plurality, why stop? Why refuse to take polysemy to the point of asemy?' (Barthes, 1989a: 324). These questions and the wider implications of the Barthesean argument bring the micro-political practices of the HE lecturer into focus. The categorization and delivery of knowledge, the protocol and format of knowledge, and the scenario of the teaching-based lecture are inevitably impacted by the ramifications of his analysis. As Barthes notes:

> The choice is grim: conscientious functionary or free artist, the teacher escapes neither the theatre of speech nor the Law staged within it: for the Law is produced, not in what he says, but in the fact that he speaks at all. In order to subvert the Law (and not simply to get around it), he would have to dismantle all vocal delivery, the speed and rhythm of words, until he achieved an altogether different intelligibility – or else not speak at all; but then he would be back in other roles: either that of the great silent mind heavy with experience and reserve, or that of the militant who in the name of praxis dismisses all discourse as trivial. (Ibid.: 311)

As a result, teaching within the HE context still generally adheres to quite typical pedagogical scenarios: the *expert* academic ejaculating a tightly surveilled and technically confined canon of knowledge on to a selected and cloistered audience of spongiform minds. *Kettled* subordinates penned into disciplinary silos, this *unidirectionary* containment is, more often than not, aligned with a closely policed consummation: the churning out of perfunctory and *safe* emulatory offerings in the form of the routine regurgitation of essays. Such automata is further engineered through the confines of forensically structured and prescribed questions aligned with expected writing styles, compulsory and expected references and contents, safe and predictable structures, and so on. Concise and technical questioning in this way further consolidates the complicit 'policing' function of the teacher/academic, as 'the interpellated subject must pretend to answer the letter of the question, not its 'address'. So a game is set up . . . the game demands a response to the content, not to the way that content is framed' (ibid.: 319). In a contemporary sense, the *academic-as-warder* scenario is further reinforced through the generation and application of legalistic and standard-izing *learning outcomes*, themselves clothed with the dense rigidities and spe-cificities of learning objectives. Any scope for radical, passionate, and creative endeavour is not only stifled but also rendered redundant and obsolete.

The Barthesean approach to text, collaborative meaning, and writing is more than a call for practitioners to seek creative alternatives, it is *political*; it chal-lenges and undermines the delimiting and exclusionary hierarchies, concentric granularities, and building blocks upon which HE continues to be built. As such, for Barthes '[t]he text is ([or] should be) that uninhibited person who shows his behind to the *Political Father*' (Barthes, 1975: 53). The radical practice of reading, interpreting, and writing through Barthesean principles contains and supposes renewable and active-political exercises, pliable tactics for the trans-gression and usurpation of imposed authority. The protective membranes, terminal knowledge, and privileged entitlement that cosset and surround the citadel of the academy are laid bare; with Barthes, fissures and footholds appear within the monolith of institutional knowledge, along with the potential to resuscitate possibilities of constructive hijack in the cultural-monogamy of its stultified environment.

In *The Rustle of Language*, Barthes reveals a facet of his own persona as educa-tor and contemplates whether he speaks in the name of 'a function? Of a body of knowledge? Of an experience? What do I represent? A scientific capacity? An institution? A service?' (Barthes, 1989a: 320). He continues by suggesting that anyone speaking in a formalized teaching situation must be (or, must become) conscious of the performative, staging, and exclusionary act of this form of com-munication; either 'the speaker chooses the role of Authority in all good faith . . . Or else the speaker is hampered by the Law which his speech will introduce into what he wants to say' (ibid.: 310). For Barthes, the traditional format of teaching is unavoidably divisive and entrenched within a political crisis, the dichotomous opposition between the unidirectionary speech act and the creative process of the reception of an idea, and the creative writing of the subjective consequences of its impact.

Within the university, conventional modes of disciplinary exposition adhere to stagnant and functionary laws; this legalism and regulation have 'always been a happy hunting ground for study in schools' (Barthes, 1970: 69). Institutional traditions, technical, colourless, and mundane writing, serve to suck the life, desire, and pleasure out of thinking; ransacked, learners are stripped of serendipitous discovery and expressive, hopeful writing. Coldly *inducted* to the formulaic constraints of technical writing, academic disciple-learners develop mechanical habits 'in the very place where freedom existed, a network of set forms hem in more and more the pristine freshness of discourse, a mode of writing appears afresh in lieu of an indefinite language' (ibid.: 78). The control and punitive regulation associated with institutionalized forms of writing and content produce a secondary effect, that of psychological order; banisters of acceptability and conformity operate on both knowledge and minds. Subjected to being processed by the powerful and shaping functions of the university, students become 'frustrated of speech; frustrated but not deprived: the student has the use of language; language is not unknown to him, he is not (or is no longer) afraid of it; the problem [is] to assume its power, its active use' (Barthes, 1989g: 150–151). In this way, once the technical empire of rules, of style and content, becomes drilled and regimented – replete with academic laws and institutional bylaws – sanctioned essayistic offerings are rendered sanitized, uniform, and desensitized. However, if writing and discovery were to emerge 'according to the subject's desire – it might constitute a very positive practice of expression . . . from the scriptor's phantasmatics, and not from a uniform and reductive law' (Barthes, 1989c: 44). Within this, Barthes suggests that the *unacceptability* of something as simple as the spelling mistake can be developed in to a political form of creative transgression (ibid.: 45). This is a seemingly obvious and simplistic point, but in fact it belies a powerful challenge to uncritical conformity and serves as a reminder that the deferential silence between 'the pleasure of the text and the institutions of the text' (Barthes, 1975: 60) is far from insurmountable. There are occasions where 'we encounter particularly 'happy' spelling mistakes – as if the Scriptor were obeying not academic law but a mysterious commandment that comes to him from his own history – perhaps even from his own body?' (Barthes, 1989c: 45). This is a politicized reminder that the parameters of the normative academic relationship between institutionally sanctioned experts and the subservient recipients of pre-packaged knowledge contain the constant and primed threat of subjective *depth-charges*. The fluidity and instability of language and association harbours a political potency where relational acquiescences, throughout the academy, can be tackled and actively shaped through the non-denominational writings of Scriptors. The fragile rigidity of brittle and porous academic rules can start to be challenged and transgressed, and the authentic process of writing *as a Scriptor* can begin to manifest as 'language *which was not foreseen*' (Barthes, 1989h: 174).

The rustle of language: Dynamic autonomy

Barthes recognizes that narrative *Scriptings* as exploratory deviances require a 'laxism' not only on the part of the institution but also within the ranks of *academic-warders* who, as commissioned representatives, are complicit in safe-guarding and upholding the principles and rules of its bureaucracy. As such, pro-dynamic practitioners who wish to embrace and pursue the muffled elements of *pro-Scriptive* and democratic learning engagement – aspects discarded by the formal practices of the university (Barthes, 1989d: 55) – must start to challenge the sham of the status quo and actively seek out alternative tactics and practices. In this sense, Barthes offers some radical and flexible tactics. However, among the academic challenges posed by the Barthesean framework is the need for individual academics and practitioners to begin to adjust pedagogical practices and expectations so as to promote and, importantly, accommodate refracted learner writings. As part of the Barthesean approach to developing pedagogical tactics, it is essential that learner collaborators are afforded the freedom to script bespoke offerings, Expressionistic explorations which may also contain and actively incorporate 'ignorances' and 'blunders'; for Barthes, these should no longer be perceived 'as aberrations or debilities' (Barthes, 1989c: 45). Incorporating the Barthesean notion of *skidding* – or 'reinterpretive skids' – the embracing of such an approach could serve to start halting the perpetuation of pupilistic prototypes, automata created in the lecturer's *own image*. In this sense, for Barthes, it is essential to remember that, as a teacher

> I speak, endlessly for and before someone who does not speak. I am the one who says I (the detours of one or we, of the impersonal sentence, are insignificant), I am the one who, under the cover of an exposition (of something known), proposes a discourse, without ever knowing how it is received, so that I can never have the reassurance of a definitive (even if damaging) image which might constitute me. (Barthes, 1989a: 12–13)

Beyond the horizon of the formal speech delivered by the teacher, 'a thousand adventures happen to it, its origin becomes confused' (ibid.: 323); connecting this to the chaotic and swirling associations of learner collaborators as recipient-Scriptors, as soon as the lecturer finishes speaking, the confines of any prescheduled narrative disintegrates and falls away to reveal a 'vertigo of the image' (ibid.: 321). In recognition of the ungrounded and meandering connections emergent within the worlds of learner-Scriptors, pro-dynamic practitioners must start to actively manoeuvre within and tactically adapt the stultifying rules of traditional academic processes so that, from within the fractured shard of a broken sentence, a *negligible trifle* can give birth to 'a whole discourse of memory and . . . reverberation' (Barthes, 1978: 200). Within the fractured interiority of a Scriptor, the minutiae of trace disturbances contain the kernel of a creative tangent, a latent and perpendicular direction which, in turn, is capable of shattering the enclosed and wasteful sphere of academic *chaff*. Through the openness of such provocation, personal and personalized driftings can emerge through 'language's illusions, seductions, and intimidations' (Barthes, 1975: 18). Through the possibility and revelation of subjective woundings or seductions, creative arrays of alternative and adventurous readings are afforded room to speak. The emergence of such pro-dynamic practices and tactics should therefore seek ways to ensure that serendipitous traces are afforded space to birth and gestate in the realms of the reader (Barthes, 1989b: 40–41). Through undisclosed and jubilatory moments, readers, as Scriptors, can retrace and revive their latencies and passions to 'dream, to remember, to understand' (Barthes, 1989c: 45). With moments of powerful revelation, emergent writings can gradually reorient towards the experience and presence of *freedom* (Barthes, 1970: 16). Through Proustian-esque moments, or what might be better referred to, in Barthesean terms, as 'experiments in rustling' (Barthes, 1989f: 78), ungrounded expositional shards of expressive and collaborative sculptings can take shape. Navigating from 'the threat of a secret' (Barthes, 1970: 20), *Scripted* ideas can develop from thought-seeds in non-linear ways. The opening up of dynamic spaces and writing opportunities in this way means that *Scriptors* can set out to grasp for a mysterious *something*, trans-audible rustles which reverberate from beyond the *formulary* of academic language. Within this context of Barthesean pedagogical tactics, it is one thing to '*talk*' of the potential of liberating the meandering and creative writings from uninhibited *Scriptors*; but it is quite another to offer actual pedagogical tactics as flexible husks, as practical techniques to be offered in ways that are open enough to be repurposed and implemented across various academic contexts. Hence, the chapter will now move to unpick and explore some culture-specific *tactics-of-freedom* from within the wider terrain of Barthes's work: incorporating the specific cultural phenomenon of photography and film.

Photograph: The studium and punctum

In *Camera Lucida* (2000), Barthes establishes an insightful and provoking analysis of the 'experience' of photographs; as part of this, he questions and explores *what we do* with, and *how we receive*, photographic images, noting that the production and experience of a photographic artefact involves the following three aspects: 'The *Operator* is the Photographer. The *Spectator* is ourselves, all of us who glance through collections . . . And the person or thing photographed is the target, the referent' (Barthes, 2000: 9). Within the spectra of Barthes's triadic schema, the particular spectrum of the spectator, and the subjective experience of the photograph, is teased out and explored in evocative and enlightening detail. Throughout each respective life course, a *spectator* gazes upon an almost infinite range of images, encountering them in all kinds of situations and contexts, such as in magazines and newspapers, but also in other myriad sites and sources – such as nostalgic porings over personal collections of photographs. Barthes suggests that the purposeful viewing of an image (or several images), or indeed an accidental and serendipitous glance at a photograph, offers moments and experiences which are characterized by very different impacts and consequences. Within this, the Barthesean spectator is subject to a bifurcation effect where the visual experience is separated by two related, though fundamentally different, responses and activities. On one hand, the spectator can be subject to a generalized and *common* experience; this *common* response to the reading of an image is a rational, *intellectual*, and possibly even a shared and cogent experience. However, on the opposing strand of the arc, Barthes highlights a very different type of spectator-encounter, the irruption of an unspecified moment, one which is invariably subjective, deeply intense, and occasionally *moving*. For Barthes, this *special* type of subjective impact is an unpredictable and chaotic shred of personal chance; such a manifestation registers initially as a tiny jubilation or 'an internal agitation, an excitement, like something unspeakable which wants to be spoken' (ibid.: 19).

To operationalize and elaborate his analysis of the two very different spectator experiences, Barthes incorporates two Latin terms: *Studium* and *Punctum*. He defines a studium-based photographic encounter as the rational type of image-based experience; with this, the spectator appreciation of an image is prompted by a general interest, a kind of cultural or intellectual reading of the photograph. Through 'a certain kind of training' (ibid.: 25), this type of encounter produces an average or standardizing effect. And to the other, more subjective, intense, and emotionally poignant experience, Barthes applies the term *punctum*. Juxtapositional to, and quite distinct from, studium, a punctum-inducing effect refers to an intense and momentary elicitation of a personal mystery; its impact generates an inner disturbance which, as Barthes attests, 'affects me at a depth and according to roots which I do not know' (ibid.: 38). The unavoidable and absolute subjectivity associated with the *punctumic* experience means that any subsequent attempt to analyse and interpret it is, 'in a certain fashion, to *give myself up*' (ibid.: 43).

Hence, the studium, or the rational and *lucid* appreciation of the photograph, means that the spectator is aware of (or certainly can become aware of) the photographer's intentions. Inevitably, the photographer captures a snapshot of visual traces; the action of isolating a moment in time encapsulates a communicable message of location, culture, and fashion, all of which can be divined and intellectualized from the social signs embedded within its context. For Barthes, the studium effect and the spectator relationship is very much associated with 'the photographer's myths in the photograph, fraternizing with them but not quite believing in them . . . And I, the *spectator*, I recognize them with more or less pleasure . . . (which is never my delight or my pain)' (ibid.: 28). With studium-*based* photographic encounters, we invoke 'the rational intermediary of an ethical and political culture' (ibid.: 26); this means that a spectator can choose to prefer, *like* or even dislike, an image, but never to lose intellectual control over the image and fall in *love* with it. Ultimately, and importantly, a rationalized understanding is brought to the context and details of the image. The studium effect is therefore, by far, the most common and likely spectator encounter; in a mundane sense, the studium emerges from the routinized and *default* form of everyday discourse where we interpret photographic images 'as political testimony or enjoy them as good historical scenes' (ibid.: 26), or we enjoy and appreciate their aesthetic qualities.

Situated against the context of the studium, of the routinized perusal of selected images, of filtered expectations and hidden cultural echelons of editorial regimes, we can still be shocked by a disruptive discovery; a moment that pierces from amidst the banality of the studious order. For Barthes, the aura of this 'glum desert' of photographic stability continues to be an image-littered terrain, with the constant potential for shards and unpredictable image-traces to break through as 'an internal agitation, an excitement which animates me' (ibid.: 20). The disruptive essence of the punctum disturbs the studium, 'for *punctum* is also: sting, speck, cut, little hole-and also a cast of the dice. A photograph's *punctum* is that accident which pricks me (but also bruises me, is poignant to me)' (ibid.: 26–27). The punctum is an inner experience which suddenly breaks beyond, or ventures deeper than the *studium*. The unique esotericism of the punctum means that it cannot be studied or sought out by rational investigation or traditional academic means; instead, it *arises* from the scene of the image and shoots out of it like an arrow. As Barthes notes, it is not 'possible to establish any kind of empirical measurement or rule of connection between the *studium* and the *punctum* (when it happens to be there). It is simply a co-presence – the punctum happens, quite simply, when it happens' (ibid.: 42). The inability to objectively categorize or stabilize the likelihood and experience of the punctum in relation to a standardized scheme or form exposes its fluidity and impact as 'a good symptom of disturbance' (ibid.: 51); it reveals the uneasiness of any punctumic articulation as being 'torn between two languages, one expressive, the other critical' (ibid.: 8).

In effect, the subjective experience of the punctum produces a consequence, which extends well beyond the capabilities of traditional academic writing and established sensibilities. A punctumic irritant – an abstracted detail from within an image – is a catalyst which can proliferate a surge of memories, experiences, and associations within a sea of swirling and subjective contexts. It is an ungrounded and chaotic principle of disorder; its initial spark, or puncture, germinates a creative and expressive journey of interpretive wandering. As Barthes suggests, in order to effectively *see* and experience the unfolding of a punctumic journey, 'the *punctum* should be revealed only after the fact, when the photograph is no longer in front of me and I think back on it . . . in order to see a photograph well, it is best to look away or close your eyes' (ibid.: 53). As such, the subjective recovery of the mystery of the image 'is achieved only in a state, an effort, of silence (shutting your eyes is to make the image speak in silence)' (ibid.: 55). Whereas the studium leads outwards, to a lexical terrain of trans-subjective familiarity, the enigmatic and personal territory of the punctum means that any emergent story or narrative is unavoidably expressive and capricious. Hence, the implosive essence of a punctumic experience can only be revealed through an exposition of freedom 'to bear me forward to a utopian time, or to carry me back to somewhere in myself' (ibid.: 40); the meanderings of any liberated *Scriptors* therefore requires a poetic, expressionistic, and anecdotal approach to writing. With this, Barthes offers a poignant example of his own punctumic encounter in relation to the impact of his mother's death. He describes the mourning-fuelled pursuit of a particular photograph, one to keep and cherish as a keepsake. Rummaging through various collected and accumulated photographs, Barthes recounts the emotional and punctumic search for a secret image, a personal hieroglyph harbouring the spirit, memory and love of his mother:

> There I was, alone in the apartment where she had died, looking at these pictures of my mother, one by one under the lamp, gradually moving back in time with her looking for the truth of the face I had loved. And I found it. The photograph was very old. The corners were blunted from having been pasted into an album, the sepia print had faded, and the picture just managed to show two children standing together at the end of a little wooden bridge in a glassed-in conservatory, what was called a Winter Garden in those days . . . I studied the little girl and at last rediscovered my mother. The distinctness of her face, the naive attitude of her hands, the place she had docilely taken without either showing or hiding herself, and finally her expression . . . (I cannot reproduce the Winter Garden Photograph. It exists only for me. For you, it would be nothing but an indifferent picture, one of the thousand manifestations of the 'ordinary'; it cannot in any way constitute the visible object of a science; it cannot establish an objectivity, in the positive sense of the term; at most it would interest your *studium:* period, clothes, photogeny; but in it, for you, no wound). (Ibid.: 67–73)

Arguably, the Barthesean notion of the punctum, and the punctumic experience, has the potential to be creatively adapted beyond the specific context of the photograph. Invoking the punctum as an informal and expressionistic mechanism, learner collaborators as *Scriptors* can be invited to explore, contemplate, and expedite thoughts, connections, and associations in relation to punctumic (versus *studious*) experiences – from among an eclectic array of memories and cultural encounters. For example, Victor Burgin (2006) effectively elaborates and extends Barthes's concept of the punctum beyond the context of the photograph; he develops it in relation to an unruly and personalized experience of memory and filmic fragments. As Burgin notes, with the punctum '[w]e may bring much the same distinction to other images from the everyday environment' (Burgin, 2006: 66). Burgin candidly explores his personal repertoire of fractured images and recurrent scenes from within the memorial archive of his favourite films. As an eclectic array of 'involuntary associations, [which] are often provoked by external events' (ibid.: 17), his filmic shards and connections are thematically chaotic and chronologically unrelated. Montages of bespoken image-sequences leap up and offer characters and fragments in transformative ways; he notes that 'If I search further in my memory of childhood I can bring to mind other types of images from films' (ibid.: 17).

For Burgin, a recollected punctumic image from the memorial legacy of a particular film can act as a catalyst, in turn prompting further connections and associations to other filmic fragments, which might otherwise have slumbered in a trove of scattered favourites. Over time, the coherence of the respective narratives drop away, and so the mysterious peculiarity of any immediate or subsequent punctumic revelations generates and leads towards 'a kind of fascinated comprehension before the hybrid object they have become' (ibid.: 59). As Burgin notes, '[c]onsciousnesses may be synchronised in a shared moment of viewing, but the film *we* saw is never the film *I* remember' (ibid.: 110). The unique and labyrinthine synapses that spark as a consequence of the initial filmic punctum generate a narrative pathway of collective unknowability. The meaning and emerging sense of the narrative journey uncover a hidden region of subjective and utopian cartography.

Barthes and film: The third meaning

This argument strikes a useful affinity with another of Barthes's essays in *Image, Music, Text* (1977), an intriguing little offering entitled *The Third Meaning: Research notes on some Eisenstein stills*. In characteristic prototypic fashion, Barthes defines and explores three separate types of meaning to be associated with the shared (and also the personal) experience of film. Focusing on an examination of a series of stills from the Sergei Eisenstein films *Ivan the Terrible* and *Battleship Potemkin* – and, with more than a passing affinity with the conceptual principles established as part of *Camera Lucida* – Barthes sketches his combination of analytical and theoretical principles.[2] The concepts that Barthes builds to explore the rational and personal encounters with his films, of course, say something about his films of choice; however, they are also open enough to shift filmic and experiential contexts, and so can be flexibly adapted by any subsequent viewer (or conceptual participant). The majority of Barthes's *Third Meaning* essay focuses on the area of serendipitous and, as he terms, *obtuse* area of personal meaning. As Barthes argues, the *third* meanings associated with the film-stills of his choice emerge beyond (and in addition to) the first two types of social and rationalized meanings, those of the *informational* and the *symbolic*. Barthes asserts that the *strangeness* and bespokenness of the third meaning, with its erratic and obstinate demeanour, means that 'I do not know what its signified is, at least I am unable to give it a name, but I can see clearly the traits, the signifying accidents of which this – consequently incomplete – sign is composed'

(Barthes, 1977: 53). In any given film-still, all three meanings are always present and 'layered as in geologic sediment', but in the third meaning the play of meaning escapes language and opens up to infinity.³

Barthes's first type of filmic meaning, that of the *informational*, refers to the intelligible realm of information which is contained and detailed within the film; this area of direct and purposeful meaning operates on a general and shared level of experience. For example, certain details within the film which may incorporate 'the costumes, the characters, their relations' (ibid.: 51). As such, these are prompts and characteristics which can be trans-personally encountered and deduced; these details constitute the imagery and immediate perception of the (indeed, any) narrative context of the film. The second type of meaning, the *symbolic*, is also associated with the shared or social aspects and readings of the film, but in some respects its symbolic meanings are slightly less tangible than the informational; for example, Barthes notes that in *Ivan the Terrible* '[t]here is the referential symbolism: the imperial ritual of baptism by gold. Then there is the diagetic symbolism: the theme of gold, of wealth' (ibid.: 51). Finally, Barthes suggests that there is a historical realm of symbolism 'in a manner even more widely embracing than the previous ones' (ibid.: 52), which touches upon and communicates differences and transitions between societal epochs.

Again, with comparisons and similarities to the dichotomy of the *studium* and the *punctum* – as explored in *Camera Lucida* – the informational and symbolic meanings are intellectual, rational, and 'obvious,' whereas the third meaning is 'obtuse'; with a scope and remit which is 'greater than the pure, upright, secant, legal perpendicular of the narrative, it seems to open the field of meaning totally, that is infinitely' (ibid.: 55). The *third meaning* of the abstracted detail of the film-still 'offers us the *inside* of the fragment' (ibid.: 67).⁴ As an obtuse and intriguing fragment, it has nothing to say of *ideology*, of the *auteur*, or of the history and industrial context of the artefact. Quite the opposite, it is a supplementary cipher which can trigger the process of free association and creativity. Within this context, the *third meaning* of the film-still is not a superficially extracted artifice amputated from the intact and coherent body of the film; it is an ethereal and potent trace which, when abstracted, can trigger an interiority of secret possibilities, the still 'is the fragment of a second text *whose existence never exceeds the fragment*' (ibid.: 67).

The emergence of a *third meaning*, and the communication of its discovery, is not schematically reducible, it opens an aperture to reveal a counternarrative. The scripted story which emerges from the surreptitious nudge and legacy of the filmic image subverts the structural meanings and narrative intentions purposefully sculpted into the film by its architects; for this reason, the third meaning in the film is 'the representation which cannot be represented' (ibid.: 64). The explosive excess of the obtuse or third meaning means that an infinity of subjective associations can emerge and meander from the artefact; the catalytic and subjective uncertainty means that it has something to do with disguise and compels the expressionistic tendencies of liberated Scriptors to engage in an interrogative reading. As such, for Barthes, 'the obtuse meaning is not situated structurally, a semantologist would not agree as to its objective existence' (ibid.: 60). Therefore, any identification or utterance of a *third meaning* is rendered, in academic terms, as technically *hazardous*, as it must surface as a subjective '*passage* from language to *signifiance*' (ibid.: 65). For Barthes, the *signifiance* of the third meaning – as opposed to signification – is an expressive defiance of any standardized, technically rigid, and regularized semantic structures; the obtuse meaning is a unique and discontinuous thread, indifferent to the formality of other ideology-related analyses or stories.

Some closing notes on the Barthesean pedagogical tactics

The possibility of adapting and implementing this Barthesean array of pedagogical tactics means that the university and the learning experience can begin to move away from the guise, process, and stasis of activity more akin to that of a museum – with its catacombs of separated and archived knowledge. The tyranny of the *studium* and the academic warder, replete with encased frameworks of functionally categorized shells of knowledge, can be transformed to a context where knowledge is collaboratively resituated and revived, inhabited, and co-produced in multiple new and fresh directions. Pro-dynamic and punctumic facilitators can engage with knowledge and liberate creative possibilities and unknown narrative undulations; through the emergent mysteries of *Third Meanings* of thoughts, ideas, and associations, bespoken knowledge-folds can emerge. In this sense, the framework and openness of the Barthesean concepts – as tactics – can be experienced as catalysts.[5] Rather than presenting Barthes and his ideas as a finite and finished body of *work*, as an indexed set of cauterized concepts, rules, and ideas – safely archived beneath a veneer of inaccessibility – they can be offered as intellectual and emotional flexes. Rather than treating Barthes as an academic endgame, as a ranking card within a game of academic *Top Trumps*, with strengths and limitations coldly compared against the assumptions, omissions, and obliquities of other theorists and writers, a different, radical, and empowered encounter with Barthes is ripe for discovery. As a liberating alternative, the *death of the author*, the *Scriptor*, the *skid*, the *punctum*, and the *Third Meaning* can be presented and approached as participatory invitations to enable learner-collaborators to start to discover, and creatively shape, knowledge, learning communities, and future possibilities in new and unforeseen ways.

Notes

1 See page 157 of *The Grain of the Voice* (taken from the 1972 interview, 'Pleasure/ Writing/Reading').
2 It is useful to note here that *The Third Meaning* was written prior to *Camera Lucida*.
3 Barthes also notes in relation to the *Third Meaning* that 'Obtuse meanings are to be found not everywhere (the signifier is rare, a future figure) but *somewhere*: in other *authors* of films (perhaps), in a certain manner of reading 'life' and so 'reality' itself' (Barthes, 1977: 60).
4 As Barthes notes in relation to this point, the still, by instituting a reading that is at once instantaneous and vertical, scorns logical time it teaches us how to dissociate the technical constraint from what is the specific filmic and which is the 'indescribable' meaning (Barthes, 1977: 68).
5 Regarding the possible pedagogical function of mass culture and ways of teaching this in a liberated way, Barthes notes, 'mass culture is perhaps fundamentally an *immediate* work or, in other words, one that lacks any ethical mediation – it is consumed that way; that is its purpose and its deep function in society as a whole . . . if such popular works one day come to be taught . . . a great shift in attitude would have to be required of teachers . . . to de-sacralise the work . . . the new *explication de texte* must enable us to use the mass work to explain their own times to students and to enable them to understand a modernity which, until now, has too often fallen outside of the education system' (Barthes, 2015a: 39).

4

Gaston Bachelard: Poetics, Space and Daydreaming

Gaston Bachelard

Gaston Bachelard was born on 27 June 1884 and died on 16 October 1962; a French professor and philosopher of science, his academic contemporaries report to have found him 'an unusual man, with an unusual career and a still more unusual mind' (Bachelard, 1994: xi). His journey into the elite and cloistered halls of the academy was far from traditional, holding a number of jobs prior to his academic ascent, ranging across soldier, postal worker, and high school teacher. Etienne Gilson notes that Bachelard 'got all the university degrees one can get and ended as a university professor; yet, unlike most of us . . . he never allowed himself to become molded by the traditional ways of thinking' (ibid.: xi). As a young philosopher, Bachelard devoted his work and thought to problems associated with the nature of science and knowledge, with a particular interest in the destabilizing implications of relativity. In 1930, Bachelard, aged 46, gained a university position and eventual professorship at Dijon; while there, he became recognized and widely respected, effectively establishing and consolidating his career and reputation (Chimisso, 2001). In 1940, this culminated in Bachelard being offered, and accepting, the prestigious position of Chair and Director at the Sorbonne Institute of the History of Science (Smith, 1982: 7).

By this time, now well into his 50s, Bachelard's academic focus and career should have been quite typical and, to a certain extent, predictably mapped. Holding a high profile and coveted position at the Sorbonne and being widely respected as a philosopher of science, the expectation would have been for him to continue writing on the same or, at the very least, *similar* subject areas. But his subsequent writings and career didn't conform to such expectations (Tiles, 1984). In 1938, the first – of what turned out to be many – of his 'literary and aesthetic' works was published, an intriguing book entitled *The Psychoanalysis of Fire* (Ehrmann, 1966: 572). Unsurprisingly, his more traditional colleagues grew somewhat uncomfortable with this radically creative *turn* (Smith, 1982: 1). Gilson again notes in the foreword to the 1964 edition of Bachelard's *Poetics of Space*:

> I distinctly remember my first reaction to it. It was: What are they going to say . . . we, all of us, the colleagues. After appointing a man to teach the phi-losophy of science and seeing him successfully do so for a number of years, we didn't like to learn that he had suddenly turned his interest to a psychoanalysis of the most unorthodox sort. (Bachelard, 1994: xii)

From here, Bachelard's focus and writing continued in this unorthodox trajec-tory, manoeuvring dramatically away from the canonical academic territories of science and reason, to those of imagination, poetry and daydreaming. John R. Stilgoe, in the foreword to the 1994 edition of *Poetics of Space*, effectively cap-tures the dramatic themes associated with this transition: 'Shells and doorknobs, closets and attics, old towers and peasant huts, all shimmer . . . in [this] transcen-dental geometry . . . focused on the house, its interior places . . . vibrating at the edges of imagination, exploring the recesses of the psyche, the hallways of the mind' (ibid.: vii).

It is to the creative challenge and philosophical unorthodoxy of the later Bachelard that this section of the book now turns; the *fuzzy* interior spaces of imagination and the creative chaos of personal reverie. Such notions offer an abundance of flexible material, malleable and open enough to be explored and repurposed as further tactics within the context of a utopian pedagogy. As such, this chapter sketches and contextualizes some Bachelardean *tactics-for-imagination* through the liberatory principle of creative reverie. The aim, and purpose, is not to offer a technically exhaustive exposition or polemical critique of the whole, or even the later, Bachelard, but instead to pose some of his con-cepts and ideas as generative tactics. Following the pattern of previous chap-ters and theoretical material, this section is also an invitation to engage with, and personally encounter, the emergent territories of Bachelardean reverie. In exploring Bachelard's concepts and ideas as polymorphous and reinterpretative ciphers, leaners and collaborators might, hopefully, be encouraged to *hear*, and, begin to articulate, their own 'geometries of echoes', emergent from within the latent traces and recollections of *old* houses and secret hideaways, or the distant apparitional mirages of hazy childhood memories.

Glimmers and limbo

In *The Formation of the Scientific Mind* (originally published in 1938 as *La forma-tion de l'esprit scientifique*), Bachelard's interests in the areas of literature, poetry and the interiority of imagination started to clearly emerge. For Bachelard, it is essential for the mind to constantly, and in all contexts, remain open and crea-tive; this is to accommodate the important facets of *wonder, beauty* and *aston-ishment*, and the productive role that they play in constructive imagination. In all of our endeavours, and this includes the pursuit of new knowledge, we must remember to ask the adventurous *whys* of a situation, as opposed to simply asking and considering the more mechanistic and technical *hows* (Bachelard, 2002: 93). In acknowledging the intensely subjective realm of interiority and the intriguing 'inner' dimension of imagination (further developed in his *Poetics* works), Bachelard recognizes that the mechanics of the realm of interiority, like that of post-Einsteinian relativistic space, evade all standardized forms and uni-versalizing systems of measurement. Bachelard's earlier works on epistemology effectively critique traditional scientific endeavours; as such, notions of *science and knowledge* constructed along *lines* of fixity and rigidly finite categories produce only stasis and stagnation where new knowledge is concerned. Hence Bachelard's later aesthetics-based works recognize and develop *reverie*, or day-dream, as an intensely subjective and non-predictable phenomenon. The highly bespoke and undulating *rhythms-of-the-imagination*, which pulse between the recollected legacies of yesterday and the open possibilities of tomorrow, mani-fest as a radical *asymmetry* where 'the past is a voice that has found an echo . . . [b]ut the future, no matter how far-reaching our desire, is a perspective without depth' (Bachelard, 2013: 31). With this, Bachelard sketches out a fun-damental distinction and schematic rupture between the assumed linearity and calculability of Euclidean three-dimensional space and that of the *strange* and quantum realm of *inner* space, the 'non-dimensional space' of interiority (Bachelard, 2011: 9). Unlike the trans-personal and mathematically fathomable space of Euclidean geometry, the elliptical dimensions of interior space warp and mutate in the ambiguous, subcutaneous zones of the imagination. Here, traditional 'spatial measurements do not apply . . . [as] size may be inverted and the miniscule may loom large' (Smith, 1982: 120). With daydream and creative imagination, Bachelard eloquently and poetically suggests that mani-fold, multidirectional *visions* can emerge from subjective reveries. From the profusion of images and symbols associated with memories, daydreams and imagination, the fluidity of interior space affords room to birth, and emanate, new articulations. Roch C. Smith usefully summarizes this Bachelardean position in relation to the quantum realm of space, 'just as the 'experiment of space' in contemporary physics was shown to transcend the commonsense, the geometric 'experience of space', and the imagination of space requires a similar transcendence' (ibid.: 131).

In its shifting complexity, the quantum dimension of Bachelardean inner space manifests multiversal microcosms of contemplation and pro-creative catalysts for prototypic and imaginative possibilities. Smith also notes that within this open system, the 'imagination does not reflect the present or the past but opens the way to the multiple possibilities of the future through poetic reverie' (ibid.: 131). The conscious and interior realm of the active imagination belongs to the realm of the daydream, 'where, the mind takes the greatest of liberties with geometry' (Bachelard, 2002: 107). Smith also usefully identifies that Bachelard's later literary works, especially his *Poetics* books, stem from (or at least the foundations of which can be rooted within) his earlier technical and philosophical works, such as *Formation of the Scientific Mind* regarding the limitations of traditional Newtonian science and Euclidean geometry (Smith, 1982: 130). In the quantum emergence of reveric fantasy, the personalized volutions of memory and creative reverie agglomerate into a gossamer-tacked web of constellated moments (or, as Bachelard terms, *instants*); a time-traversing biographic register of accumulated personal events. This is further corroborated in his 1932 work *Intuition of the Instant*, where Bachelard notes that 'the mind is the receptor of a myriad incidents . . . In its labour of knowledge, the mind manifests itself as a series of discrete instants' (Bachelard, 2013: 10). Ethereal apparitions of reveric *accidents* emerge as a shifting architecture of cumulus or cirrus proto-forming clouds of fractured inconsistencies. In an anticipatory and productive sense, such anecdotal fractions and revelatory instants also contain a proliferation of *lacunae*, as 'in between the fractures, gaps and spaces a vertical relativity gives pluralism to these mental coincidences' (Bachelard, 2000: 104).

The mind, and its Janus-type faculties for non-linear imaginings, is an ultra-sensitive time-detector; its dynamic abilities can shift instantaneously between caches of mental fugues and accumulated instants, unfettered by the constraints of metric time and history. Unpredictably, we re-attune to the intrigue and emergent shards and splinters within the swirling constellations of memories and associations, detecting moments which murmur from within intra-connected and hermetic silos. In *Dialectic of Duration* Bachelard asserts that within the internal nexus and pluritudes of time, we can detect patterns and connections almost without effort; to do this, 'all we need to do is turn aside from all practical chores and all social cares, and listen to time's cascades within us' (ibid.: 81). Through the personal and serendipitous process of daydreaming, intense and bespoke *instants* are liberated to accidentally re-emerge and flourish; new and as yet unknown spaces and territories of possibility can rush and manifest as 'jerks and rushes of feeling' (ibid.: 82). Unavoidably, these *reveric* thought impulses emerge as rejuvenated reinterpretations, as they are subject to shifting, dynamic and colourful manipulations and time-refracted adjustments. Loaded with anticipatory possibilities, reveries and incidents of creative imagination are born of many spaces, times and *instants*; as such, to reimagine 'is to absent oneself, to launch out toward a new life' (Bachelard, 2011: 3). Cartographies of reveric meanings, with their shifting sand-tracks and fuzzy territories, can only be divined by the host defying external or proxy attempts to hijack or reduce them to a linear sequence of technical points. The psychic echoes or *glimmers* in *limbo* (Bachelard, 2004: 112) must be traced out as personal, Expressionistic and asymmetrical beginnings. The highly subjective and deeply personal minutiae of reveric irruptions therefore render any attempt to predict or routinely systematize them as inevitably doomed to inadequacy or failure (Bachelard, 2000: 84–85).

To *hear* things from within the infinite expanse of interior space, we need to learn to recall wishful affinities from among the flotsam of slumbering instants; mental offertories of shards and images offer fresh opportunities to actively engage in the reveric-sculpting of alternative thought-images and future scenarios. Bachelard would assert that every human being is hungry to speak, to register their existence, to *make a mark* and deposit some kind of legacy for the world; the more conscious that this need and hunger becomes, the more that human activity 'wants to write, that is, to organize dreams and thoughts' (Bachelard, 2011: 249). To allow our imaginations, our dreams and our thoughts to speak, we need to hatch and grow increasingly proficient in utilizing an active *will to* creatively navigate the quantum interior (ibid.:49). Instead of relying on the artifice of the dreams and utterances of other *writers*, to confirm our reveries and permit us to live in our reimagined past, we need to fathom, and hone, our own liberated and productive imaginations, so that the revival of past and anticipatory reveries take 'on substance again' (Bachelard, 2004; 119–120).

House, fairytale and forest: Metaphors
for empowered imagination

In its external or *concrete* manifestation, the physical house and home into which we are born and nurtured provide an initial perspective and subsequent *grounding-context* for lived and outer-spatial experience. But for Bachelard it also impacts profoundly in the quantum space of interiority, offering a *form* or a shaping-function to the inner psychic realm. In the quantum realm of inner space, the stratified or concentrically enclosed layers of the house operate as a sort of 'psychic-jig', a guiding mechanism that lends an array of images and symbols to the subconscious journey of internal discovery. The house of our earliest years and recollections 'is more than an embodiment of home, it is also an embodiment of dreams. Each one of its nooks and corners was a resting-place for daydreaming . . . a house of dream-memory . . . lost in the shadow of a beyond of the real past' (Bachelard, 1994: 15). The Bachelardean house analogy suggests that, as with the external house, where we physically ascend, conceal and explore, so it is with the locations and recesses of the *inner* 'psychic' house; in the house of interiority, the dreamer

> constructs and reconstructs upper stories [in] the attic until they are well con-
> structed . . . when we dream of the heights we are in the rational zone of intellec-
> tualised projects. But for the cellar, the impassioned inhabitant digs and re-digs,
> making its very depth active . . . [w]hen it comes to excavated ground, dreams
> have no limit. (Ibid.: 18)

Within the liberated framework of this Bachelardean scheme, the pro-creative faculty of imagination should be unleashed so as to increasingly facilitate departures *beyond* the ordinary course and routine of everyday life. The *Poetics of Space* establishes the evocative argument that the inner-dream-world is a universal, though fluctuant, characteristic of the human psyche; the world of interiority becomes shaped by memories and experiences from within the houses and homes of our past; as such, the house posits lingering reveric *essences*. As he notes, the house and its legacy of thought-traces become 'a sort of airy structure that moves about on the breadth of time . . . open to the wind of another time. It seems as though it could greet us every day of our lives in order to give us confidence in life' (ibid.: 54). A latent though potent mix of instants and moments, they re-emerge as whispers of astonishment amid contemplative moments of recollection and daydream.

For Bachelard, memory-traces from the house of our childhood register a mental causeway which elevates the legacy of hopeful thoughts and associations up and beyond the detritus of everyday banality. Therefore, when we reminisce and speak about the distant shadows of the house, we choose the images and associations, and so it begins to reveal more about *us* than it does about 'it' (ibid.: 1). In addition to this, in *Air and Dreams* Bachelard notes that when a strange memory or mirage of a daydream emerges to fascinate and cajole us, it also brings with it an uplifting and empowering quality; as such, when an image, wandering daydream or thought emerges, we should consider the *torrent* of words and associations that it unleashes and allow ourselves to detach them from 'the all too stable background of our familiar memories' (Bachelard, 2011: 3). In the quantum house, we can build and re-construct in prolific and unbound ways the fluidity and organic entity of the creative dream world; this is the realm of adventures and exploratory expeditions. As liberated dream builders, we can experience a revival of secret hopes and topophilic associations; triggered by solitary *ascents* into attic rooms, ventures into wardrobes and dens, or other inglenook-type hideaways. While the physical places of memory, legacy and location may no longer be accessible or may no longer exist, the rekindling of an original *warmth* can radiate from within the remnant traces of the psychic-spaces of such cherished and hazy moments. Locations of wish-infused solitude serve as reminders that these 'other' places did once exist, along with the hopeful *dream-land* adventures from within them. As Bachelard notes on this point:

> The old house, for those who know how to listen, is a sort of geometry of echoes. The voices of the past do not sound the same in the big room as in the little bed chamber, and calls on the stairs have yet another sound. Among the most difficult memories, well beyond any geometry [is] the sweet smells that linger in the empty rooms, setting an aerial seal on each room in the house of memory. (Bachelard, 1994: 60)

Other familiar and even *absurd* representations of houses are also of interest and importance for Bachelard; for example, ice palaces, towers without entrances, candy-houses, or castles in the clouds, such as those portrayed in fairytales. Vortical associations create extensions which connect to dream-rooms of possibility; these, in turn, lead out afresh towards new unexplored territories of reverie. Of particular relevance, Bachelard identifies the various representations of surrealistic 'miniature' which recur throughout fairytale stories, as these serve to decipher an interior expression of a recurring reveric mystery. Places of

interior beauty where cunning heroes solve riddles and escape from dark for-
tresses, and brake through enchanted walls (ibid.: 150). The absurd, the surreal
and the strangely familiar nature of '*fairytale-building-scapes*' offer a particularly
ripe and potent source for creative contemplation and reveric freedom; here,
unadulterated hope and the most beautiful simplicity of childhood possibility can begin to murmur and reappear. With striking similarities to Blochian
principles, Bachelard suggests that visual or textual representations of fairytale
huts or houses provide a miniature gateway; as the soft golden light streams
from its hidden interior, the window becomes the house's *eye*, which pours forth
its enclosed light, which filters through and warmly emanates to the 'outside'
(ibid.: 34). Bachelard confides that simplistic or fantastic portrayals of the hut,
or miniature house, ignite the fires of his imagination; such personal encounters
cease to remain at a distance or as a mere representation; on the contrary, '[i]ts
lines have force and, as a shelter, it is *fortifying* . . . the print house awakens a
feeling for the hut in me and, through it, I re-experience the *penetrating gaze* of
the *little window*' (ibid.: 50). The mystery of the fantasy or fairytale *house* and
its dream-geometry intermittently beckons to our ever-lurking tendency to daydream and gently provokes wishes to recapture an idealized intimacy from some
location in the past. Although absurd, the miniature of fairytale imagery can
also serve as a reminder that an unquantifiable, unfathomable *immensity* dwells
'within', that to psychically meander beyond the source of a fairytale house and
into the inner realm of creative reverie catalyses a re-discovery of a treasured
place of daydream, one that is timeless, immense, yet also intimately familiar.
The quantum space and dream-geometry of the house can also be associated
with disjuncture or estrangement, for example, when a journey into the 'forest' leads away from the comfort and shelter of the house, and the trail home
becomes covered by snow. In the creative and constructive realm of dream-
geometry, the immensity of the metaphorical forest expresses and facilitates a
way of going *deeper and deeper* into a limitless world where established frameworks of knowledge lose prominence. Here, Bachelardean *immensity* has little to
do with the geographical dimensions of a sprawling and densely wooded area.
Instead, to 'experience the forest' in this way is to open up to the presence of the
unwritten nature of *immediate immensity* (ibid.: 189).

The open and fluid form of the house, in its various guises, thus allows for
personal permutations and reinterpretations to occur in new and fluctuating
ways. Due to the *metaphoric* and open essence of the imaginary house, 'missing meanings' continually refresh in ways that can be deformed and adapted.
The asymmetrical quantum *space* of interiority allows for personal reveries to

'peer' through and defibrillate extinguished promises by providing thought-conduits, doorways for subjective remembrance. Lost or slumbering images of the house can offer reveric portals and imaginative approaches to reanimating latent *instants*, as subjective time dimensions become increasingly 'freed'. Relative time-pulses and memories bring into view the unmade openness of the uninhabited future, un-navigated and yet to be defined. Unveiled exits leading to the lost immensity of the inner 'forest' await the revival of dormant daydreams. Reaching 'in' to the forest, and towards a *beyond-to-somewhere-else*, can begin to facilitate hopeful transgressions. The deeply subjective tactics associated with the Bachelardean themes of daydream and imagination can permeate and revive the personal realm of thought; through revelatory moments and uncovering of the mysterious, hidden promises of overcoming associations and ideas can proliferate. *Sparks* of possibility can reignite a twinkling of ideals, hopes, dreams, and symbolic encounters, which, in turn, hint towards a promise of 'awakening'.

The possibility of childhood: A Bachelardean pedagogical tactic

In *Air & Dreams: An Essay on the Imagination of Movement*, Bachelard notes that reveric flight and anticipation is 'associated with hopeful words, words that have an immediate future within us, and allow us suddenly to discover a new, exhilarating and lively idea, an idea that is our own, like a new treasure' (Bachelard, 2011: 12). Poignant and relevant to this, in *The Formation of the Scientific Mind*, Bachelard refers to the importance of the creative reconception of childhood (a theme that is developed in more detail in his *Poetics of Reverie*) as an additional and treasured trove of latent possibility. As an *idea* and evocative image, the creative, prototypic idea of a new, rewritten or refreshed childhood becomes a key and corroborative transpersonal thought-vehicle with a potency to ignite the future-grasping stretch of the imagination. Bachelard notes that many of the threads of our embedded and archived histories lead back to influences and expectations established and imposed by '*others*'; many of which continue to linger and haunt us. These pivotal pressures continue to bind and influence us as 'we end up resembling ourselves. We gather all our beings around the unity of our name' (Bachelard, 2004: 99). The potential of childhood, constituted of fragments, and the halcyon times of an indefinite past evokes a *messy sheaf of vague beginnings*. Through an accumulating and aggregating story, we can experience moments of illumination, moments when we suddenly, fleetingly start to understand an emerging message (Bachelard, 2013: 3). The tiniest of fragments can reveal a multiplicity of devolutionary instants teeming with creative possibility (ibid.: 18). This is where we also locate another type of house, the '*Other-House* is, the House of an *Other-Childhood*, constructed with all that *should-have-been* upon a being which was not and which suddenly takes a notion to be and constitutes itself as the home of our reverie' (Bachelard, 2004: 121). Traces of a possible childhood can emanate out of the shadows, such a childhood 'in the mists and glimmers . . . gives us a certain layer of births . . . reverie looking for childhood seems to bring back to life lives which have never taken place, lives which have been imagined' (ibid.: 112). A map of an alternative universe can appear beyond a place that dwells within the cracks and small recesses of old walls, or beyond a few lines on the ceiling that chart a new continent' (Bachelard, 1994: 144). A new-found childhood, a childhood reanimated, is latent in each of us as 'a state of new childhood . . . which goes farther than the memories of . . . a childhood which was not well finished, and yet which was ours and which we have doubtless dreamed on many occasions' (Bachelard, 2004: 106).

Within the memory spectrum of our latent childhood, reverie can afford a fantastic freedom, which can fuel and morph fantastical and hopeful ascents; more than this, the posited seeds and reveries of childhood continue to harbour and glimmer, a powerful beauty, a mystery which 'remains within us, at the bottom of memory . . . the beauty of a flight which revives us' (ibid.: 101). The Bachelardean framework thus asserts that potent echoes remain deep and unspoilt within us; as such, an archaeology of actual and creative *childhood* fragments can help us to reminisce and descend so deeply that they can begin to shed the shackles of our imposed histories; they can serve to 'liberate us from our name' (ibid.: 99). Thanks to the *imaginary*, the psyche's experience of the novel and phantasmagoric childhood of reverie is essentially *open* and *elusive*. A potential childhood always remains, and 'like a forgotten fire, a childhood can always flare up again within us' (ibid.: 104). This suggests that a whole childhood of renewed imagination and hopeful possibility remains to be constructed and, in the process of reimagining it, invoke 'the possibility of recovering it' (ibid.: 100). The atmosphere of another time, beyond the matter of spent memories of actual and previously lived childhoods, prompts us to seek and divine the mystery of our unknown being, somewhere amid 'the sum total of all the unknowable elements that make up the souls of a child' (ibid.: 16). Through disruptive and glimmering fragments, prophetically hopeful stories of alternative and redemptive possibility are 'not purely and simply registered but reconstructed with a faithfulness which has been thought and willed, and sustained by reasons for coherence which are specific to the learner' (Bachelard, 2000: 94).

From unexplored, unarticulated reaches, it becomes possible for the pro-liferation of previously unknown thought-flashes and creative possibilities to emerge. Subjective murmurs of emerging memorial *instants*, connected by unique associations, have an unpredictable fluidity and as such defy more con-ventional pedagogical methods; creative and reveric encounters of hazy pos-sibility cannot be subjected to standardized academic structure, analyses and mode of interpretation. Roger (2014) notes that hierarchically polarized and technico-objective approaches to learning serve largely to create lifeless disen-chantments and pseudo-objectivity devoid of substance and subjective relevance (Roger, 2014: 35). Disengaged from the wonder of childhood spirit, routinized 'habit' with its sibling of bored unproductivity can be juxtaposed and confronted with the essence and life, 'of the creative imagination' (Bachelard, 2011: 11). As Bachelard notes, an 'image learned in books. Supervised and criticized by teach-ers, blocks the imagination' (ibid.: 11).

In a traditional teaching and assessment scenario, the imposition of inter-pretive authority, from an emotionally and reverically uninitiated bystander, serves to deflate and institutionally funnel the pluralistic complexities posed by Bachelardean polyphonic and multidimensional voices. As a productive contrast to a particular type of learning, the work of Bachelard emerges as a powerful pedagogical antidote; Bachelardean reverie, imagination and child-hood can be geared towards the reinvigoration of the mind through its ability to reflect and innovate. As such, a 'genuine, cultivated teacher is therefore not someone who knows everything and holds a great sum of knowledge, but rather a teacher who thinks, who reflects, who guides others in their reflection, and who is able to sustain a permanent state of learning' (Roger, 2014: 35). Learning to escape from the comfortable discipline and carceral rigidity of mental habits formed by the strategies, expectations and familiar experiences of the institu-tion means 'observing one's own thought, and being aware one is examining one's own evolution and one's own transformation' (ibid.: 36). To excavate and explore memories, dreams and reveric excursions, to reconnect to childhood reverie, should involve the recovery of primordial possibility. A returning to pre-linguistic images and traces, infused with the pollen of a time that existed prior to the entrenchment of names, labels and authoritative expectations occurs; with this, places and spaces beyond the predictable body and psyche of the organiza-tion shimmer and inspire (Bachelard, 1994: 10). Creative re-invokations of a place where we didn't yet resemble *what we*, in turn, *became* can awaken the promise of liberation from all such stultifying categories (Bachelard, 2004: 99). For Bachelard, the recovery of the magic of childhood memory and reverie is a challenging, though ultimately restorative, activity, a kind of *call-to-(poetic)-arms*. Emergent childhoods from within pro-creative imaginations do not reflect the present or the past, but rather, through poetic reverie, open up new pathways and potential journeys towards multiple possibilities on the horizon of the future (Smith, 1982: 131). A reimagined *future*-childhood of latent possibility offers open themes or vague metaphorical canvases upon which fractured learning transitions can emerge, prompting non-linear learner collaborator engagements within an open framework of *Expressionistic* possibility. The informal embrace of a phenomenological topophilia can be developed to accommodate the free-play of quantum space and – to invoke some Barthesean terms here – punctumic thought-skids. Bachelardean tactics of reveric exploration within the context of a utopian pedagogy are sympathetic to the notion that learners enroute to their emergent discoveries are free to engage in a process of discovery and self-transformation. Hopeful excavations and revitalizing rediscoveries may, ultimately, contribute towards transforming the learner's mind and self-image. The a-symmetrical and intimate depth of interior-space prompts the necessity to invert or sublimate personal contemplation into the inner-realms of reverie; reminiscences and rediscoveries harmonize with the quantum rhythms and reverberating pulses of childhood, with its echoes of wonder and creative possibility (Bachelard, 2004). With Bachelard's inner-space, we bring the recognition of the fractured, irregular and disconnected sources of personal creativity.

On return to the distant, inner-house of memory, we can re-learn to speak of the roads and cross-roads that slumber beneath the undergrowth of lost, yet magical places. Creatively and actively, learner collaborators can reconstruct the residual essence of childhood daydreams, with their reverberations, resonant-aromas and *sentimental* repercussions of the past. When rummaging amid the latent remnants of childhood dens and wardrobes, a hopeful recovery of reveric possibilities can emerge, a resurgence of 'everything that it could have been' (ibid.: 101). Through personalized and creative processes of exploration, self-generated and self-directed wonder-arousing questions can open up towards as-yet untold directions, ideas and expressions. As such, the reveric freedom associated with the Bachelardean pedagogical tactics unveils the dormant territory of past memories, the immanence of hope and the future potent possibilities of untethered and creative articulations. The usual proscenium of academic performance must thus be destabilized so as to enable individual collaborators to inter-weave journeys towards their own traces, each manifestation of a hieroglyphic beacon containing an immanent desire to *touch* a forgotten magic once again. Through unpredictable fluidities and associations, a profusion of multiplicitous voices and relative permutations thus emerge; Bachelardean pedagogical tactics and heterogeneous proliferations generate an infinity of multilayered, interweaving and fluctuating stories. The splintered and fractured narratives which emerge as a result of this facet of the utopian pedagogical experience generate a flux of personal voices, which, in turn, as part of a community of meandering thinkers, further germinate personal and creative expression.

Part II

Pedagogical Strategies
for Creative Possibilities

Dérive and Détournement: Pedagogical Strategies for Creative Engagement

Guy Debord (1931–1994), a French Marxist theorist and intellectual *provocateur*, became the leader of a group of artists and intellectuals, who came together to form the *Internationale Situationniste* in July 1957 (referred to throughout this chapter as the *Situationists*, or the *SI*). The founding members of the SI amalgamated from two-and-a-half existing groups, the Movement for an Imaginist Bauhaus, the Lettrist International and the London Psychogeographical Society (Wark, 2015: 61).[1] From the outset, the focus of the collective was to critique and challenge the stagnation and boredom of the increasingly technologically driven consumer society. Coverley (2010) notes that the foundation and ethos of the group was inspired by a key and influential pre-Situationist text entitled *Formulary for a New Urbanism*; the tract, written in 1953 by a 19-year-old Ivan Chtcheglov, contributed towards the political activism of the SI and fuelled its hunger for the pursuit of change. Throughout the piece, Chtcheglov attacks any form of resignation or apathetic retreat from radical or critical life, even – or especially – within the confines and surroundings of the modern and mundane *City*. As a rallying call, he offers a venting swirl of ideas which focus on replacing our functional and sterile existence 'with a magical awareness of the wonders that surround us' (Coverley, 2010: 84); as he notes:[2]

> We are bored in the city, we really have to strain to still discover mysteries on the sidewalk . . . And you, forgotten, your memories ravaged by all the consternations . . . no longer setting out for the hacienda *where the roots think of the child and where the wine is finished off with fables from an old almanac.* That's all over. You'll never see the hacienda. It doesn't exist. *The hacienda must be built.'* (Ivan Chtcheglov, *Formulary for a New Urbanism*). (Knabb, 2006: 1)[3]

At the 1957 founding meeting of the Situationists, Debord issued his manifesto for the group, with the unwieldy title of *Report on the Construction of Situations and on the Terms of Organization and Action of the International Situationist Tendency*;[4] in particular Debord notes that '[t]he crisis of modern culture has led to total ideological decomposition. Nothing new can be built on these ruins . . . as each judgement clashes with others and each individual invokes fragments of outmoded systems and follows merely personal inclinations' (Debord, 1957). Using this as part of their constitutional basis, the tactics and counterstrategies subsequently developed by the Situationists were aimed at challenging and disrupting the mundane routine of everyday life. As part of this, they considered it essential to establish 'physical – as well as psychological – activities, to produce new concepts, new ideas, and new knowledge' (Wark, 2015: 58). As part of their emerging focus, the Situationists adapted, applied and advocated the wider implementation of a set of distinctive practices, those of the *dérive*,[5] *détournement*,[6] and *potlatch* (or, the notion of the gift).[7]

In his later work, the *Society of the Spectacle* (1970), Debord emphasized the necessity for a continued development of a Situationist-infused praxis to counter the extent to which the subjective experience of everyday life was being cast adrift; Debord asserts that 'without language, without concepts, and without critical access to its own past . . . misunderstood and forgotten' (Debord, 1970: Para: 157) everyday life is smothered by the consumer *spectacle*, with its false memory of the past and phony purchasing of the present. Skwarek (2014) notes that Debord's important and quite particular use of the term 'spectacle' refers to the explosion of consumption, not only as a way of marketing and distributing goods within and across society but also as a deeper and more infectious way of framing the consumer experience of everyday life. The spectacle then becomes the 'inverted image of society in which relations between commodities' (Skwarek, 2014: 24) supplant the connections and relations between people. For Debord the spectacle is to be understood as a trans-dimensional *totality*, where the habits and processes of consumption become both 'the result and the goal of the dominant mode of production. It is not a mere decoration added to the real world', it becomes the very heart of society (Debord, 1970: para 6). The personal experience of everyday life, while loaded with longings, dreams and desires to create a better life, is drained of scope and possibility for wider political expression. Other than engaging in the superficial and empty practice of consumption, the transformatory potential of everyday life becomes stripped of dynamic and critical possibility. For Vaneigem, in *The Revolution of Everyday Life* (2006), we must consider 'the incredible diversity of *anyone's* dreams . . .

landscapes of the brilliant . . . [where] Every individual is constantly building an ideal world within himself, even as his external motions bend to the requirements of soulless routine' (Vaneigem, 2006: 191). With the intention of harnessing the momentum and latent power behind these themes and disappointments, Debord, in *One Step Back*, asserts that we 'have to find concrete techniques to revolutionize the setting of everyday life' (Debord, 2004a: 26).

Consumption and everyday life

For Debord – and the wider Situationists – cultural, artistic and political concerns need to be defibrillated in order to confront and tackle the malaise and critical idleness generated by the stupefying excesses of consumption. The spread of the society of the spectacle, with its advertising, marketing and catchy slogans, is further assisted by the spread and increasing adaptability of technology; in conjunction with overwhelming levels of bureaucratization, all of these forces and practices converge to create a social and economic machinery which interpellates all facets of human concern and activity. Debord notes that in the abyss of unending consumption, the everyday impact of these developments and pressures reduces 'people's independence and creativity' (Debord, 1961: para 18). In support, Coverley notes that the superficial emptiness of modern life is obscured 'behind an elaborate and spectacular array of commodities . . . immersion in this world of rampant consumerism leaves us disconnected from the history and community that might give our lives meaning' (Coverley, 2010: 102). As a consequence, the everyday experience of culture, leisure and relational habits grow increasingly desensitized to the human ramifications of consumer-bent fractures; in the void left by the fragmentation and disappearance of previous social and political architectures, personal life and wider socio-political meaning become flaccid and alienated. Flamboyant perpetuations of glitzy gimmicks, superfluous slogans and grandiose fashion inventions mask and deflect attention away from the wider impact of helplessness-inducing apathy. Passive and individualized consumers, furnished with spectacles and clichés, become structurally defined and disempowered; as disconnected aggregates, they become cast adrift as grains of sand blustered by the gusts, whims and priorities perpetuated by globalized and faceless capitalist forces. For Debord, the society of the spectacle 'tends to atomize people into isolated consumers, to prohibit communication' (Debord, 1961: para 16); a related and emasculating consequence of this is that the potential for any transformative political action also dissipates and recedes 'behind the development of the modern potentialities of produc-tion' (Debord, 2004b: 29). Mentally infested and usurped by the reach and grip of technology, the psychological onslaught of this fuzzy-tinselled tyranny has conspired to generate a *historical crisis* where even 'the simple exercise of critical thought' becomes impossible (ibid.: 37). Vaneigem corroborates this by noting:

> The consumer cannot and must not ever attain satisfaction: the logic of the con-sumable object demands the creation of fresh needs, yet the accumulation of such false needs exacerbates the malaise of men confined with increasing dif-ficulty solely to the status of consumers. Furthermore, the wealth of consumer goods impoverishes authentic life. It does so in two ways. First, it replaces authentic life with *things*. Secondly, it makes it impossible, with the best will in the world, to become attached to these things, precisely because they have to be *consumed*, i.e., 'destroyed'. (Vaneigem, 2006: 162)

The banality of everyday life

Debord claims, in *Perspectives for Conscious Alterations in Everyday Life* (1961), that this historical – that is, contemporary and future – crisis means that everyday life is now 'organized within the limits of a scandalous poverty' (Debord, 1961: para 11). This transition towards the obliteration of meaning-ful politics and political action has been far from accidental, it is the result and inevitable conclusion of historically organized patterns of human exploitation. Consequently, the atomized behaviour of isolated consumption generates a per-functory state of *smooth conformity*, where the spaces of everyday activities and experience operate in 'a sort of reservation for good natives who keep modern society running without understanding it' (ibid.: para 15). The superficial values and passive activities generated by the consumer process of exchanging money, in valuation and payment for skills and goods, permeates 'peoples everyday rela-tions with themselves and with their fellows' (Vaneigem, 2006: 88). One of the detrimental consequences of this is that any notion of authentic, socialistic and altruistic giving is increasingly exorcised from the cultural repertoire.

In *Basic Banalities* (1963), Vaneigem argues that the power associated with liberal, capitalistic and bureaucratic structures is now such that its reign of men-tal dominion extends across all areas of 'the press, television, stereotypes, magic, tradition, economy, technology' (Vaneigem, 1963: chapter 17). Such heinous mastery at the hands of consumer-peddling *overlords* enslaves its subservient subjects 'with words to the point of making them the slaves of words' (Vaneigem, 2006: 103). Vaneigem further warns that far from merely garnering a culture of disenfranchised apathy, the wider consequences of consumer acquiescence are far more severe, as 'he who thinks for you judges you; he reduces you to his own norm; and, whatever his intentions may be, he will end by making you stupid – for stupidity doesn't come from a lack of intelligence, as stupid people imagine, it comes from renouncing, from abandoning one's true self' (ibid.: 243). In *Comments against Urbanism* (2004), he adds that it is *in* the activities and environments framed by consumer-based values and bureaucracies that 'you lose your shadow, and end up losing yourself by dint of seeking yourself in what you are not' (Vaneigem, 2004: 121); in our metronomic states of mental and physical routine, we route-march towards death as the 'radiant ascent of the soul towards heaven is replaced by inane speculations' (Vaneigem, 2006: 92). Institutionally hemmed and channelled, in this objectified life,

> We are poisoned by the spectacle. All the elements necessary for a detoxification (that is, for the construction of our everyday lives) are in the hands of specialists . . . We are living in a space and time that are out of joint, deprived of any reference point or coordinate, as though we were never going to be able to come into contact with ourselves . . . The space of everyday life, that of one's true realization, is encircled by every form of conditioning . . . Our freedom is that of an abstract temporality in which we are named in the language of power (these names are the roles assigned to us), with a choice left to us to find officially recognized synonyms for ourselves. In contrast, the space of our authentic realization (the space of our everyday life) is under the dominion of silence . . . and the only answer cybernetic society has to offer us is to become spectators of the gangrene and decay. (Vaneigem, 1963: para 20–23)

Despite the fact that individually we crave dynamic and vibrant everyday environments in which we can foster regenerative activities of self-realization, we are stranded in a parched political wasteland which oscillates between the unfortunate extremes of life-negating thirst or superficial satiation through banality. For the Situationists, the only way to *arouse the masses* from the standardizing rhythms of capitalistic regimentation is to expose and reveal the rupture between its systemically imposed and vacuous constructions and the poverty of everyday experience robbed of participatory and socialistic possibilities (SI, 1960b: para 5). In relation to this challenge, Vaneigem notes that collectively we 'have nothing in common except the illusion of being together . . . but real community remains to be created' (Vaneigem, 2006: 39). The activist stridency more typical of Situationist-based confrontation and antagonism brings the pessimism of the consumer analysis back around to more proactive theoretical climes. As McDonough (2004) notes, for the SI, the banality and dominated spaces of *everyday* life still contain *flotsam* of resistance, as '[d]istinctions and differences are not eradicated; they are only hidden in the homogeneous space' (McDonough, 2004: 249). In recognition of the lingering possibilities of new and latent permutations, the SI strategies act as direct responses to the relentlessly deconstructive nature of the consumer society; the *dérive* and *détournement* become micro-political techniques pitted against the psychological *Lethe* inseminated by the juggernaut of consumption. As a form of *potlatch*, the SI concepts and practices can be revisited, revised and offered as mechanisms to target, morphogenically disrupt and 'contest the organization of the society of the spectacle itself' (ibid.: 254). Inciting fractured and creative heterogeneities, the SI strategies were (and can be) geared towards infiltrating and reclaiming the slumbering residue of individual autonomies.[8] As Vaneigem notes, despite the spatial confinement and puppeteering of roles and activities, subjective life always 'filches a small portion of the time that sweeps it on . . . [and] seeks to create the unitary space-time of love, of poetry, of pleasure, of communication' (Vaneigem, 2006: 227). As part of this, and to counteract the powerful routines of consumerized space, the *Situationists* promote the practice of 'inhabiting' any and all corporate-consumer-dominated environments. Ensnared within political, architectural and bureaucratic spaces, bespoke and non-conformist voices can shift direction and rhythm and grate against the regulatory structures of formal establishments. Resuscitated, individual *dériveurs* can mentally uncouple from the constraints of conformist routine, sever the umbilical hold from governmental bureaucracies and, in doing so, begin to *detour* beyond the expectations of organized compliance.

The dérive

In his instructional tract *Theory of the Dérive* (1958), Debord defines the Situationist take on this concept and establishes it as one of the foundational principles of SI practice; as he suggests, 'the *dérive* [literally: drifting], [is] a technique of rapid passage through varied ambiances. Dérives involve playful-constructive behaviour and awareness of psychogeographical effects, and are thus quite different from the classic notions of journey or stroll' (Debord, 1958: para 1). For Debord, in one sense then, the notion of the dérive is associated with the physical act of purposeful *wandering*; it is about actively transiting from psychic states of flatline conformity – behavioural and mental habits programmed over time, resulting in flâneurs or voyeurs of life – to engage in the active avoidance of uncritical physical routine. Illustrating the elasticity of this facet of the dérive, Debord notes that the conscious and intentional dérive or *meander* can take place 'within a deliberately limited period of a few hours, or even fortuitously during fairly brief moments; or it may last for several days without interruption' (ibid.: para 12).[9] However, the purpose and application of the dérive is not confined to a specific set of practical instructions for 'getting lost' in the city with a view to discovering secret enclaves and new locations; it is more fluid and transcontextual than this.[10] As Wark (2015) notes, the Situationist adaptation of the concept can also refer to

> 'derivare' [which] means to draw off a stream, to divert a flow. Its English descendants include the word 'derive' and also 'river'. Its whole field of meaning is aquatic, conjuring up flows, channels, eddies, currents, and also drifting, sailing or tacking against the wind. It suggests a space and time of liquid movement, sometimes predictable but sometimes turbulent. The word dérive condenses a whole attitude to life. (Wark, 2015: 22)

Therefore, the Situationist dérive also refers to a shift or transition in a state of mind; in this sense, it is a mechanism to challenge oneself, to resist the compulsion to conform to established expectation and stultifying thought patterns. Debord clarifies this by noting that the dérive can be 'precisely delimited or vague, depending on whether the goal is to study a terrain or to emotionally disorient oneself' (Debord, 1958: para 14); as a result, the diverse and molten characteristics of the dérive overlap and morph. Ultimately, it is quite impossible to rigidly define either of the loose and intersecting permutations of the dérive (or indeed, the concept as a whole) in a stable or 'pure state'. Kofman and Lebas (2000) further articulate the opaqueness and instability of dérive and remark that, as both a political and psychological strategy, it encapsulates more than just the creative re-mapping of a location and that, as a technique, it is more than just a liberated form of thinking and communication. Fundamentally, by invoking multiple pursuits in search of new voices and new ideas, the Situationist dérive entails 'the production of a new aesthetic' (Kofman and Lebas, 2000: 83).

As a counter-strategy and mode of contemplation, the dérive can be adapted to almost any situation, with the aim of jolting passive spectators out of ruts of banality and routine. The dérive serves to resituate the spectator as a subversive actioner, a potential 'revolutionary following a political agenda' (Coverley, 2010: 97). The constructive actions of a dériveur can manifest as adventurous and meandering lone voices with various styles and expositions, which 'neither collapse back into the dead time of routine, nor ossify into [a] mere artifact' (Wark, 2015: 103).[11] Replacing the figure of the Baudelairean or Benjaminian flâneur – a passive stroller and hapless receptor of environments – the *dériveur* is an active, purposeful and resistant rebel. As a micro-political act and response to being objectively positioned, dériveurs are *free radicals*, catalysing and unleashing non-linear geometries of fragmentary expression. As a key Situationist challenge, Debord proposes that the dérive and the activities of the dériveur be transposed and translated to all forms of human relationship and organization. But such an application is far from routine; the SI tract *Instructions for an Insurrection* points out that one of the greatest obstacles to implementing this as a transformative strategy is the need to establish 'new types of human relationships . . . by methods yet to be experimented with' (SI, 1960a: para 4).

Therefore, adapting the dérive as a Situationist strategy into educational spaces and environments means that a new architecture of associations needs to emerge so that they can be reinhabited by the wandering and creative meanders of individual dériveurs. In this sense, the dérive, as an open and flexible approach to thinking and organizing, must be creatively resituated so as to alter the wider framing of knowledge and the specific activities of the *learner*. In doing so, co-constructive possibilities can start to emerge in ways that can directly change and alter the ways in which the pedagogical parameters of curricular space is shared and experienced. Each dériveur can start to challenge and change the ways in which they navigate and encounter learning environments to create learning spaces with the potential for new connections and discoveries, which remain 'open-ended for all participants' (McDonough, 2004: 261–262).

Détournement

As was briefly highlighted earlier, the notion of détournement – basically, to *detour* – identifies re-interpretive cultural practices. To restate Coverley's definition from above, to détourne is to seek out 'a word, statement, image or event from its intended usage and to subvert its meaning' (Coverley, 2010: 95). Détournement entails the political poaching of aspects, or segments, of published cultural works; the idea is to hijack the ossified isolation of the piece or pieces in order to use them to create and produce new and previously unintended meanings. There is no particular size, shape or context that must be associated with, or attached to, the source of a détourned object; as Wark notes, it could 'be a single image, a film sequence of any length, a word, a phrase, a paragraph' (Wark, 2015: 40). What matters is that, as a result of the refracted subjective association, a fresh and creative direction becomes unpredictably jettisoned.

The SI tract *Détournement as Negation and Prelude* identifies two related aspects to the practice of détournement; initially, the object being *détourned* must be stripped of its false and reified original context and ownership, this is in order for it to be perceived as just another fluid and contributory building block of culture. Secondly, once stripped of its false value, it should influence or become part of a 'brand new ensemble', a new creative expression and fresh artefact of cultural work (SI, 1959: para 1). Any chosen or adapted cultural fragments thus serve to act as a point of departure. The source of the original artefact (with its associated cultural past) is de-composed and rendered unimportant; as such a 'reinvested' cultural expression emerges from the creative *detour*, which produces 'a negation of the value of the previous organization of expression. It arises and grows increasingly stronger in the decomposition of the original' (ibid.: para 3).

Détourning a piece of writing or other segment of pre-existing cultural product is the 'opposite of quotation' (Wark, 2015: 40). Traditionally the rigid and authoritative process of quotation entails the insertion of a *piece of the past* into a newly emerging 'here-and-now'; however, it is executed within the strategic confines of an institutional setting in a specific and legislated way. Importantly, quotation maintains the identity and legal separation of the existing work and retains the security and identification of its privately owned and corporate shackles. The original and owned work must always be aligned with its author. In comparison, to détourne is to resist authorial expectations and corporate standards; again, as with the dérive, to engage in an activity of détournement is to adopt a micro political and subversive stance geared towards challenging corporate standards of ownership and control. Ultimately, détournement embodies a 'challenge to private property, it attacks the kind of fetishism, where the products of collective human labor in the cultural realm become a mere individual's property' (Wark, 2015: 40). As a form of *expressive* subversion, the hijacking of existing culture and its associated artefacts is targeted at disrupting the consumer world of packaged and privatized order. As a strategy, it can take a torn fragment (or an assemblage of disparate fragments) from an *original* context, and develop it (or them) into a whole new and personally refracted piece of culture work. Through reinterpretation, détournement liquefies the artificial petrification of a cultural product into a false truth and untethers the guy-ropes of its quotidian stagnancy, so that the corporate hold over the work is weakened; this in turn facilitates alternative and polyrhythmic new voices.

Dérive, détournement and pedagogy

Despite the relative brevity of the existence of the SI as a group, and with the unorthodox parameters and expectations attached to the inner core of its membership, the Situationists generated a significant and lasting impact.[12] Their cause and activities contributed towards the 1968 Paris student uprising, and their writings and ideas inspired the Punk and post-Punk cultural movements. Furthermore, their emphasis on technology, consumption and the consumer society means that their essays, tracts, concepts and concerns harbour a haunting and contemporary relevance; not least of which in relation to the increasing commodification, consumption and debt associated with the realms and privileges of HE. In contemporary social, political and educational environments, austerity (and the consequences of austerity) continues to dominate and, along with this, social inequality and economic exclusion also continue to exponentially increase. Politically and educationally it may appear futile to even consider beginning to try to challenge the immensity of this macro consumer-driven Leviathan; the human collateral damage, encircled and swallowed within such powerful forces, may appear to have little or no democratic or radical alternative. All too familiar now, HE environments are being infiltrated with consumer-based narratives and expectations. HE students increasingly *pay* for their degree; attached to this come the array of consumer expectations: readily available data, clear and accessible course and modular details, equitable and uniform standards and assessments. Inadvertently – or otherwise – these tendencies serve to increasingly generate a state of pedagogical mediocrity: institutionally regulated and uniform knowledge, routinely channelled and churned out. As a response to these developments and pressures, the framework and exploratory techniques associated with Debord and the SI present a rustic and raw arsenal of counter-strategies as potent and flexible vehicles open enough to creatively re-enthuse the somnambulistic state of consumer-pummelled subjectivities.

One of Debord's central arguments in the *Society of the Spectacle* is that all environments are inevitably shaped (or will be shaped) by the principles of *consumption*; contemporarily the university is no longer exempted from the immediacy and worst excesses of the shaping force and impact of these develop-ments. The Academy is restructuring to effectively align itself with the processes and expectations associated with offering a *commodity*, which its market of iden-tified consumers then set out to 'buy' as a premium priced academic product. In doing so, the constituent roles and subjectivities within the university are being re-aligned to activities and values more conducive with conspicuous consump-tion (supported by a whole range of routines with the purpose of standardizing and controlling the *product*). It is in relation to this increasing commodification and *spectaclization* of education that the Situationist concepts of the dérive and détournement can be targeted and primed as *ammunition* to tackle and target the shaping and confinement of pockets of knowledge, the peddling of a wider *university* lifestyle and the corporate routinization of pedagogical techniques. Consequently, Knabb (2006) claims that the reconstruction of universities along the lines of large business corporations is reducing them down to institutions of *efficient ignorance*. Increasingly, as uncritical organizations, the financial and bureaucratic purpose of the university is running the risk of generating a 'mass production of uneducated students who have been rendered incapable of think-ing' (Knabb, 2006: 410–411). The security of budgets, markets and the university 'brand' means that 'the anarchy of individual construction has been officially sanctioned, and taken over by the authorized organisms of power' (Vaneigem, 2004: 121–122). Subjected to university processes of routine and conveyance, the castrated role of the consumer student is characterized increasingly as a pas-sive witness who at most engages in instructional and ceremonious façades as a 'rehearsal for his ultimate role as a conservative element in the functioning of the commodity system' (Knabb, 2006: 408–409). Pedagogies of imposition and instruction serve to construct, dupe and regurgitate students in the guise of production-line operatives serving a 'paternalistically entrenched cultural mire of subservience and deference' (ibid.: 310). Within any – and all – such con-texts, Debord would assert that any (or maybe all) educational practitioners who think that they cannot conceive of, and engage in, methods of radical transfor-mation only serve to support and prop up the corruption and contagion of the status quo (Debord, 2004c: 53). Inducing a 'mental menopause', the conformist student in the university of consumption listens

> respectfully to his masters, conscientiously suppressing all critical spirit so as to immerse himself in the mystical illusion of being a 'student' – someone seriously devoted to learning *serious things* – in the hope that his professors will ultimately impart to him the ultimate truths of the world. (Knabb, 2006: 411)

The increased *businessification* of the academy, with its strategies and its bureaucracies, means that the previous role of the university as the hub of academic
freedom and criticality, in pursuit and creation of dynamic and innovative
knowledge for the *public good*, is increasingly abandoned. The most that can
be expected from the *consumer university* is the increased and professionalized
catering for markets, brands, consumer tastes and the 'quality' control of target-
aligned curriculum and assessments, reinforced and policed with equitable
standardization. Along with this, the previous role of the HE lecturer (as maverick, critic, innovator) is increasingly annulled; the dramaturgical assignment
expected of the standardized instructor of knowledge consists of the 'consider-
ably less noble function of sheep-dog in charge of herding white-collar flocks to
their respective factories and offices in accordance with the needs of the planned
economy' (ibid.: 411). The ubiquity of these pressures and changes means that
any educational practitioner – and indeed student – interested in pro-dynamic,
Situationist practices must confront the problem of establishing a free and non-
specified dynamic creativity within the strategically reductive context of the HE
institution with its standardized systems of regulation and disciplinary control.
Importantly, university populations cannot resist and revolt against anything
without first tackling the infantilizing practice of packaging and standardizing
pre-masticated knowledge.

Hence, malleable pedagogical counter strategies consisting of adaptable facets of the dérive and détournement are all the more necessary. The sanitized
spectator environments of the modern (and expensive) university, with its *step-
by-step* 'knowledge-by-numbers', can only produce curricular voyeurs. Wark
notes that this poses a problem for knowledge, and asks 'what if one challenged
the organization of knowledge itself? What if, rather than knowledge as a representation of another life, it is that other life?' (Wark, 2015: 41). Essentially, rather
than continue to induct fledgling followers into tranches of bordered readings
and *policed* interpretations of knowledge, pedagogical embracings of the dérive
and détournement as counter strategies must be developed so as to elicit spontaneous traces and caches of hidden associations. Vaneigem notes that all such
approaches are essential, as spontaneity 'is the true mode of being of individual
creativity . . . unpolluted at the source and as yet unthreatened by the mechanisms of co-optation . . . The instant of creative spontaneity in the minutest possible manifestation . . . is a unitary moment, i.e., one and many' (Vaneigem,
2006: 194–195). Practitioners must therefore set out to discover, creatively
experiment with and implement new pedagogical frontiers, as '[n]o one can
develop in freedom without [first] spreading freedom in the world' (ibid.: 247).

The counter strategic spontaneity of the dérive can be co-opted so as to generate and open up new forms of learning labyrinths, to build a bridge between the disparate and burbling non-linear worlds of the singular imagination and the wider environment of curriculum and practice. Whetting the pedagogical appetite with the wisp of a pragmatic technique, Vaneigem suggests that individual and creative meanders can be kick-started by an expansive range of détourned cultural goods such as music, film and literature (ibid.: 19). But rather than passively consume the contents of the cultural material, he urges that fragments must be extracted and used as catalysts to incite spontaneous and creative associations towards new and vibrant diversions. As educational dériveurs, learners can still (and maybe always will be in a position to) manoeuvre thoughts and connections beyond the banisters of the *educational spectacle*.

Through alternative possibilities latent with such strategies, knowledge, thinking, learner engagement and the wider purpose of education can set out to confront the practices and pressures dictated by the architecture of edu-business and the capitalist environment. Rather than accept and obey the imposition of consumer expectations as a *categorical imperative*, pedagogical practice can be opened up to the principle of the 'aimless stroll (*derive*), the results of which may then form the basis of a new cartography characterised by a complete disregard for the traditional and habitual practices' (Coverley, 2010: 90). To experience and pursue pedagogical co-constructions of micro moments and events of creative discovery, practitioners and students must first start to engage in the challenge of developing and inhabiting tactics and strategies of alternative and transformatory practice. Resisting the pressure to conform to the new role of business, *all* can start to resist and call into question the emerging practices of a system based upon the routine fulfilment of pre-assigned tasks and outcomes. Pedagogical practice – in the form of flexible counter strategies – based upon the principles of the dérive and détournement can begin to challenge, through experiential discovery, the standardizing practices of rote and regurgitative learning. For Debord, this poses problems associated with fathoming how to reproduce *ourselves*, as opposed to the things and practices that enslave us (Debord, 2004d: 61). This is not about creating a set of typical instructions and measurable objectives with a view to implementing a Situationist pedagogy; as Debord notes in *One More Try If You Want to Be Situationists*, 'there is no 'situationism' as *doctrine*', as such, we should resist the habit of exhaustively predefining knowledge, practice and outcome prior to any explorative experimentation (Debord, 2004b: 49). Negating pre-specified formulas and institutional narratives based on grades and final awards, a Situationist-esque experimental pedagogy can lead towards practices and developments that are as yet to be defined. The potential for the pedagogical adaptation of these principles and counter strategies means that conversations, narratives, learning-practices and expectations within and across university contexts can be resituated to start to resist the poleaxing mental consequences of the consumer university. The counter strategies for subjective discovery and empowerment can reinvigorate untapped passions and visions of possibility; as Debord notes:

> The revolution in everyday life, breaking its present resistance to the histori-cal (and to every kind of change), will create the conditions in which the . . . critique and perpetual re-creation of the totality of everyday life . . . must be under taken in the present conditions of oppression, in order to destroy these conditions. (Debord, 1961: para. 34–35)

The dérive and détournement can be openly and freely gifted as flexible peda-gogical alternatives which can be resituated in any number of different ways to facilitate creative permutations and opportunities for discovery. Untethered renovations of personal voices, moments and situations can emerge to provoke wonder and nudge longing, astonishment and *renewed expectations* to the fore of the explorative learning experience. Conjoined with the array of concepts and tactics previously covered in relation to Bloch, Barthes and Bachelard, the Situationist-based counter strategies of dérive and détournement can form the basis for a wider pedagogical framework; the flexibility of this framework, in turn, can be infused and inhabited with a proliferation of non-linear and per-sonalized expressions. It is possible for fresh academic and democratic oppor-tunities to unfold, where learners are free to collectively embark on adventures, to divine and rearticulate refracted pasts, and begin to posit them as unspent traces of possible futures. As Vaneigem notes, Situationist counter-strategies are essential and potent, as they can be used to construct the present in ways that can 'rectify the past, to change the psychogeography of our surroundings, to hew our unfulfilled dreams and wishes out of the veinstone that impris-ons them, to let individual passions find harmonious collective expression' (Vaneigem, 2006: 234). The insights presented by Bloch, Barthes and Bachelard become the tactics and specific vehicles through which the step-change and experiential revolutions of everyday life can begin to emerge. Coupled with the pedagogical counter strategies offered by the Situationists, the Blochian, Barthesean and Bachelardean tactics become the bread-crumb trails through which non-linear echoes of interiority and new possibility start to emerge. As flexible mechanisms of curricular engagement, they can be malleably implemented and subjectively received in ways that can recognize and enable fractured searches for latent nubs of expressive hope. Through the wider, open and flexible spaces afforded by the dérive, learner collaborators can set out to détourne conceptual fragments and their own troves of poignant shards; and through the work of Bloch, Barthes and Bachelard, they can start to re-inhabit and repurpose flexible parameters of expressionistic learning spaces. Equipped with these tactics and counter strategies, pro-dynamic practitioners and learner-collaborators can start to challenge and depart from the staid, pre-specified and fatalistic consumer-infected present and start to conceive of new practices for new futures.

Notes

1   For a detailed breakdown of the founding (and subsequent) members of the SI, go to www.notbored.org/members.html
2   The brief though strident little tract incited the germination of a set of *SI* ideas and strategies, which were to be taken forward and developed across the fifteen years of the group's existence.
3   Coverley (2010) and Kofman and Lebas (2000) note that Chtcheglov's *Formulary for a New Urbanism* wasn't actually published until 1958. Chtcheglov/Ivain was part of – and contributed to – another of Debord's pre-Situationist groups, the Lettrist International group (which was in existence from 1952 to 1957). Chtcheglov was also referred to by his pseudonym 'Gilles Ivain'. James Nice (2011) provides a detailed account of the Situationist foundations of Tony Wilson's Manchester-based Factory Records and highlights the influence of Chtcheglov's text – and the wider *Situationist* writings on the formation of Manchester's Factory Records and the *Hacienda* Night Club.
4   Debord's manifesto is referred to throughout the remainder of this chapter as *Report on the Construction of Situations*.
5   This concept (and the concept of détournement) is defined and explored in more detail later in the chapter; but, by way of an initial definition, Coverley (2010) notes that the theory and practice of the dérive refers to experimental behaviours which strive to invoke 'a technique of transient passage through varied ambiences' (Coverley, 2010: 93). Adding a little clarity to this, Wark (2015) asserts that the 'dérive is the experimental mapping of a situation' (Wark, 2015: 57), one that allows *dériveurs* to follow impromptu and unpredictable discoveries; from the desire to explore and wander, new places and new experiences can emerge. Coverley (2010) also usefully notes that the notion and practice of the *dérive* has a long and varied history – one that predates the Situationists. As such, it is appropriate to note that

Debord and the SI didn't originally conceive of the dérive, but they developed and enhanced it as a key Situationist and political strategy.

6 Coverley (2010) again notes that détournement is a method which encounters and tackles – with a view to creatively transforming – entrenched, established and routinized cultural practices, knowledge, or artefacts. To *détourne* means to seek out 'a word, statement, image or event from its intended usage and to subvert its meaning . . . *Détournement* creates new and unexpected meanings by hijacking and disrupting the original' source of published culture (Coverley, 2010: 95).

7 Wark clarifies that *Potlatch* was a key Situationist concept and a practice which refers to an *authentic* kind of gift or donation, something that is freely passed on and given to another party – but with a political purpose. The Situationist notion of potlatch meant that time, materials, texts and energy were given away 'in order to acquire reputation' (Wark, 2015: 71). A key example of Situationist potlatch is that none of the SI Journals, essays, or other texts were ever subject to copyright (essentially, the SI gave them away); in this sense, the entire work of the 'Situationists International was a grand potlatch' (Wark, 2015: 71).

8 Debord notes that 'all the desires that have been frustrated by the functioning of social life . . . of the profound richness and energy abandoned in everyday life is inseparable from awareness of the poverty of the dominant organization of this life' (Debord G., 1961: para 18).

9 Debord also offers the following insight into the physical dérive: 'In spite of the cessations imposed by the need for sleep, certain dérives of a sufficient intensity have been sustained for three or four days, or even longer. It is true that in the case of a series of dérives over a rather long period of time it is almost impossible to determine precisely when the state of mind peculiar to one dérive gives way to that of another' (Debord, 1958: para 12).

10 Written descriptions can be no more than passwords to this great game (Debord, 1958: para 18).

11 Debord questions, in relation to this point, 'What is private life deprived of?' Quite simply, of life itself, which is cruelly absent. People are as deprived as possible of communication and of self-realization. Deprived of the opportunity to personally make their own history (Debord, 1961: para 23).

12 The Situationists were active and in existence for a relatively short period of time, between 1957 and 1972. Wark (2015) notes that in its entirety, the SI only ever consisted of seventy-two members, with an average of twenty to thirty at any point in time. This was down to the fact that membership within the SI was challenging and unpredictable; philosopher and Situationist collaborator Henri Lefebvre recalls that in order to *distil* the group to a pure core, Debord ruled the SI with an unforgiving style, expelling *non-conformist* members for often

obscure reasons (Ross, 2004: 268). Kofman and Lebas (2000: 82) note that the architect and Situationist member Constant Nieuwenhuys (referred to as Constant in his Situationist texts) was expelled by Debord for actively and ideologically contributing to a town planning project (this was problematic, as one of the key tenets of SI membership was to 'never work').

6

Bye Bye Badman: The Redemption of Hope through Popular Culture

The New Year celebrations were over, it was now 1994 and deep into the winter cycle; daylight only managed to emerge for about six or seven hours each day in short and cold-muffled stints. I remember this time quite lucidly. January, in its entirety, was regulated by the metered tapping of clock-time and the electrical pulsing of motors through heavy industrial machinery. I was a textile weaver, working for a wet-felt and paper-dryer manufacturer in the north-west of England. The factory buildings, a 20th century pastiche of weaving sheds, warehouses and treatment rooms, bridged a stagnant-smelling Blakewater tributary. Throughout January an abundance of customer orders meant that compulsory overtime working was required, 12-hour night-shifts, 6 pm to 6 am, six days a week. I would arrive ten minutes prior to the start of the shift, take my place in the orderly queue along with the other weavers and operatives, and wait in line to clock-in. The familiar and slightly bitter smell of oil, chemicals and fine, airborne textile spores permeated the coolness of the atmosphere; in here, regimented lines of bright white electric lights obliterated the probing winter darkness outside. The shuttle-beds of the superlooms ranged from a mere 5 meters (at the smaller end) to the intimidating loom number seven, an imposing 25 meters wide; these mechanistic colossi torpedoed heavy 1-meter shuttles from side to side. The noise was damagingly loud, and this necessitated the wearing of ear protectors when the shed was in full operation.

For weeks I hardly saw, or felt, the light brush of daylight; arriving home, somewhere around 06.30 in the morning, I'd sit in the still darkness, and then I'd eat a little; in advance of my partner and young daughter surfacing, I'd unfold into bed and, in the drab mirk-lit silence, escape temporarily into fits of broken sleep. This state of somnambulistic reclusiveness meant that I rarely saw them depart for their respective worlds of work and school on the other side of the short winter day. By the time I surfaced, in the mid-afternoon, lurching shadows cast by the weak and dissipating daylight were already in retreat across our late-Victorian mid-terraced house.

Each evening as she returned from work, conversation was scant and stunted. The necessity for human connection quickly dissipated as days and weeks of little physical and verbal contact ate away at the wound of our relational rupture. An hour or so to eat, catch-up with snapshots of news on the TV, followed by stuttered sentences of estranged functionality, this all circuitously brought us back round to 5.30 pm, where I'd exit to repeat the routine.

In the locker room, I'd thread my rustic, hand-made weaving pouch, respective tools, and *Sony Walkman* on to my leather belt; amid joking and banter, I'd congregate and wait with the others for our night-shift dispatches. The shift foreman would descend the narrow wooden stairs from the small office mezzanine and issue loom allocations and fabric schedules. Collectively, we would then spill into the shed and receive a technical debrief from the departing day-shift weaver. Prior to initiating the mechanized thunder, my thoughts and senses would be submerged into the isolating inner-foam of my red plastic ear protectors. After checking the loom, fabric and shuttle for damaged warp and remaining weft, I would initiate the motor, pick the first shuttle across, and then depress the all-important play-button on my *Walkman*. As the picking-arms and reed crashed and rocked through each slow-moving minute, the snug-fitting ear phones, secreted inside each of the plastic half-domes, dulled and disguised some of the rumbling machinery. Once a weaver's routine has been learned, drilled and conditioned, the tasks can be carried out with swift accuracy; predictable repetition ensures an efficient mastery over the whole process. Gripped inside the plastic and per-cushion sealed world, I had little else to do other than to listen; so I listened and thought.

More than sixty-five nocturnal hours per week is a lot of mental space to fill; listening to the same, familiar array of artists, albums, songs and lyrics can become equally repetitive and mundane. So I sought out new and much needed musical material to add to and vary the long night's playlist. As part of the search, I discovered one of my partner's cassettes which had been left and shut away in one of the drawers of accumulated rubbish in the kitchen; I'd seen the cracked cassette case in there before, the vibrant, chaotic artwork on the front cover had intrigued me; it was the *Stone Roses* seminal album from 1989. My brief stint in the army as a young soldier from 1987, followed by a rapid and troubled exit in 1989, meant that while I had been familiar with the band, and some of their songs, I hadn't yet been fully acquainted with the whole of the album.

On the evening of this musical find, my shift schedule placed me on to one of the more modern and computerized looms, the 8-meter machine number twelve, the newest, most technological and efficient machine in the shed. The particular fabric and respective fine-gauge weft meant that a good *two* minutes elapsed between each bobbin change and weft-patch. The loom was running smoothly, and the vulnerable warp strands on each side of the flat looped fabric were spaced appropriately and holding well; from the moment of clicking 'play' on the *Walkman*, I immediately loved the *Stone Roses*. Embraced by the industrial-tinged echoes of John Squire's guitar and the prophetic drawl of Ian Brown on *I want to be Adored*, the first three bobbin changes went by almost without notice, the flow continued with the more upbeat *She Bangs the Drums* before drifting gracefully in to the ethereality of *Waterfall*. The Expressionistic reversal of *Don't Stop* offered a disruptive welcome to the vibrating picks and rhythms pulsing through the raised metallic platform.

And then, something happened! An unexpected moment impacted me so intensely that I had to shut down the loom; the music and cloaked lyrics of *Bye Bye Badman* punctured through to something. Rewinding this particular song a number of times, I couldn't quite make out many of the lyrics, but that didn't matter, the chorus was clear, and this was the segment of the song that wounded me. A sluice-gated chest-rush of emotion poured forth, and the song and the lyrics of *Badman* continued to explode as a source of fascination. For a period of time my loom remained motionless as I rewound, played and replayed the song.

With friends on the shift, I'd grown to love, analyse, and discuss *Pink Floyd*, the *Sex Pistols*, *Joy Division* and *New Order* – among many others. The styles and lyrical metaphors created by these bands established and cemented a coded bond between like-minded working-class dreamers, aspiring escapologists funnelled and hemmed-in to a low-paid and soulless environment. But, unlike the imaginative space generated by *Floyd*, and the working-class, anti-establishment post-punk Factory bands, *Joy Division* and *New Order*, *Badman* was beyond all of this. *Badman* was different, something deeper dwelled here, and it continued to provoke and stir. I grew obsessed and intent on deciphering the lyrics, spending time at home playing the song, writing and rewriting the words, sporadically attempting to decipher some sort of hidden code; I became a culture-detective on the hunt to locate the source of the intensity and psychic disruption caused by the song.

Where we shall land no more

February offered a welcome break from the compulsory overtime, and the shift returned to a more standard 5-day pattern, Monday to Friday, 10.00 pm till 6.00 am. This created a little space in the evening to become reacquainted with my daughter. We both started to look forward again to my reading her a bedtime story, and we continued with the nightly reading of J. M. Barrie's *Peter Pan*. One particular Saturday evening, I can recall tucking her into her duvet; and in the gentle glow of her night-light, she shuffled towards the wall, and I perched on the side of her bed. We located the folded corner of the most recently read page and continued with the story. As her beautiful eyes started to close, I continued to read, silently, until I reached a particular paragraph, which unleashed another unexpected culture-*punch*; a brief and poignant sentence which read: '[on] these magic shores children at play are forever beaching their coracles. We too have been there; we can still hear the sound of the surf, though we shall land no more' (Barry, 2015: 6). My undisclosed and vacuous ache sensed that this, along with *Bye Bye Badman*, was another culture detonation of an unfolding and hiero-glyphic message.

I descended the stairs and seated in the dining area, the soft yellow under-lights of the cupboards cast an atmospheric shadow across a disordered and scattered array of papers on the table. My partner is out, again, I'm not entirely sure when, or if, she'll be home. With my musical mantra playing through the enclosed and crystal clarity of the earphones, I decide to *detect* and uncover the lurking secret of the place where I *shall land no more*; could this be the location and hiding place of the *Badman*. Intermittently closing my eyes, I start to scrib-ble, and sketch meandering free-associative notes; searching and grasping at the fleeting irruptions emerging from within a hazy mirage of *lost time*. Through an emotional reservoir, *Badman* starts to appear and make sense; he's a ciphered sentry at a long-forgotten doorway. I peer further into the reverie and detect the face of what appears to be a multifaceted *Badman*. I recognize him, he took something long ago, something that has remained lost and locked away ever since; traces of daydream debris, desperate longings for escape, all meander back to a deposited and lingering silence. The mask shifts, and through the refrac-tion, the related face of an accomplice is revealed; the *Badman* is also humilia-tion, heaped on to a now distant self, struggling to make sense of a lifeless and technical system of school-based rote-instruction. With each ridiculed and daily sequence of unintentional errors, he makes me ascend the public spectacle of the dreaded chair, to reach the ultimate pinnacle of shame, the table. I then see that the *Badman* is a tripartite oppressor, he is also the *Hyde Park* bombing and the battle for the *Falklands*, a war-damaged veteran who's indiscriminate and vicious rage regularly rained down and into the disintegrating world of a lost and alienated teenage soldier.

I find myself gazing inward, towards the lingering shadows of violence, theft and implosion, I eventually arrive at the destination of an old memory; it's a house from my childhood, I'm familiar with its uneven, stone covered back yard and dank, disused coal-shed. And I'm there, on a cherished and battered red-and-yellow plastic tractor spinning pedals attached to either side of the black front wheel. Riding round in circles, I have my favourite silver NASA jacket on, *army* trousers, and a black felt cowboy hat with a silver starred badge attached to the front. Suddenly he looks back, and I want to tell him that the *Badman* isn't his fault. I want to run in there and grab him so that we can escape down to the shoreline where we can set sail together. But I can't move, no breath can escape my mouth. Instead, I blow a whispered thought over to say sorry for the wasted and lost years that he's been dragged through, followed by the years of oblivion and silent rage. And then the lingering shadows, peering from within the coal shed, start to shrink and disperse. I move towards him and take hold of his hand, he kisses my cheek, turns and walks away; I can see his silver NASA jacket glint as he climbs up the double-stone step and leaves through the unbolted back-gate.

Under the paving stones, the beach

My sister telephoned to speak to me; she'd heard that I was a little down and struggling living alone. She was at university in Sheffield and said that she needed to pass a quick message on to me. I returned her call, and across the distance she recited Charles Bukowski's poem *The Laughing Heart* to me. It was beautiful, and I cried. She said that I must go to watch a newly released film, *The Shawshank Redemption*.

It's October now, mid-afternoon on a crisp and clear Saturday. I hadn't heard of this film; not many people had. No huge bill board postings, a far-from impressive start at the box-office; the old cinema, located in the historical neo-Gothic corn-exchange in the centre of the town was the perfect setting. A small handful of people dripped in to the showing and spread out chaotically around the musty, vacuous auditorium. This was a prison film unlike any other that I had seen before; a powerful flowering started to bud around the loosening joints of my chains. And as I hear and listen to Red's final words on his bus journey to meet Andy, a cathartic release pours out. Concealed, among the red velvet seats at the back of the now empty auditorium, I wave bye bye to my *Badman* and leave him sitting in the shadows of darkened history. I depart and, in the crisp autumn of the evening, set off to pursue the revival of a daydream, a gradual and adventurous journey towards long-delayed hope and transformation.

Alluvial skids

A number of years after these esoteric and transformative encounters, I discovered that the *intended* meaning of the song *Bye Bye Badman* (by the Stone Roses song writers Ian Brown and John Squire) was about the French student riots and general strikes of Paris in May 1968. Uncovering the seeming 'authentic' or original meaning ascribed by the songwriters, I was struck by the irreconcilable difference between Brown's and Squire's quite specific motivation and the very different interpretations that I had subsequently elicited. Initially I was disappointed, as my apparent misinterpretation of the song and lyrics had grown to represent not only painful and destructive associations but also, ultimately, redemptive and empowering triumphs. Personally ingesting the *call-to-arms*, I had risen up against, thrown stones at and bid farewell to my *Badman*. How could it be that my profoundly personal misunderstanding and subsequent strange connections to the song had served to excavate such intense reflections and the eventual facilitation of the conquest of lingering and incarcerating adversities? The unfolding impact and change that this song had generated within me was real and undeniable. The song continued to grow as an important part of my personal folklore, and the disjuncture between the two narratives continued to intrigue and puzzle me.

As part of my later unfolding academic journey, I was to discover a Roland Barthes essay *Death of the Author* (1977); this enigmatic little essay started to gestate a personal resolution to my nagging *Badman* 'problem'. The potency and shifting relevance of *Bye bye Badman* continued to mutate as part of a creative metamorphosis of associations. In a Barthesean sense, the original authors had inscribed and unleashed an initial cultural artefact; essentially, the song contained a text that could never belong to only one singular and universal meaning. With *Badman*, something in the psychic *ether* glinted and emerged beyond the authority of the original text; in the shifting spaces and times of my experience, memories and disappointments, the hieroglyphic fluidity of the artefact spoke to me, and not the controlled, abstracted singularity of the 'author'. As a liberated and amateur *Scriptor*, the *skid* of my misinterpretation opened up a disruptive crevasse;[1] beyond the pharisaical legalism of retracing an objective *pure* origin, the shifting terrain of dynamic instants, shored up on the alluvium of my quantum interiority, started to give *form* to the mirage of a distant hope. An incomplete utopian territory started to slowly distil and make sense; against the thwarted disappointments of the past, a future of alternative possibilities started to stutter and emerge beyond the trace of the text.

Something's missing

For Bloch, beloved, intimate stories operate as secret cultural catalysts, ciphers of hope which decode and uncover the mystery of incognito utopian possibilities; as such, my reflection and creative recounting of *Badman* was not just recounted for the routine of the telling; quite the opposite, it became a malleable and détourned palimpsest, a narrative mechanism which started to clothe and articulate a transformative story. My thoughts and meditations on the trace impact of *Badman*, and the ways in which it became a beautifully harboured story, unveiled a deeper and embedded reason as to why it *cajoled* the awakening of poignant *secrets*. The embryonic utopian gestations revealed painful disappointments, but along with these, the cultural sources also started to whisper the constructive empty space of anticipatory hope. The metaphoric mystery of the self-encounter with *Badman*, with its shadows of incompleteness and the shock of the empty space, resonates with an evocative story recounted by Bloch in *Traces*, entitled 'Pippa Passes'.[2] This story offers an example of a cultural trace, a recounted encounter as a culturally mediated metaphor which, according to Bloch, has a poignancy which can revive the vacuity of *other* thwarted or missed opportunities:[3]

> Our friend sat in the tram car . . . and across from him a girl, who he barely looked at, about whom he noticed only her peculiarly large pale blue eyes, noticed them dimly while talking to his companions. He had to notice, actually, for those eyes watched him steadfastly, not enticingly; rather, they were round and lonely, truly like stars . . . Now chance came to his aid: the man dropped his ticket. He picked it up from the floor, thereby lightly brushing the girls knee – truly so lightly and awkwardly, so inadvertently in that narrow space . . . Soon the tram stopped, as the stars of her eyes rose again (or perhaps had never set); my friend stepped off with his companions while the girl observed, now with a truly mysterious expression, and the tram disappeared in the direction of the

park. The man claimed not even to have watched the taillights, so uninterest-ing did the matter seem to him, and so calm did he feel. But no sooner was he seated at the table than there came, in the midst of the cafe, while he was still listening to light news . . . a crash that almost buried him: love exploded on a timed fuse. Illusion began to operate, and the girl within it became the beloved, the one just lost, and neglected, hopelessly gone, with whom an entire life sank. A beautiful, long life, never lived yet deeply familiar, which he recalled almost in a hallucination, and which lacked nothing but its tiny beginning . . . one can understand the next few days, which he described, unreservedly open and agitated, days of wandering, of madly pacing off the tram route, the often repeated trip at the same time along the same route, the search for the pearl in the haystack. (Bloch, 2006: 59–61)

The moment of shock and melancholic astonishment as part of the narrative also has an Expressionistic utopian potency beyond the authored text. Bloch suggests that subjective flashes emanate from beyond the story; a hieroglyphic utopian shimmering on the cusp of the 'darkness of lived-moments'.[4]

Indomitus ideology

Theodor Adorno, a friend and close associate of Ernst Bloch, wrote an essay enti-tled *Ernst Bloch's Spuren* (1991), which, as a piece of work, set out to critique Bloch's work on the *trace*. Adorno explains that as a philosophical strategy the Blochian trace refers to the deposits of culture-infused memories and narrative legacies registered and accumulated during childhood and youth. For Bloch, as we have seen, these remnant phantasms have the potential to shock a liberatory and reconstructive *encounter with the self*; the subject, confronted with the reali-zation that s/he is not yet complete, 'appears as something unreal, something that has not yet emerged from potentiality, but also as a reflection of what he could be' (Adorno, 1991: 205–206). It becomes clear, as Adorno's analysis continues and develops, that he does not agree with Bloch's liberating and transformative position in relation to culture, trace and the utopian potency of memory. For Adorno, all popular culture, with its simplistic mechanisms, image-sequences and narrative structures, serve only to generate 'mimetic impulses which, prior to all content and meaning, incite the viewers and listeners to fall into step as if in a parade' (Adorno, 2001: 183). Therefore, film, music and other popular cultural sources, subjected to the critical filter of an Adornean and wider *Culture Industry* critique, render the pre-*constructed* relationship between the duped consumer and the capitalistic cultural artefact as one of alienated and alienating control. The creatively disempowered and atomized recipient is entirely 'subject' to the torrents and currents of the mass consumption society. Within this *culture-as-manufactured-ideology* approach, cultural material is a ubiquitous force which renders the audience as an almost passive mass, purposefully positioned beyond the facilities of reinterpretation or re-negotiation. Capitalist-consumerist, cultural and ideological agendas ensure a repetitive and recognizable formula, where from the beginning 'it is quite clear how it will end, and who will be rewarded, punished, or forgotten' (Horkheimer and Adorno, 1969: 125). The anonymous power structures which linger behind the public facing cultural product ensure that '[b]usiness is their ideology . . . the power of the culture industry resides in its identification with a manufactured need' (Adorno, 2001: 137).[5]

Adorno, Horkheimer and the persuasive canon of the *Culture Industry* are not the only critics to adopt such a cynical approach; Jack Zipes, as part of his work on folk culture and fairytales, corroborates this position and suggests that the highly controlled and technical way in which mass-produced and mass-mediated culture is manufactured renders the spectator as a cultural shell, subject to a universal and sanitized spectacle of the story. Culture produced and disseminated in this way effectively arrests the potential of any political potency to the confines of a techno-universal narrative (Zipes, 2002: 20). For Zipes, mechanistically mediated stories do not prompt reflexive agency or collective bonding (as would have traditionally been the case with storytellers and folk-tales); instead, through automated systems of production and distribution, they establish a 'total' meaning, one that over-arches and influences the non-active audience (Zipes, 2006: 193–212). Henry Giroux further supports this critical, ideological position using the example of the intimidating matrix of the globalized Disney *machine*; he calls for parents and cultural workers alike to be aware and to become consciously critical of Disney's purposeful conservative agendas and tactics. He asserts that there is a need to learn how to guard ourselves and others against the subtle strategies and subliminal identity-moulding techniques emitted from within the Disney oeuvre (Gillam and Wooden, 2008: 7). Furthermore, he proposes that we learn to scrutinize the underlying ideological codes within and across cultural products; in doing so, we can learn to differentiate and separate the manufactured ideology and false desires 'and subject positions that define for children specific notions of agency and . . . possibilities in society' (Giroux, 2001: 97).

It would be difficult, not to mention *questionable* and problematic, to deny the corporate, capitalistic and profit-seeking agendas purposefully generated and aggressively marketed by powerful and multinational culture-making companies. Certainly, the theme and message of my analysis here (and throughout this book) is not to disregard or negate the persuasive influence and ideological potency of mass, consumer based, popular culture. It is, rather, to navigate towards a quite different, perpendicular dimension of quantum and interiorized space; a liberated territory *left-of-ideological-field*, where the chaos of subjective creativity is afforded a voice beyond the linearity and stasis of *culture-work-as-ideology*. Critical of universal-ideological positions, Griffin (2000) points out that *text-poaching* is a practice that has always taken place within different cultural circles; recognizing that not every viewer, at all times, accepts and endorses cultural representations of conventions and norms, '[r]ather, they choose their own way, enjoy certain parts more than others and sometimes enjoy these parts in diverse fashion' (Griffin, 2000: 49). The coercive might, authorial potency and ideological reach generated by the agents, and distribution matrixes of popular cultural works, may not be as seamlessly universalizing as the ideological critics suggest. To successfully execute such a level of mental and ideological conformity would need a constant, carefully crafted and ubiquitous process, one whose impact would need to closely survey and control all subjective facets of narrative impact. As Barthes argues in *The Pleasure of the Text* (1975), it 'is not very useful to say 'dominant ideology', for the expression is a pleonasm: ideology is nothing but an idea . . . But I can go further subjectively and say: *arrogant ideology*' (Barthes, 1975: 47). Without detracting entirely from the pertinent points raised by the ideological critiques of the *Culture Industry*, the reflexive frameworks of Barthes and Bloch enable non-linear and more nuanced connections and analyses to emerge. Beyond the text, and beyond the ideology, empowered *Scriptors* can seize the perpendicularity and openness of Expressionistic space in order to détourne flakes and catalytic *skids* from culture-trace remnants. Recognizing and accommodating complex myriad and multidimensional threads, which striate from the *hieroglyphic* metaphors of culture-works, creative reinterpretations can form beyond traditional academic formulas.

Denken Heisst Überschreiten[6]

For Bloch, mundane and mass produced cultural material, including some of his own favourites, such as cowboy films and the Wild West, detective stories, and of course fairytales (see Bloch, 1993; Dayton, 1997; Zipes, 2002), have the potential to provoke traces of thoughts, hopes, and daydreams towards the edge of the predictable, the known, and the familiar. The recurrent (as Bloch would call them) *utopian* ciphers of liberation, love, hope, and even death continually manifest across all kinds of culture sources and artefacts; such themes have the potential to kick-start self-encounters, anticipatory and fleeting considerations, of *Not-Yet* attained hopes and opportunities.

Bloch's shifting category of the Not-Yet is sympathetic to the wild variations and psychological affinities, which intertwine with eclectic montages of popular cultural associations. The Not-Yet establishes, and continues to establish, new and emergent connections, as relativized human time(s) continue to move forward towards the open and undisclosed future. Incrementally shifting and drifting, the interiority of subjective 'Now' time can become tinged with the fleeting hue of hope and daydreams, and progress towards moments and events that have yet to come into being. As Bloch states, 'the immediate fleeting Now is too little, it fades and makes way for the next, because nothing in it has yet been properly achieved' (Bloch, 1986: 313). Art and culture–infused stories nudge magmatic trace emergencies which psychically murmur of *something* from beyond the original source; in doing so, creative inner moments take us beyond the static context and specifics of ideology. Korstvedt (2010) clearly summarizes this aspect of Blochian thinking, in that art and culture 'provide access to the inner-realm, and this is needed, for in the 'darkness of the lived moment' . . . we encounter something that reaches beyond and can break through not only the error of the world, but the prison house of the existentially specific' (Korstvedt, 2010: 36–37). The wider Blochian suggestion here is that an ideological or *cultural surplus* latently dwells invisibly on the periphery of a utopianly communicative cultural source. Beyond the immediate intention, theme and authority of an artefact or piece of culture work, a malleable utopian hieroglyph of transformative possibility ethereally lingers. This cultural surplus is where the subjective yearnings ache for new forms of existence, alternative worlds and possibilities without alienation; as Bloch suggests, 'every act of anticipating identifies itself to the utopian function, and the latter seizes on all possible substance in the surplus of the former' (Bloch, 1986: 150). Again, Korstvedt provides a useful synopsis here:

In *The Spirit of Utopia* [Bloch] proposes that although many forms of knowledge are socially or culturally determined, and thus learned by observation, certain 'archetypal figures of the human landscape' (Bloch lists love, hatred, hope, despair, states of the soul) are innate, free from social or material conditioning, and therefore do not depend on any empirical knowledge. For this reason, the experience of these archetypal figures carries with it 'an ontic surplus value' of symbolic intention, which depends not on the existing world but subsists in its 'own self-presence'. (Korstvedt, 2010: 53)

Recognition of the cultural surplus means that new tales can be thought and brought forth from the ideological debris and traces of the past; thwarted hopes and incomplete experiences, and wishes that have Not-Yet been completed, can be retold as constructive scenarios that have *yet* to come into being. The utopian function chaotically provoked and subjectively manifested through the hermetic spring of the cultural surplus is fluid, and must be re-discovered by each separate subjective encounter. Memories and traces embedded in subjective pasts give form to unspent anticipations. The cultural surplus, evoked from the ethereal periphery of the culture-work, contains seeds of Not-Yet-conscious (*noch-nicht bewusst*) utopian material. Geoghegan (1996) concisely sums up the role of the Not-Yet-conscious as part of the creative utopian process:

> Bloch isolates three stages in the process whereby the Not-Yet-Conscious becomes a creative force in the world: incubation, inspiration and explication. Incubation is the period of active fermentation where the new material is developing, much of it beneath the surface of consciousness, until a point is reached when it bursts into the conscious world. This is the moment of inspiration, a sudden lucid moment of illumination. (Geoghegan, 1996: 35)

Geoghegan (1996) also notes that another crucial aspect of the Blochian approach to understanding hope and utopia is the way he uses metaphor. For Bloch, the world contains a secret, one that is continually expressed through art and culture in metaphorical form; as such, it is the inevitable task of the human to decipher the traces of this secret and, as detectives, continually work towards achieving the essence of its form. Art is therefore not a copy or imitation of the world that exists, but it is instead the gradual revelation of what it could be. Cultural and artistic creation is the human-inspired mechanism by which the *Not-Yet conscious* is brought gradually to the *Front* of consciousness (Bloch, 1986: xxxii). Within this generic notion of art and culture, subjective wish-landscapes emerge to re-awaken the posited traces of a yearned-for-future that is yet to be.

Bloch (1993) uses the term *Novum* (or new) to identify an encounter with genuine, new possibility; momentary *Nova* erupt into consciousness, as we are shocked into recognizing the possibility of future newness. The utopian tendency, or surplus, inherent within all art forms should not be regarded as unfathomable mirages of impossible ideals, but rather as abstracted indicators of

future utopian states. As Roberts (1990) informs us, the Blochian way of thinking establishes a

> thought-experiment that can be embarked upon by anyone, the Blochian
> system clears space, [it] opens possibilities and refunctions the past in the
> name of the future. As such Bloch articulates indispensable middle ground
> between nostalgic regression into the past and capitulation of the coming . . .
> Bloch re-awakens a lost past through the category of the hidden future and
> exploits the idea of the possible so as to threaten all ideological rigidities.
> (Roberts, 1990: xv)

Telling stories

As part of this, art and literature and other cultural forms generally must be
understood and considered as essential facets of a utopian pedagogy; memory
and traces of cultural surplus can serve as powerful reminders of a *distant* and
non-quantifiable territory somewhere beyond the mundanity of everyday life.
Routine, daytime activities can be mysteriously punctured by the experience of
a strange recognition of vague familiarity (such as *Badman*). The possibility of
completion, somewhere in the future, beckons and awakens the shock of 'all the
past disruptions of this kind, all the aborted beginnings of our life in general .
. . This too is suffused by a feeling of recovering something once possessed –
and by a feeling, quite motionless in itself, of re-entry' (Bloch, 1998: 202–205).
As a pedagogical strategy, *Scripted manifestations* can emanate from within the
chaotic-temporal terrains of inner-worlds; for learner collaborators, infectious
symbolisms and traces can be détourned from the initial context of the infinite realm of cultural artefacts and experiences. Beyond the purposeful architecture and ideological parameters of manufactured art or culture-works, *third
Meanings* and associations can emerge. Unsettled latent and incognito possibilities wait 'for us in the future rather than bind us to the past' (Bloch, 2009: 221).
Such a practice of bespoke discovery would be, and is, deeply and unavoidably
subjective. However, within the context of a utopian pedagogy, deeply subjective
does not equate to objective irrelevance or incoherence.

Blochian, Barthesean, Bachelardean and Debordean infused learner encounters and analyses of poignant legacies and cultural artefacts, in conjunction with
respective, emergent traces, can be posed as opportunities, invitations, to *dérive*
and *Expressionistically* wander towards interpretations of their own nudges

and Not-Yet material in open and creative ways. The style and content of collaborative *trace*-philosophic refractions can take detours beyond the confines of the technical and universalizing contexts of ideology. Therefore academic custodians and institutional gatekeepers should resist the default temptation to incarcerate 'the' reinterpretive *skids* and détourned meanings of creative learners, and instead, nurture the hieroglyphic, utopian intrigue of the fresh stories being discovered, detected and ultimately told. Drawing upon and incorporating Bloch's notions of astonishment, shock and the self-encounter, subjective analyses – hooked on to multivariate cultural and memory montages – can be autonomously framed as emergent utopian reflections.

Avoiding the perpetuation of a top-down imposition of authoritarian knowledge, learner/collaborator trace-manifestations, and creative readings can become liberated as open-ended processes (which should remain open and liberated). Interpretive *skids'* misinterpretations and reinterpretations can manifest as chaotic flourishes and new narrative offshoots. Learner manifestations should remain, then, as active sites to be *Scripted*. In approaching abstract-utopian essences and temporalities of cultural surpluses in this way, pro-dynamic practitioners and learner collaborators can avoid the pseudo unilaterality of authorial revelation. Instead of uncovering a purposeful and rigid architecture of ideology, creative learner Scriptings can expressively explore and open up to previously hidden traces and heritages; hopeful reflections and ideas for transformed and alternative futures can prompt further geneses of untold stories. Embryonic and chaotic unfoldings such as these offer rich pedagogical possibilities; as cascadent continuations, they can continue to engage the hermeneutic capacities of contemporary and future collaborators.

Notes

1   Usefully, Barthes, in *Roland Barthes* (1977) notes that the amateur is (someone who engages in painting, music, sport, science, without the spirit of mastery or competition), the Amateur renews his pleasure *(amator:* one who loves and loves again); he is anything but a hero (of creation, of performance); he establishes himself *graciously* (for nothing) in the signifier: in the immediately definitive substance of music, of painting; his praxis usually involves no *rubato* (that theft of the object for the sake of the attribute); he is – he will be perhaps – the counter-bourgeois artist (Barthes, 1977: 52). And in *The Rustle of Language* (1989), Barthes argues that 'a theory of 'skidding' is necessary *precisely today*. Why? Because we are in

that historical moment of our culture when narrative cannot yet abandon a certain readability, a certain conformity to narrative pseudo-logic which culture has instilled in us and in which, consequently, the only possible novations consist not in destroying the story, the anecdote, but in *deviating* it: making the code skid while seeming to respect it' (Barthes, 1989h: 175).

2   It is significant that Bloch takes the title of this short story from Robert Browning's poem *Pippa Passes* (in 'Bells and Pomegranates [1841]), where a beautifully young and innocent girl ethereally wanders through the streets of Asolo (in Italy). Singing, as she goes, she attempts to influence the 'troubled' residents that she encounters to redeem their problems and woes with virtues of hope, love and kindness.

3   What is pertinent for Bloch in this story is how 'thematically' such a story has the flexible potential to nudge or prompt comparative traces from within the listener or reader (in our own reading of this – and other stories – in *Traces*). Thus, our own nostalgic shock-traces which become kick-started out of memorial slumber, as a result of encountering and meditating upon this story, is of importance.

4   Bloch, E. (2000) *The Spirit of Utopia*, chapter 4: 'The Shape of the Inconstruable Question' – the segment entitled: 'Again the Darkness (of the Lived Moment) and its Mutual Application to Amazement'; pp: 199–208.

5   Adorno, discussing the notion of utopia with Bloch, argues that 'dreams themselves have assumed a peculiar character of sobriety, of the spirit of positivism, and beyond that, of boredom'. What I mean by this is that it is not simply a matter of presupposing that what really is has limitations as opposed to that which has infinitely imaginable possibilities. Rather, I mean something concrete, namely, that one sees oneself almost always deceived: the fulfilment of the wishes takes something away from the substance of the wishes . . . instead of the wish-image providing access to the erotic utopia, one sees in the best of circumstances some kind of more or less pretty pop singer, who continues to deceive the spectator in regard to her prettiness insofar as she sings some kind of nonsense instead of showing it, and this song generally consists in bringing together 'roses' with 'moonlight' in harmony. Above and beyond this, one could perhaps say in general that the fulfilment of utopia consists largely only in a repetition of the continually same 'today' (Bloch, 1993: 1–2).

6   This is a key Blochian slogan which translates as 'thinking means venturing beyond'; see Roberts (1990: 33).

7

The Wisdom of the Crowd:
Liberating Creativity

Incubation, inspiration and explication

The previous chapter, *Bye Bye Badman*, made *passing* reference to the tripartite Blochian schema of *Incubation, Inspiration and Explication*; for Bloch, this conceptual triptych identifies an essential intra-subjective and trans-personal process of elicitation, a cumulative process of aspirational thoughts and imagined alternative scenarios. As Bloch notes, incubation, inspiration and explication 'belong to the ability to travel forward beyond the previous edges of consciousness' (Bloch, 1986: 122). Within the context of this triptych, incubation, as the first stage, refers to fleeting reveric moments, lingering *traces* which meander on matrical threads and striate towards memorial legacies of dormant hope. With incubation, 'there is a powerful intending, it aims at what is sought, what is dawning' (ibid.: 122). Incubation in this sense means to *brood* on the musty nudges of sepia-hued nostalgias, to harbour and gestate an embryonic *form* of *something* on the cusp of conscious thought. In a Blochian sense, such encounters and shards are often draped behind melancholic whispers, archived disappointments and incomplete latencies of thwarted personal journeys and adventures. Such refracted bubbles of incubation are associated with an *at-a-distance* recognition of desires and wishes for 'things to be different, to be better, to be more beautiful' (ibid.: 117). In the deep inner realm of hopeful-incubation, thoughts and associations teeter on the horizons of contemplative daydreams, oceanic shimmer-ripples of redemptive possibilities. As such, for Bloch, the stage of incubation is loaded with *Not-Yet-Conscious* splinters of transformative possibility (ibid.: 119).

Occasionally, lucid and persistent material (the incubated *stuff* of recurring daydreams and imaginary scenarios) can spill over into the next stage – that of inspiration; here utopian longings grow and establish as a more acute awareness of previously stunted opportunities and begin to appear as unspent possibilities that have *Not-Yet-Become*. In a literal sense, to *inspire* means to 'inhale', as though to breathe-in a divinely imparted truth, or, in a more secular sense, to experience a momentary *breath-snatch*, an involuntary physiological response to the unexpected shock of revelation. Flourishing moments of *inspiration* can increase as uncanny nuggets of familiarity and expand in their utopian potency the more they are deliberated. With this, subjectivities progressively identify with the missing aspects of reminisced and lingering contexts. Buoyant upon forward-cusping torrents of the future, moments of inspiration grow as wonder-probing aches; as Bloch notes, the inspiration stage manifests initially as a disconcerting flash or apparition, '[t]hat is why the expression *inspiration* [. . . is] used to describe this; it indicates the abruptness, the illuminating and inspiring stroke, the sudden insight' (ibid.: 123). For Bloch, inspiration is a stage and process of clarity and *quickening*, one that can inwardly grow and proliferate to such an extent that its powerful anticipation must also be released or *explicated*. With its explication 'out' into the world, the previously hidden impulse for hope is birthed, externalized and sent forth as a concrete confession of hope, its linguistic or cultural message becomes the 'final act of productivity', in the agonizing, blissful work of *explication*' (ibid.: 125).

Within the context of this current and unfolding work, the Blochian triptych is important; in terms of developing alternative tactics and counter strategies as part of a utopian pedagogy, it offers an effective and sympathetic framework, one that can contextualize and facilitate the previously established concepts, methods and ideas. Operating within the parameters of *Critical Pedagogy*, Henry Giroux and Peter McLaren acknowledge that a key intention embedded within the principles of Blochian philosophy is for the collective quanta of utopian aches to be translated into pragmatic options (so as to facilitate constructive change and alteration within the context of everyday life). As such, a pedagogical translation of the Blochian triptych can serve to acknowledge and map a growing awareness of the limitation of 'what exists' as an additional counter strategy; incubated *rumours* can operate in conjunction with inspired stories and narratives. Acting as utopian barometers of what 'might be' explications of anticipatory hope can also be afforded space for the expression of hope (Giroux and McLaren, 1997: 147). Usefully, Giroux and McLaren highlight a close and productive affinity between Paulo Freire's work on pedagogy and Bloch's work on utopia and the Not-Yet. Fundamentally, both Bloch and Freire aspire to target and nurture the human *something* that lies 'latent in the present, something immanently future-bearing that can be grasped in the flickering moment of anticipatory consciousness' (ibid.: 147–148). Giroux and McLaren also recognize that the more oblique and elliptical aspects of Blochian philosophy gain fortuitous ground in this partnership; Freirean praxis in particular addresses the problem of 'real world' practical implementation more completely than Bloch, as for Freire, 'both theory and practice [are] mutually constitutive and animating aspects of the process of becoming more fully human' (ibid.: 155). Further reinforcing this connection, Freire, in *Pedagogy of the Heart*, iterates a vein of argument which contains more than a passing affinity with the Blochian philosophical project. Freire notes that proactive manoeuvres that seek to reach out to and grapple with transformed 'tomorrows' are problematic; however, in order for any degree of potential or incremental change to take place, any such tactics need to be creatively and tenaciously pursued. To build a better tomorrow, it is imperative that 'we build it through transforming today. Different tomorrows are possible . . . [but] it is necessary to reinvent the future. Education is indispensable for this reinvention' (Freire, 2000: 55).

In a pedagogical sense, Freire establishes a direct connection with the purpose and function of active hope; new and democratic parameters in a climate of non-linear discovery and confidence can open up learners to a self-induced momentum, propelled by a desire to tackle and overcome externally imposed limits and constraints. As Freire notes, *hope* 'is rooted in men's incompletion, from which they move out in constant search . . . carried out only in communion with others. Hopelessness is a form of silence, of denying the world and fleeing from it' (Freire, 2005: 91). Within this context, both Bloch and Freire corroborate and assert that 'hope co-operates with possibility in fashioning freedom . . . As such, hope is to be conscripted by social agents in order to contest the gangsterism of the spirit so common in this era of consumer capitalism' (Giroux and McLaren, 1997: 157). In order to pursue pedagogy as a mechanism for transformation, liberation and social justice, it is essential that active, militant and constructive hope be one of its key foundations. To enable new and fresh generations of *hungry* thinkers to start to confront and grapple with the problems of the future, there needs to be a recognition that radical shifts and changes – to the consumerized and consumerizing guise of education – be incited and accommodated. San Juan in the *Foreword* to Peter McLaren's *Pedagogy of Insurrection* notes that Critical Pedagogy must be seen as an essential weapon 'in the age of the wars of terror, planetary surveillance, legal torture, genocidal drone assassinations'; and with this, there needs to be 'a rearming of the collective spirit to explore possibilities for resistance and transformation of social life' (San Juan, 2015: xv).

Furthermore, McLaren notes that consumer capitalism 'has made us feel alone together and homesick at home . . . we want to engage in acts of self-creation, [but are] forced to act in self-preservation' (McLaren, 2015: 395) in order to survive in a system of dehumanizing competition. Importantly, Freire also understood that any form of *liberation pedagogy* cannot, in itself, offer perfect or final answers. Any form of radical praxis must 'emerge from continuous struggle within specific pedagogical sites and among competing theoretical frameworks' (ibid.: 159). This remains necessary, as Giroux in *Rethinking Education as the Practice of Freedom* notes:[1]

> Each classroom will be affected by the different experiences students bring to the class, the resources made available for classroom use, the relations of governance bearing down on teacher–student relations, the authority exercised by administrations regarding the boundaries of teacher autonomy, and the theoretical and political discourses used by teachers to read and frame their responses to the diverse historical, economic, and cultural forces informing classroom dialogue. Any understanding of the project and practices that inform critical pedagogy has to begin with recognizing the forces at work in such contexts and which must be confronted by educators and schools every day. (Giroux, 2011: 162)

Within such environmental constraints, a utopian pedagogical strategy based upon nurturing active hope and aligned with an openness and fluidity of tactical practice should fashion and cascade an array of 'mental' and organizational *options*. Loaded with democratic possibilities, a utopian pedagogy can serve to influence and shape a wider contagion of transformative ideas; as such, it is essential that in order to sow the seeds of alternative pedagogical manoeuvres, educators and learners must fight to co-construct new forms of educational space and meaning. The more that practitioners continue to provide 'people with programs which have little or nothing to do with their own preoccupations, doubts, hopes, and fears' (Freire, 2005: 96) – and, in doing so perpetuate a bureaucratic desert of functionality – the less likely it is that change of any kind can start to emerge and unfold.

Enabling democratic and creative transgressions

bell hooks, in *Teaching to Transgress* (1994), and Heart to Heart: Teaching with Love (2003), reaffirms Freire and Giroux's charges surrounding the exclusionary and emotionally devoid practices of distantiated and fact-based teaching. Usefully, hooks reflects on her own negative experiences as both an undergraduate and graduate student, and argues that the alienating and boring environments mirrored the imposition of curricular cannons and knowledge tranches which bore no relevance to her cultural contexts, interests or concerns. For hooks, the architecture of the typical classroom, bolstered by the format of the traditional lecture – with its restrictive flow of rigid *knowledge-as-static-information* – was used

> to enact rituals of control that were about domination and the unjust exercise of power. In these settings I learned a lot about the kind of teacher I did not want to become . . . It surprised and shocked me to sit in classes where professors were not excited about teaching, where they did not seem to have a clue that education was about the practice of freedom . . . I longed passionately to teach differently from the way I had been taught since high school. The classroom should be an exciting place, never boring. And if boredom should prevail, then pedagogical strategies were needed that would intervene, alter, even disrupt the atmosphere. (hooks, 1994: 5–7)

Problematically for hooks, as part of her subsequent journey into academia as a career, she discovered a lack of interest among her colleagues – an active resistance even – to incorporating freedom and *excitement* as part of the HE experience. In *Heart to Heart*, hooks aligns the relational distance and emotional stunting of the traditional university, with its pre-existing and entrenched hierarchies, with the legacy of an outmoded and exclusive system. Embodying intimidating echelons of power and control, the traditional HE environment renders the student experience as one based upon fear, where students 'fear teachers and seek to please them. Concurrently, students are encouraged to doubt themselves, their capacity to know, to think, and to act' (hooks, 2003: 130). Rather than learning to communicate – and collaborate – as *comrades*, students are pitted against each other as adversaries, as part of a competitive struggle for victory; individuals vie to snatch the coveted and institutionally sanctioned prize of being the *one* 'smart enough to dominate the others' (ibid.: 131). The endemic values of power, hierarchy and exclusivity easily infiltrate and influence the role and activities of the lecturer and operate to constrict and stifle the space of learning. Ensconced in a scaffold of expected behaviour and performance, the innovative and maverick tendencies of the lecturer are defaulted to the security of familiarity; practitioners, through time constraints and other bureaucratic pressures, adhere to and reinforce a wary, emotionless and *safe* distance from the objectified student.[2]

Creative autobiography: A practice for wandering

The curricular principles and *everyday* practices of a critical or dynamic pedagogy – such as a utopian pedagogy – must recognize and factor-in to its strategy the support and action of all participants. To influence and shape an *open learning community*, the recovery of hope and anticipation must be accessible and creatively habitable by all. Furthermore, the development of a micro community of collaborative and democratic support must also generate freedom and excitement through vibrant and fresh learning experiences. The capacity to accommodate and openly develop bespoke ideas, fuelled by novelty, must also supportively and sensitively evoke a wider group interest in hearing others' voices, as 'any radical pedagogy must insist that everyone's presence is acknowledged' (hooks, 1994: 8). Incorporating the excitement of discovery and the *pleasure* of learning, all aspects of teaching and pedagogy can become shared and, in microcosm, initiate formative acts of democratic challenge against practices which generate boredom and apathy. As part of this, a utopian pedagogy should be flexible enough to allow for spontaneities and multidirectional shifts in meaning, rhythm and direction. Furthermore, educating or leading learners towards the freedom to create and to personally excavate – through excitement – the openness of knowledge production and its democratic possibilities means that all participants (including the lecturer / teacher) must engage with and *practice* these principles. As hooks notes:

> When education is the practice of freedom, students are not the only ones who are asked to share, to confess. Engaged pedagogy does not seek simply to empower students. Any classroom that employs a holistic model of learning will also be a place where teachers grow, and are empowered by the process. That empowerment cannot happen if we refuse to be vulnerable while encouraging students to take risks . . . I do not expect any students to take any risks that I would not take, to share in any way that I would not share. (Ibid.: 21)

Freire, Giroux, McLaren and hooks all emphasize the need for innovative pedagogical approaches, with the purpose of recognizing and ultimately enabling personal transformation. In order for learners to engage collaboratively with freedom and compassion – love even – and grow in confidence and excitement about personal connections and discoveries, it is essential that a meaningful practical process and externalizing 'end-point' be built in to the utopian pedagogical approach. Learners must be able to not only incubate inspirational aspects of alternative learning but also, importantly, materialize and *explicate* (*speak out*) their discoveries. This means that learners must be liberated to not only think in alternative ways but also act and create work in alternative ways, to expressionistically inhabit and interpret traces and reveries within the context of their own lives, stories and hopes. In order for *inspired* fragments and refracted notions of the Not-Yet to emerge, widely disparate and diverse populations of learners with varying troves of personal and poignant experiences must be afforded space to dérive and détourne their cherished traces of cultural biography. To incorporate chaotic and unpredictable permutations of cultural reference points, hopes and experiences, an alternative approach to producing, assessing and ultimately grading work must be made available. To accommodate this, I propose the development and implementation of a type of assignment that reflects – and is conducive with – the styles, expectations and ethos of critical and utopian pedagogical principles.

The setting of pre-determined essay questions (aligned with distantiated, objectified knowledge and instructional learning outcomes) purposefully stitch learners into dichotomous theoretical oscillations, which also operate to perpetuate subservient roles within a *scandalous* poverty of hope and creative possibility. A utopian pedagogy requires a process of learner discovery and knowledge production that moves away from this format. By incorporating an alternative practice of *Creative Autobiography*, learners can be afforded a self-determinate and expressionistic space, which can accommodate non-linear and refracted cultural connections and creative explorations.[3] As a mechanism, Creative Autobiography presents a *real world* practical activity that can embrace and facilitate the pedagogical strategies of the dérive and détournement; at the same time it can offer opportunities for liberated and subjective reinterpretations of the Blochian, Barthesean and Bachelardean conceptual tactics. As part of the Creative Autobiographical journey, a learner collaborator can produce a personal-creative work which recognizes and reflects the uniqueness of their bespoken voice; the non-prescriptive openness and invitational format of this approach also means that it remains fluid enough to embody multi-gendered, ethno-cultural and socio-economic contexts within an infinite array of cultural reference points. Ultimately, the strategies and tactics sketched out as part of the earlier stages of this work exist to disaggregate and dissolve; the openness of the concepts that cascaded in a wider context of wandering and reinterpretive freedom means that they serve as catalysing husks. Learners should not be grounded or situated as disempowered narrators of irremediable theoretical oscillations but instead be initiated into a micro puzzle of creative revival through the discovery, incubation, inspiration and explication of unnarrated hope and latent possibility. In tandem with the pedagogical strategies of freedom, dérive and détournement, Creative Autobiography means that learners and their projects can engage in creative departure and wander beyond the springboards of preliminary concepts and tactics.

The format of the Creative Autobiographical mechanism should not be presented as a rigid or densely prescribed activity; instead, participating learners can be invited to engage with tactics and counter strategies in ways that enable the construction of flexible and reflective accounts of emergent thoughts and experiences. Reinforcing the spirit and principles of the pedagogy, Creative Autobiographical projects should be generated primarily through personal exploration; this can be further explored and reinforced through constructive dialogue with the tutor (or wider academic team). Furthermore, the trans-creative and open format of the Creative Autobiographical activity means that the formative themes, connections and narratives can be gathered and presented in a diversity of modes and formats; the incubated and explicated work of learner-collaborators must be compatible with their respective culture, identity and area of interest. While personal and creative freedom is the main focus of the Creative Autobiographical technique, the following themes or prompts can be offered so as to kick-start each learner experience:

- From week 1 of the programme of study, learners should be prompted to begin the construction and development of a 'Creative Autobiographical' piece of culture and memory work. The idea is for learners to cumulatively and progressively construct a personal and reflective archive or portfolio of thoughts, cultural connections and nostalgias. This could be based upon their own 'favourite' experiences of 'culture' (in its widest sense). In doing this, learners will increasingly reflect upon and write about different aspects of their cultural biographies and archives, and explore – via Bloch, Barthes and Bachelard – what they feel they represent. In turn, learner collaborators will be invited to begin to consider their cultural artefacts and experiences in empowered ways in relation to the counter strategies.
- The counter strategies of the dérive and détournement, incubation, inspiration and explication, in conjunction with the conceptual tactics offered by Bloch, Barthes and Bachelard should be utilized as the basis and progression of the *autobiographical* exploration.
- Key to this learning experience, learner-collaborators must be afforded the openness and freedom associated with an *expressionistic* space to

enable them to explore and increasingly articulate the key themes and metaphors contained in the cultural artefacts of their choice (equipped with the strategies and tactics on offer). Learners should be encouraged to consider and creatively articulate 'why' the permutations of their cultural connections – and personal, subjective encounters – have become (and remain) popular in the personal realm of memory and association. Furthermore, they should be encouraged to consider the extent to which their own cultural threads are reveric vehicles loaded with reminders or 'traces' of inner yearnings for wider connection, hope and, ultimately, future transformation.[4]

The Creative Autobiographical project as a mode of utopian pedagogical praxis is aligned with the first two principles of the Blochian triptych, those of *incubation* and *inspiration*. The expressive space made available for each learner opens up to a fractured portal of interiority, which means that the subjective serendipities of trace, punctum and reverie can formulate and proliferate in non-linear ways for each learner collaborator across the programme of study. However, while Creative Autobiography effectively facilitates the first two principles of the Blochian triptych, the third principle, that of *explication*, still remains to be addressed. Producing a personal artefact in the form of a Creative Autobiographical project and portfolio means that learners must also be presented with an opportunity to externalize their respective discoveries. This is important from a Blochian triptychal point of view, but also within the confines of a mainstream programme of study; a final piece of work – in the form of a tangible artefact – must be produced. In order to enable this, I propose the format of a bespoke presentation. Again, in keeping with the democratic and creative openness of the utopian pedagogy, the criteria for the presentation must dovetail with the fluidity of the Creative Autobiographical formula and process. This means that the criteria within which the *learner-presenters* are expected to operate – in order to create their tangible and explicatory end point – should also embrace and reflect the subjective bespokenness of the prior journey and activities.[5]

The wisdom of the crowd

The multiplicitous nature of a *swarm* of Creative Autobiographical artefacts, produced within the context of the utopian pedagogical method (and explicated through the personalized mechanism of the presentation), poses significant problems for the objective grading of the work. The application of an empiricized judgement by a sole academic *expert* to an individual student on the basis of a deeply personal journey – full of Expressionistic *skids* and punctumic divergences – is profoundly problematic. Therefore, in order to protect and secure the integrity of personal creativity emanating from each learner, a collaborative Peer Assessment process aimed at assessing, grading and feeding back on each piece of work can be developed. This effectively replaces the restrictive approach of the lone and powerful *expert*.

As part of the latter section of this chapter, a Peer Assessment scheme has been devised which involves and incorporates the whole group of learner participants; the Peer Assessment scheme – and wider utopian pedagogy – therefore shifts the emphasis away from 'individual risk' and alternatively creates a supportive *collective* where comrades as co-explorers of traces and possibilities experience the unfamiliar alternative of group support.[6] With regard to the more mechanistic processes of university bureaucracy, as part of the group Peer Assessment activity, each student still receives a grade – albeit generated by the accumulated and averaged grades and feedback from the group as a whole (inclusive of the grade/feedback generated by the tutor). James Surowiecki notes in *The Wisdom of Crowds: Why the Many are Smarter than the Few*:

> Under the right circumstances, groups are remarkably intelligent, and are often smarter than the smartest people in them. Groups do not need to be dominated by exceptionally intelligent people in order to be smart. Even if most of the people within a group are not especially well-informed or rational, it can still reach a collectively wise decision. (Surowiecki, 2013: xiii–xiv)

With Surowiecki's argument – whose book explores an impressive array of successful and intriguing collaborative group experiments and examples – we can challenge the traditional approach to leading, organizing and managing groups of learners (with the expert lecturer dominating the group and making unilateral decisions and impositions). The traditional position of dominatory leadership inevitably defaults to principles of linearity and control and stifles creative and innovative voices which, as a result, tend to remain unproductively latent within the wider collective. Following Surowiecki's argument, in order for an authentic process of Peer Assessment to work in a meaningful way, *true* democratic freedom must be the basis of the collaborative and decision-making mechanism.

Ultimately, there is no point in making a group of learners part of a collaborative structure if they are not afforded an authentic and egalitarian method of aggregating their feedback and opinions. Surowiecki states that participants 'should be allowed to make decisions. If an organization sets up teams and then uses them for purely advisory purposes, it loses the true advantage that a team has: namely, collective wisdom' (ibid.: 190). This means that rather than allowing a student group a tokenistic role in a process of Peer Assessment – for example, where a Peer Assessing activity accounts for only a negligible proportion of a specific assessment grade – their activities should have an equal and influential remit, and in so doing, play a direct role in engineering the whole grade available for a specific assignment. Surowiecki states that creating and affording such a mechanism serves to establish a 'wise crowd'. He summarizes the following ideal characteristics of the wise crowd and the organizational principles required for an authentic collaborative decision-making process:

1. Diversity of opinion: each person should have the freedom to offer thoughts, contributions and information (however *eccentric* this may be);
2. Independence: An open environment is essential, which embraces and ensures that emergent group thinking is not determined or stifled by the narrow opinion of a small minority – or of an individual;
3. Decentralization: Individual collaborators must be able to offer their opinions and incorporate their *local* knowledge in useful, meaningful and productive ways;
4. Aggregation: A transparent mechanism must be devised, which can translate the heterogeneity of private judgements into a meaningful collective decision (principles adapted from Surowiecki, 2013: 10).

As part of this scheme and approach, the following draft module handbook sets out a range of hypothetical parameters through which an academic, or a small team of academics, and supporting practitioners can collaborate with learners to democratically exercise the utopian pedagogical experience. In addition to proposing the weekly lecture themes and topics, the handbook also contains advice, guidelines and a rubric to afford and implement a Peer Assessed and mutual process of decentralized, collective assessment and feedback. Draft Peer Assessment grids, booklets and grading formulas are also available towards the end of the draft handbook. These ensure that the whole group can arrive at an accumulated and averaged grade for each learner-participant.

Hope, Utopia and Creativity
A (draft) Module Handbook[7]

Programme Overview, Aims and Activities

The module can be broken down into the following main 'parts': initially the module will provide students with an overview of the ethos and philosophy of the module, along with an introduction to the main pedagogical theorists and strategies for student engagement throughout the module – namely, via the theorists Paulo Freire, Henry Giroux, bell hooks, and Guy Debord and the Situationists, (the dérive and détournement). This will be followed by introductions to ideas and concepts (and *tactics*) associated with Ernst Bloch (key works: *Traces, The Spirit of Utopia, The Principle of Hope, The Utopian Function of Art & Literature*); Roland Barthes work associated with *The Rustle of Language, Camera Lucida, The Death of the Author, The Third Meaning*; and, Gaston Bachelard's *Air & Dreams: An Essay on the Imagination of Movement,* the *Poetics of Space* and the *Poetics of Reverie.* These strategies and tactics are to be utilized as a basis for the exploration and articulation of learner connections to cultural elements (of their choice). Emphasis is to be placed on the above theorists' strategies and tactics – and ways in which they articulate personal (subjective) connections to everyday culture.

Equipped with the pedagogical strategies and conceptual tactics, learners are then invited to explore their own choices of cultural artefacts (film, literature, music and/or other wider cultural examples and genre). As part of this, students – *as learner-collaborators* – can begin to creatively apply the theoretical frameworks and ideas discussed above. Learners are provided with an *Expressionistic*, analytical and creative freedom to explore key themes and metaphors contained in their cultural artefacts of choice; they are encouraged to think about their connections – and why, as personal favourites, they remain so poignant and popular. One of the main intentions of this module is to encourage students to consider, and try to make sense of, their own experiences of cultural 'moments' (inclusive of wider art-forms, such as music, theatre, books, and so on). For the assignment, students will be expected to establish their own projects and titles and, using the conceptual framework(s) provided throughout the module, creatively explore the themes of their chosen works.

Creative autobiography

From week one, learners are invited to begin to construct and develop a 'Creative Autobiographical' project in the form of a piece of culture or memory work. Based upon their own 'favourite' experiences of 'culture' (in its widest sense), learners should construct a personal and reflective archive or portfolio of thoughts and nostalgias. As we cover more of the concepts, tactics and strategies, learners will increasingly reflect upon and write about different aspects of their chosen cultural materials and what they feel they represent. Invoking the strategies of dérive and détournement, in conjunction with Blochian, Barthesean and Bachelardean tactics, learner-collaborators are encouraged to consider the extent to which their own cultural threads are potential vehicles for expressing reminders or 'traces' of inner yearnings for wider connection, hope and ultimately transformation. The qualitative methodological approach of Creative Autobiography does not adhere to a specific structure or format; instead, participating learners construct flexible, reflective accounts of their thoughts, connections and experiences (with the module and cultural artefacts) in modes and formats compatible with their respective learning styles and interests. Reinforcing the spirit and principles of the module, the creative portfolios will be generated and accumulated through negotiation with the tutors/researchers.

See the following key texts for further details and information on Creative Autobiography:

Crowther, G. (2016); Goodson, I. and Gill, S. (2013); Hunt, C. (2013); Kelley, D. and Kelley, T. (2013); Robinson, K. (2011); Stanley, J. (1998).

Learning outcomes

By the end of the module, students should be able to provide evidence of the following 'learning outcomes'; these include competence in the skills needed to verbally and textually express their ability to do the following:

1. Creatively engage with the pedagogical strategies associated with the Situationist notions of the dérive and détournement.

2. Explore and apply an array of theoretical materials, strategies and concepts associated with Paulo Freire, Henry Giroux, bell hooks, Guy Debord, Ernst Bloch, Roland Barthes, Gaston Bachelard, and Henri Lefebvre.
3. Critically appraise personal values and experiences in light of the theorists studied.

Weekly lecture programme

Week one (3 hours)

Overview of Module (Theory and Intention)
Introduction to the module (and handbook)
Creative Autobiographical (CA) process/approach
Student engagement, assignment and creativity (Peer Assessment)
The ethos and pedagogical Context of the Module:
    Paulo Freire: Pedagogy of the Oppressed; Pedagogy of Hope
    Bell hooks: Heart to Heart Learning with Love; Teaching to Transgress
    Peter McLaren: Pedagogy of Insurrection
    Henry Giroux: Critical Pedagogy; challenging the capitalist/consumer
       environment
    The Situationists: The theory of the Dérive; Détournement

Week two (3 hours)

Ernst Bloch: The Principle of Hope; Everyday Culture, Utopia and the
    Not-Yet
    Ernst Bloch: The 'spirit' of utopia
    Hope: Trace and the detective
    Expressionism: Art and Literature as symbols of hope and
       transformation
    Deciphering Utopia using Bloch's concepts and the Creative
       Autobiographical process

Week three (3 hours)

Ernst Bloch: The Utopian Function of Art and Literature
    Marxism: Poetry and the Philosophy of Music
    The Blochian Fairy Tale and longing for *Heimat* (Home)
    Blochian *Expressionism* (connecting Bloch with the dérive and
       détournement)
       Bye Bye Badman: The Redemption of Hope through Popular Culture

Week four (3 hours)

Roland Barthes: Punctum – Uncovering Personal Cultural Encounters
  The Death of the Author
  The Rustle of Language
  Photography and the punctum
  Film and The Third Meaning
    Creative Autobiography:
      Encountering and *Recording* Punctumic Moments via 'Creative
        Autobiography'
      Making sense of Barthes' concepts in personal and creative ways
      Reflections on emerging Combinations: the dérive, détournement,
        Bloch and Barthes

Week five (3 hours)

Gaston Bachelard *with* Marcel Proust and Walter Benjamin
  House/Home and its representations
  Bachelard: Poetics of Space
  Language: memory, nostalgia and creativity
  Reverie (and the open imagination)

Week six (3 hours)

Henri Lefebvre and Rhythmanalysis:
  Henri Lefebvre: multiple rhythms and voices
  Rhythmanalysis: Space; Everyday Life and Dynamic creativity
    Uncovering personal connections to Space and Memory

Week seven (3 hours)

Creative Autobiography, Peer Assessment – personal directions:
  Introduction to the Peer Review processes – documentation and grading criteria
  Enabling personal creativity within the university context
  Surowiecki's The Wisdom of the Crowd
  bell hooks – Heart to Heart (community of supportive learning)

Week eight (3 hours)

Activities in preparation for the 1-2-1 meeting: whole group discussion in
    relation to the following:
  Discuss developing ideas(s) and possible materials and artefacts – how
    to develop and finalize the Creative Autobiographical portfolio and

presentation materials, and bring to the respective 1-2-1 meetings, to be
scheduled across the next four weeks

Explore possible theoretical and conceptual connections to Bloch's utopian
framework, Bachelard's reverie, and Barthes' punctum (etc.) along with
the counter strategies geared towards developing Expressionistic freedom

The portfolio, the presentation and the Peer Assessment process

Scheduling of 1-2-1 meetings across the next four weeks (individual students
to meet with tutor[s] to develop and consolidate ideas and connections –
recommended minimum of 20 to 30 minutes discussion with each
learner collaborator)

Weeks Nine, Ten, Eleven and Twelve (12 hours in total)

1-2-1 appointments to discuss Creative Autobiographical portfolios and
Bespoke Presentation ideas

Weeks Thirteen, Fourteen and Fifteen (9 hours in total)

Peer Assessed Presentations

Creative Autobiography – Presentation Guidelines

The coursework assignment and assessment element of this module is a student presentation; learners are to draw upon the content produced as part of their Creative Autobiographical projects and portfolios: examples, materials, and interpretations are to form the basis of a 20-minute presentation. Each learner is to conceive, design and deliver their own title and themes. In order to produce these pieces of work, students are advised to follow and actively engage with the following guidelines.

The lecturer (and wider academic team) will plan at least one period of informal discussion with each presenting student; this will contribute towards the production of the learner portfolio and presentation. Students will be given space to discuss and consolidate their emerging ideas and clarify connections between their personal examples and the module material.

Students are given creative freedom to interpret, understand, represent, associate and suggest the topic and themes to be contained in their presentation (and descriptive document).

Details and protocol for each presentation:

1. Each individual student presentation should last for 20 minutes.
2. The presentation will be assessed using a collaborative Peer Assessment scheme.
3. The presentation will be assessed against the Peer-Assessment criteria (as set out in the Peer Marking booklet).
   i. The tutor will distribute the Rubric, Peer-Assessment paperwork and detailed marking criteria in advance of the presentations (and will provide opportunities for detailed briefings, questions and discussion).

'Rubric' for Peer Assessment of (Alternative Education) presentations

Due to the unique, bespoke nature of the student presentations negotiated and produced as part of this programme, it is inappropriate for a lecturer to individually apply a judgement to the personal innovations associated with each student work. In order to enhance and protect the personal creativity that each student (and the group as a whole) is invited to enter into, the following Peer Assessment scheme and rubric, has been devised; the aim is to shift the grading process away from expert authority and 'individual risk', and alternatively award *each* presenting student with a grade generated by the accumulated and averaged responses and feedback from the group as a whole.

The following 'rubric' has been developed to facilitate and safeguard a rigorous and transparent Peer Assessment process. As part of this, the whole student group, and the module academic team, can collaborate and arrive at a standardized grade for each presenting student:

1. All presenting students are entitled to Peer Assess each other's work (using the grading sheet/criteria produced and provided by the module tutor/team)
2. As part of the collaborative Peer Assessment process, the tutors' grades will serve two functions; first and foremost, they will serve as a constituent grade, cumulatively contributing towards the overall grade produced by the entire Peer Assessing group. Secondarily, they will also be used as a 'comparator/control' grade, should any significant individual or collective anomalies occur

3. The array of individual grades, produced by the accumulated scores and feedback comments on the Peer Assessment score sheets, will be compiled and averaged to produce an 'overall' grade for each presenting student

4. All Peer Assessed grades and paperwork will be made available and/ or sampled for a 2nd internal marker, and then verified by an External Examiner

   a. It is essential that all Peer Assessors provide their names (and signatures) on the front page of each Peer Assessment sheet; without this, their grades cannot be included or counted as part of the final grade decision

   b. Should the 1st marker, and/or 2nd marker, and/or the External Examiner deem that the grading on any individual Peer Assessment grade sheet(s), or the accumulated grades for the group as a whole, produces an incongruous grade, the ultimate decision and authority to include, and/ or adjust, and/or exclude those grades rests with them

5. All of the paperwork (signed PA booklets, Excel spreadsheets, etc.) will be stored and made available for scrutiny by an independent External Examiner

Hope, Utopia and Creativity
Presentations – Peer Assessment/Grade Sheet[8]

Instructions to Peer Assessors	Letter Grades & Numerical Equivalents	
Instructions to Peer Assessors:	**Letter Grade**	**Numeric Equivalent**
1: Before Peer Assessing any work, participants should read through (and ensure that they understand) the Peer Marking Criteria – below. All of the presentations to be Peer Assessed in this session will need to be graded against the generic Peer Marking Criteria and the Lettered/Numerical grading system (located to the right of this page). Each presenter's performance – as judged against the array of grades and criteria – must correspond to these:	A+	24
	A	21
	A-	18
	B+	17
	B	16
2: Presentation Assessment Criteria 1, and Presentation Assessment Criteria 2 (below) require you to allocate a 'Letter-Grade' for each category; the Letter awarded for each aspect of the presentation should reflect the grade that you feel the presentation is worthy of.	B-	15
	C+	14
	C	13
	C-	12
3: In doing this, you will produce two different grades (Letters) for each of the two Presentation Assessment Criteria (complete this for each presentation that you watch/assess during this session).	D+	11
	D	10
	D-	9
4: At the end of each presentation, you should translate the letters into their numerical equivalent, add them together and divide them. You will then be able to calculate your overall grade for the presentation.	F1	7
	F2	4
	F3	2
	F4	0
5: Finally, at the end of each presentation you must also produce (write some) feedback in the form of a brief explanation – as to why you allocated the grade that you did – in the space provided at the end of each Peer Assessed presentation.		
For validation purposes, it is essential that you provide your name/signature here – otherwise your grades cannot be included. In signing this booklet, you also identify that you have been made aware of (and agree to) the Rubric underpinning this Peer Assessment process: **Peer Assessors Name**: **Peer Assessors Signature**: **Date**:		

Hope, Utopia and Creativity: Peer Marking Criteria

1		Excellent
	A+ A A-	Work shows excellent breadth and depth of all aspects of theory, adaptation and examples; exceptionally structured with coherent arguments and convincing connections. Excellently and confidently presented, with clear and accurately articulated materials – effectively translated and 'put across' by the presenter. Excellent understanding of all of the requirements and aspects of the presentation. Clear evidence of independent thinking, development of ideas and original contributions. Strong and creative use of (détourned) concepts. Highly individual though accessible presentation; overall, excellent standard of presentation – enjoyable, accurate and provoking.
2i		Good – Very Good With Few Weaknesses
	B+ B B-	Work shows very good breadth and depth of aspects of theory, adaptation and examples; with a good, robust standard of connections being made. Generally clear and logical approach to ideas; good evidence of ability to engage in evaluation of personal experiences in relation to the theory and concepts covered as part of the module. Generally competent, systematic analysis of connections, with no major weaknesses. Good understanding of assignment requirements, with clear/well-structured presentation of argument. Evidence of development of concepts/ideas, good use of ideas and presentation processes and techniques. Very good standard of presentation, enjoyable and accessible.
2ii		Average – Above Average With Some Weaknesses
	C+ C C-	Generally good levels of knowledge and understanding; largely relevant development and application of ideas – but with some limitations to the engagement of peers in relation to theory and personal experiences. Adequate analysis of relevant ideas, but with some apparent weaknesses (e.g. not a fully developed application of détourned concepts). Satisfactory presentation of argument, experiences and ideas, with some weakness in clarity and/or structure. Adequate presentation, overall, work completed to a satisfactory standard.

3		Satisfactory, Several Significant Weaknesses, Limited Work
	D+	Little knowledge/understanding of relevant ideas, lack of ability to
	D	engage in theoretical and comparative discussion; some attempt
	D-	to analysis, discuss and apply détourned theory and/or concept
		to a personally developed example. Some attempt to draw out
		connections and ideas, but with weaknesses in coherence and
		clarity. Few theoretical influences, weakly developed. Overall,
		limited idea development, poor use of materials and presentation
		framework.
F		Fail
	F1	While some basic knowledge of some relevant topics and issues
	F2	were implicitly evident, the presenter did not effectively address
	F3	the requirements of the assessment. Work is largely descriptive
	F4	and uncritical with some unsubstantiated assertion. Analysis
		is minimal or contradictory. Insufficient understanding and/
		or creative application of the given concepts. Irrelevant use of
		artefact(s) and incomplete and flawed explanation of meaning
		and context. Treatment of the subject was directionless and
		fragmentary.

Presentation/Presenter 1

Name of Student Presenting: _____

Presentation Criteria '1':

Present a snapshot of a reflection – or reflections – on the influence and/
or impact of an example of cultural material (or the impacts of several cultural materials), and the ways in which they have shaped or impacted the
presenter

- The presenter may make reference to film and/or music and/or literature
  and/or 'art' examples (or other wider examples of cultural experience). The
  presenter should also make reference to the strategies covered as part of this
  programme of study
- It is important to remember that the areas of personal experience and
  culture (in its widest context) can be interpreted by the presenter in a
  wide-ranging context. Some non-exhaustive examples might be: music and
  memory; home and longing; photography and place

Presentation Criteria 1	Letter Grade	No.	Description	Honours Class
Circle the appropriate letter (to the right) that you feel best reflects the presenter's performance – in relation to the above presentation Criteria 1: As judged against the detailed Peer Marking criteria (above)	A+	24	Excellent	1st
	A	21		
	A-	18		
	B+	17	Good	2:1
	B	16		
	B-	15		
	C+	14	Satisfactory	2:2
	C	13		
	C-	12		
	D+	11	Weak	3rd
	D	10		
	D-	9		
	F1	7	Marginal Fail	Fail
	F2	4	Fail	
	F3	2	Poor Fail	
	F4	0	Very Poor Fail	

Presentation Criteria '2':

Presenters must make theoretical connections to at least one of the following: Guy Debord, Ernst Bloch, Roland Barthes, Gaston Bachelard, Henri Lefebvre. Presenters should also make reference to – and analyse – an array of conceptual tactics associated with their artefact and chosen theorist(s)

- This list of theoretical frameworks is not exhaustive – (presenters may incorporate additional theoretical perspectives not listed above – based upon the curricular content of the particular programme of study)

Presentation Criteria 2	Letter Grade	No.	Description	Honours Class
Circle the appropriate letter (to the right) that you feel best reflects the presenter's performance – in relation to the above presentation Criteria 2: As judged against the detailed Peer Marking criteria (above)	A+	24	Excellent	1st
	A	21		
	A-	18		
	B+	17	Good	2:1
	B	16		
	B-	15		
	C+	14	Satisfactory	2:2
	C	13		
	C-	12		
	D+	11	Weak	3rd
	D	10		
	D-	9		
	F1	7	Marginal Fail	Fail
	F2	4	Fail	
	F3	2	Poor Fail	
	F4	0	Very Poor Fail	

- Letter for Presentation Criteria 1: _____

- Letter for Presentation Criteria 2: _____

- Averaged Grade (using the numerical values): _____

Provide a brief explanation of 'why' you reached your decision:

Excel spreadsheet – example of accumulated Peer Assessed grades: averaged, with comparator 1st and 2nd marker lecturer grades

	Stdnt Mrkr 1	Stdnt Mrkr 2	Stdnt Mrkr 3	Stdnt Mrkr 4	Stdnt Mrkr 5	Stdnt Mrkr 6	Stdnt Mrkr 7	Stdnt Mrkr 8	Stdnt Mrkr 9	Stdnt Mrkr 10	Stdnt Mrkr 11	Stdnt Mrkr 12	Stdnt Mrkr 13	Stdnt Mrkr 14	Stdnt Mrkr 15
Array of Student / Peer Grades															
Presenter		12	13	15	18	14	16	14	15	16	17	16	14	17	16
Presenter	24		16	21	21	17	21	21	18	21	18	16	24	21	18
Presenter	16	17		12	13	15	14	17	14	15	16	14	14	17	12
Presenter	14	16	17		18	13	14	15	18	16	15	17	18	16	18
Presenter	15	18	16	21		16	17	18	21	24	15	16	18	17	24
Presenter	15	16	19	15	18		17	21	17	16	16	15	16	17	18
Presenter	17	15	20	18	16	17		18	17	17	17	17	15	18	21
Presenter	9	14	11	12	9	12	16		14	15	13	14	9	11	12

A version of this draft 'Hope, Utopia and Creativity' handbook can be accessed online and downloaded from: http://www.slideshare.net/CraigHammond/hope-utopia-creativity-draft-module-handbook1

Note: In the above image, the two grades (per peer marker) are accumulated from each Peer Assessment booklet, and then combined in to one grade (for each marker). Each peer assessed grade is then inputed to the spreadsheet; as can be seen, all grades – including the grades for the 1st and 2nd academic staff/peer markers – are accumulated and averaged to generate a single grade for each presenting learner collaborator.

										Staff Grades Combined		Overall Grade	
Stdnt	Stdnt	Stdnt	Stdnt	Stdnt	Stdnt	Stdnt	Stndt	Staff	Staff	Staff	Staff	All	Overall
Mrkr 16	Mrkr 17	Mrkr 18	Mrkr 19	Mrkr 20	Mrkr 21	Combined	Grade	1st Mrkr	2nd Mrkr	Combined	Grade	Combined	Grade
18	13	16	14	15	16	15	B-	18	18	18	A-	17	B+
Stdnt	Stdnt	Stdnt	Stdnt	Stdnt	Stdnt	Stdnt	Stndt	Staff	Staff	Staff	Staff	All	Overall
Mrkr 16	Mrkr 17	Mrkr 18	Mrkr 19	Mrkr 20	Mrkr 21	Combined	Grade	1st Mrkr	2nd Mrkr	Combined	Grade	Combined	Grade
20	24	21	21	24	18	20	A-	18	24	21	A	21	A
Stdnt	Stdnt	Stdnt	Stdnt	Stdnt	Stdnt	Stdnt	Stndt	Staff	Staff	Staff	Staff	All	Overall
Mrkr 16	Mrkr 17	Mrkr 18	Mrkr 19	Mrkr 20	Mrkr 21	Combined	Grade	1st Mrkr	2nd Mrkr	Combined	Grade	Combined	Grade
16	13	15	13	15	16	15	B-	12	14	13	C	14	C+
Stdnt	Stdnt	Stdnt	Stdnt	Stdnt	Stdnt	Stdnt	Stndt	Staff	Staff	Staff	Staff	All	Overall
Mrkr 16	Mrkr 17	Mrkr 18	Mrkr 19	Mrkr 20	Mrkr 21	Combined	Grade	1st Mrkr	2nd Mrkr	Combined	Grade	Combined	Grade
20	18	14	16	15	18	16	B	16	17	17	B+	16	B
Stdnt	Stdnt	Stdnt	Stdnt	Stdnt	Stdnt	Stdnt	Stndt	Staff	Staff	Staff	Staff	All	Overall
Mrkr 16	Mrkr 17	Mrkr 18	Mrkr 19	Mrkr 20	Mrkr 21	Combined	Grade	1st Mrkr	2nd Mrkr	Combined	Grade	Combined	Grade
17	18	21	16	16	24	18	A-	16	15	16	B	17	B+
Stdnt	Stdnt	Stdnt	Stdnt	Stdnt	Stdnt	Stdnt	Stndt	Staff	Staff	Staff	Staff	All	Overall
Mrkr 16	Mrkr 17	Mrkr 18	Mrkr 19	Mrkr 20	Mrkr 21	Combined	Grade	1st Mrkr	2nd Mrkr	Combined	Grade	Combined	Grade
16	17	15	16	16	21	17	B+	16	18	17	B+	17	B+
Stdnt	Stdnt	Stdnt	Stdnt	Stdnt	Stdnt	Stdnt	Stndt	Staff	Staff	Staff	Staff	All	Overall
Mrkr 16	Mrkr 17	Mrkr 18	Mrkr 19	Mrkr 20	Mrkr 21	Combined	Grade	1st Mrkr	2nd Mrkr	Combined	Grade	Combined	Grade
24	18	16	17	17	18	18	A-	18	20	19	A-	18	A-
Stdnt	Stdnt	Stdnt	Stdnt	Stdnt	Stdnt	Stdnt	Stndt	Staff	Staff	Staff	Staff	All	Overall
Mrkr 16	Mrkr 17	Mrkr 18	Mrkr 19	Mrkr 20	Mrkr 21	Combined	Grade	1st Mrkr	2nd Mrkr	Combined	Grade	Combined	Grade
14	15	11	17	14	9	13	C	11	13	12	C-	12	C-

Notes

1   The Freirean pedagogical framework is pivotal for an understanding of Giroux's developmental work on Critical Pedagogy and mainstream higher education in the United States; as Giroux notes on this point: 'Freire became an essential influence in helping me to understand the broad contours of my ethical responsibilities as a teacher. Later, his work would help me come to terms with the complexities of my relationship to universities as powerful and privileged institutions that seemed far removed from the daily life of the working-class communities in which I had grown up' (Giroux, 2011: 159).

2   hooks notes in relation to this point: 'Even though students enter universities at similar levels of capability and skill, it is not assumed that the classroom will be a communal place where those skills will naturally lead to overall excellence on the part of all students. Competition rooted in dehumanising practices of shaming, of sado-masochistic rituals of power, preclude communalism and stand in the way of community' (hooks, 2003: 131).

3   This method and approach was inspired and influenced by Dr Gail Crowther's PhD and subsequent research into Sylvia Plath, see also Gail Crowther (2016) *The Haunted Reader and Sylvia Plath.*

4   This approach has been influenced by Mike Neary's notion of the *student as producer,* which emerged out of the recent crisis of meaning and purpose within higher education, as a result of being increasingly framed by an ever narrowing focus on marketization via the commercialization of students as consumers. Creative Autobiography produced by *students-as-producers* emerges as a fresh approach, which resituates – through direct empowerment – the student as an active collaborator in knowledge production. Re-engineering the relationship between teaching, research and knowledge, undergraduates become a part of the academic project of the university. For Neary and Amsler (2012), this establishes the subversive possibility of students 'occupying the curriculum, or of appropriating the social space and time of education'. This also resonates with the 'emotionally connected' principles as set out in bell hooks' chapter in 'Teaching Community': *Heart to Heart: Teaching with Love.*

5   Example skeletal prompts and presentation marking criteria – aimed at recognising and explicating the autobiographical journey – are contained in the sample programme/module handbook at the end of this chapter.

6   In order to assuage queries or consternations from university 'quality' departments, and to safeguard against the event of *tactical* foul-play within the system, a draft rubric has been developed with a view to facilitating and safeguarding a rigorous and transparent Peer-Assessment process. This is available as part of the draft 'Hope, Utopia and Creativity' module/programme handbook I have successfully

implemented in the Peer Assessment scheme, paperwork and aggregated feedback for the last four academic years.

7   For any dynamic practitioners interested in incorporating or adapting either a whole module based on implementing the strategies and tactics of this utopian pedagogy – or, excerpted, adapted aspects of the framework – a draft programme is set out in the following handbook. This draft module/programme of study is a hypothetical hybrid based upon amalgamated aspects from two existing Lancaster University, UK, validated (Level 6, 15 Credit) modules that I have written and implemented for a number of years.

8   The Lettered/Numerical grades and boundaries (located on the right-hand side of this page) are the current standardised grading mechanisms as used by Lancaster University, UK, and University Centre Blackburn College (at the time of press).

Part III

Learner Stories, Reflections and Projections

8

A Garland of Rhythms

The polyrhythmic complexity of space, everyday life and memory

Incubated, inspired and explicated artefacts birthed from the subjective and non-linear *expressions* of remembrances, aches and hopes produced by each learner collaborator can be articulated as part of a philosophical context of *everyday life*. As such, the relative and complex experiences which emerge from the Creative Autobiographical process – prompted by dérives and détourned aspects of cultural splinters – can be further consolidated as part of a multifaceted and polymorphous utopian ontology. In order to tease out and develop this, this chapter will incorporate conceptual aspects from Henri Lefebvre's three-volume work *Critique of Everyday Life*, along with sympathetic and supporting elements from his writing on *Rhythmanalysis*; this, in turn, will be constructively fused with the established Blochian material on hope and utopia. Further framing and bolstering the kaleidoscopic mosaic which constitutes the utopian pedagogy, the Lefebvrean praxis of *rhythmatics* will also align (implicitly as part of this chapter) with the Barthesean, Bachelardean and Debordean philosophical foundations of *complexity* and temporal experience.

In comparing and, to an extent, combining Lefebvrean and Blochian space-time fractures and tangents, more traditional approaches to understanding and defining the experience of space, time and memory are challenged and philosophically reframed; subject to a treatment of proliferation, the whole notion of everyday life and experience can be conceived and considered in different ways. Challenging standardizing approaches to rigidly defined measurements of linear time (for example, through the use of chrono-metric tools such as clocks and calendars), subjective interiorities and *relativized* enclaves of strange, scattered and multispatial worlds can form and emerge. For Blochian and Lefebvrean-esque understandings, the relative experiences of *space* and *time* consist of acute worlds, inner-dimensions which shift and lurch between non-linear pastiches. This contrasts, fundamentally, to more traditional and metronomic rhythms associated with externally imposed and regimented symmetries emanating from the ticks and rhythms of clock time. Stuart Elden, in the introduction to *Rhythmanalysis*, notes that, for Lefebvre, times *complex* essence is that of a shifting fluidity, its separated and intra-personal reference points render it non-calculable in traditional terms; just as 'Cartesian geometry is a reductive way of understanding space, so too is the measure of time, the clock' (Lefebvre, 2010: 11). Lefebvrean time is therefore resistant to epistemological abstractions which claim to identify and seamlessly ensure trans-personal uniformities.[1]

For Lefebvre, the *typical* experience of everyday life is one of constant bombardment; infiltrated by pressures and homogenizing pulses, standardizing thought patterns emanate throughout and across external spaces. Unleashed and perpetuated via communicative compulsion, the dynamic potential of everyday life, with its individualized rhythms of plurality, is hijacked and caught up in a *theatre* of political performance; as a result, everyday life is characterized by an ongoing conflict, caught between the qualitative rhythms of interiority and 'processes imposed by the socio-economic organization of production, consumption, circulation' (Lefebvre, 2010: 73).[2] The shunting of normalizing routines throughout the daily networks of myriad social contexts and institutions serves to dilute and stifle the potential for *de Certeau-esque* tactics and the wider germination of non-conformist actions. The ubiquitous pressures operate to such a degree that generally we only become conscious of our differing pulses and arrhythmic patterns 'when we begin to suffer from some irregularity' (ibid.: 77). Further elaborating this, Lefebvre clarifies that we can experience time as 'biological or physical time, as psychological duration, or finally social time' (Lefebvre, 2008b: 128). The different guises and manifestations attached to the separate zones and quanta's of time are characterized by competing pulses and rhythms; this is most pronounced where the qualitative experience of psychological duration, or *internal* time, is concerned; as Lefebvre notes, here 'rhythms are multiple and interfere with one another qualitatively: heartbeats, breathing, being awake and asleep by turns, being hungry and thirsty, and so on' (ibid.: 128–129). The everyday dimensions of psychological duration and its refracted spaces of interiority mutate and morph in relative, deformative and complex ways; departing from the generalized spaces of society with its architected cathedrals of spaces, flows and lines – with its expansive spaces of transport, consumption and areas of collective habitation – any assumptions attached to the notion of 'real' or 'authentic' space become deconstructed and shown to be 'produced in accordance with certain schemas developed by some particular group within the general framework of a society' (ibid.: 135). Echoing tactics reminiscent of Debord and the Situationists, Lefebvre proffers that despite the tidal surges of social time, micro polyrhythmic reverberations still *nag* and emanate from within the shifting spaces of interiority. This means that the subjective and complex experience of space, time and memory continues to harbour kernels of democratic potential ripe for the activation of tactical voices and rhythms beyond the emotionless and tactless distance of external metrics. Although hidden and suppressed, subjectivities can still manifest a shifting diversity of rhythmic relations; hence, intersecting and competing pulses can form or *sync* into micro-unities of complex pluralities. This is why Lefebvre's notion of fractured time and the subjective quantas and dimensions of space are important. As a multiplicitous essence, Lefebvrean everyday time, conceived and perceived as a qualitative entity, reaches and sprawls beyond externalized, linear and quantitative metrics.

With this, we start to shift from the nurtured and defaulted expectations of daily life as something that must be constructed and regulated by external pressures and organizations; instead, we start to engage with the idea that the subjective and interior realm of everyday life is something to be proactively recognized and micro-democratically produced.[3] The Lefebvrean *turn* recognizes the fractal orchestration of *garlands* or *bouquets* of internal rhythms; aspiring rhythmanalysts must therefore resist the disciplined urge to '*jump* from the inside to the outside of observed *bodies*'. Instead, 'by integrating the outside with the inside' (Lefebvre, 2010: 20), they must learn to listen to the garlands, bundles and bouquets of interior rhythms and the associated fractal formations of their bespoke directions. It is worth quoting Lefebvre at length on this issue:

In everyday life, ancient gestures, rituals as old as time itself, continue unchanged – except for the fact that this life has been stripped of its beauty. Only the dust of words remains, dead gestures. Because rituals and feelings, prayers and magic spells, blessings, curses, have been detached from life, they have become abstract and 'inner', to use the terminology of self-justification. Convictions have become weaker, sacrifices shallower, less intense. People cope – badly – with a smaller outlay. Pleasures have become weaker and weaker. The only thing that has not diminished is the old disquiet, that feeling of weakness, that foreboding. But what was formerly a sense of disquiet has become worry, anguish. Religion, ethics, metaphysics – these are merely the 'spiritual' and 'inner' festivals of human anguish, ways of channelling the black waters of anxiety – and towards what abyss? And if beauty has disappeared from everyday life, what of its great mystical heroes? No, the mystic hero is virtually extinct. Everything is calculated on a cut-price basis. A penny for heaven. A little bit more (but as little as possible!) to pacify the 'poor'. (Lefebvre, 1991: 213)

Proust and the beauty of time

It is necessary, and will be useful as part of the wider context of this study, to extend the Lefebvrean formulary and recognize a key influence that impacted upon and shaped his approach to space, time and rhythms. A key and early influence on Lefebvre was Marcel Proust, whose highly subjective, diverse and eclectic *raconteuring* of time and memory served to provide an effective and enticing foundation.[4] It is well worth a brief excursus into the Proustian world of time and experience in order to develop a brief appreciation of the beauty and relevance of his *search for lost time*. In his meandering twelve-volume work *In Search of Lost Time*, Proust (2003) develops and explores what he refers to as *fortunate moments* (*moments bienheureux*) and *involuntary memories* (*memoire involontaire*); with these concepts Proust attempts to decipher and make visible ways in which memory and nostalgia combine to operate in strange and polymorphous ways. Through the intersecting intricacies and interweaving legacies of often banal everyday encounters, Proust narrates the minutiae of everyday life and produces a detailed account of subjective recollections. While much of the writing can be read as functional though often evocative and reflective detail, the formula and routine of the work is interspersed with hidden and revelatory jewels: the unexpected eruption of involuntary memories and fortunate moments. Through seemingly insignificant triggers, emotive accounts, through often moving moments of recognition, chaotically jolt back into conscious awareness. A dominant theme that runs alongside Proust's *fortunate moments* is the enchantment and stridency of childhood and youth, and the ways in which forgotten pockets of wonder-inducing experiences unexpectedly puncture the reveric meanders and disappointments of adulthood. In the final volume, *Time Regained*, Proust brings to the fore a poignant nostalgia and confides to the reader an ache to re-experience and *feel again* some of his earlier, more enchanted and happier times. Recollecting time spent in Venice and the creative, aspirant person that Proust *remembered* himself to be during those times, it is clear that his remembered, younger self embodies a hieroglyphic mystery, a mental avatar hermetically concealing an elixir of optimism and hope. With age and the accumulation of years, his creative ambition dissipates and sinks beneath the threshold of conscious existence; and with this the secret of his life-affirming essence and passion for life also disappears.

In a move to revive his former, younger self and attempt to rekindle an element of creative astonishment and inner wonderment, Proust attempts to resuscitate the past by seeking out and looking at photographs from an earlier time spent in Venice.[5] However, the perusal of his selected images produces only further disappointment; the lifeless *stills* fail to evoke and revive the desired psychic renewal of the coveted content. The shapes and shadows in the photographs prove only to be artificial replicas of previous light-captured moments; the vibrant *spirit* of the *life* that Proust so desperately craved remained lost to somewhere in the past. Despite his withdrawal from life, Proust's narrated character accepts an invitation to the party of a family friend, the Princess de Guermantes. Arriving in the cobble-stone courtyard at the mansion, he alights from the carriage and is immediately forced to stumble out of the way of an oncoming vehicle; as he steps back, he trips on an uneven cobble-stone. Reacting to steady himself, he finds that the moment is suddenly flooded with the inexplicable and overwhelming feeling of happiness. As Proust explains, this unexpected and unfolding event was the involuntary bursting forth of a forgotten memory, a moment in which he immediately recognized a vision; it was 'Venice . . . the sensation which I had once experienced, as I had stood upon two uneven stones in the baptistery of St. Mark's had, recurring a moment ago, restored to me complete . . . all [of] the . . . sensations linked on that day' (Proust, 2003: 224). Lost and embedded *somewhere* in the rubble of the Proustian past, a latent and ruptured phantasm of an enchanted and wonder-struck 'younger self' was defibrillated; the implosive collision of the two different time-worlds meant that his contemporary and temporal dimension was involuntarily punctured by the psychic ingredients from a different and more astonishing time. This previously forgotten and hidden experience (loaded with wonder, hope and anticipation) momentarily synchronized with the older, benumbed and disillusioned Proust. Where the Venice photographs had failed, the unpredictable and unforeseen cobble-stone *stumble* succeeded in recovering the multifaceted shower of a past happiness infused with panoramic and visceral enchantment.

Usefully, Walter Benjamin's essay *The Image of Proust* (1999) suggests that the Proustian recollection of a previous life is not necessarily the re-experiencing of 'it' as it was *actually* lived; rather, it is the recollection of shards of possibility, fragments jolted by a momentary association. Therefore, the event *'that was'* is creatively remembered through a patchwork piecing-together of remnant time-segments, a memorial assemblage constructively reconceived within a temporally unique context. Analogizing the Proustian refraction of memory and melancholic nostalgia, Benjamin proposes that there is 'something of the detective in Proust's curiosity' (Benjamin, 1999: 205). Indeed, Proust is a *detective* par excellence, a private detective on the hunt for the *trace* of a person whose mysterious disappearance has left only a fading echo. And as a trace-detective, when the spectre of an *involuntary memory* reveals itself, he pursues the *not-immediately-apparent* root of the mysterious sign and uncovers its disappearance in the *fall* from youth and childhood. Benjamin further develops his Proustian adaptations on memory and nostalgia in his essay *Unpacking My Library*. Here, Benjamin, having travelled and lived in different and transient locations for a number of years, evokes, in poetic detail, the anticipation and eventual unpacking of his personal book collection; as he tells us, 'I am unpacking my library. Yes, I am. The books are not yet on the shelves, not yet touched by the mild boredom of order . . . I Must ask you to join me in the disorder of [the] crates that have been wrenched open' (ibid.: 61). Guiding us to the intimate interior and mental biography of the book collector, Benjamin recounts the context and memorial cartography associated with the acquisition and textual imbuement of each cherished book. Through his archive of personal traces, a bespoke and experiential *story* of meaningful events is told, ascribed by location, smell and emotional imprint. The root of the drive to collect books, he confides, is a secret striving for rejuvenation; with each new addition (especially worn and aged books), an inner desire is reinforced, a compulsive ache to rejuvenate the shadow of *something* lost to the past. The excitement and anticipation that Benjamin reveals, as he works through the disordered unpacking of his book collection, articulates the bursting forth of a 'childhood' *springtide-of-memories*. As he fittingly suggests:

> I am on the last half-emptied case and it is way past midnight. Other thoughts fill me than the ones I am talking about – not thoughts but images, memories. Memories of the cities in which I found so many things . . . memories of the rooms where these books had been housed, of my students den in Munich, of my room in Bern . . . and finally of my boyhood room. (Ibid.: 68–69)

With Proust and the *Benjaminian-Proust*, we find a corroborating theme, one that prompts the emergence of subjective time-irruptions which emanate from within the relative *worlds-of-experience* and recollection. Through their confessional aches they take us with them along winding and non-linear jour-neys, *back* towards a nostalgic idea of incompleteness; and as Benjamin sug-gests, 'Proust . . . did it such a way that everyone can find it in [their] own existence' (ibid.: 205). This doesn't mean that we get a glimpse of 'the' *actual* spent and archived pasts of the authors; as Benjamin suggested, the retrospec-tive and creative gaze of nostalgia means that it never existed in quite that way. As a *hieroglyph-of-recollection*, the recognition of a revisited moment becomes something quite different. As a creative world, it extends chaotically beyond the immediacy of the moment and into the chaotic, fractal mind-space of the witness.

We can also relate and usefully elaborate the *Lefebvrean-Proustian-Benjaminian* approach to space, time and nostalgia with Ernst Bloch's work on déjà vu. For Bloch, the disorientating experience of the déjà vu is always bor-dered by a sense of shock; its occurrence interrupts and disrupts the stability and routine of everyday life. As a seemingly forgotten and fleeting fragment, the intensity of its resurfacing content ruptures through the relative temporal experience of the present. A troubling event, its uncanny resemblance, of having lived the exact same moment somewhere in the past, prompts a mental scouring for the source. However, for Bloch, the déjà vu experience does *not* equate with or locate an encounter that has been lived through before. As Bloch notes:

> Authentic déjà vu . . . is characterised by the reliving of an experience that has never been lived through before . . . no external occurrences are remembered in déjà vu. Rather, what is activated is merely an *inner state* that has been touched upon previously in an identical fashion, in much the same circumstances . . . Thus it seems plausible that in authentic déjà vu only the *intention*, not the con-tent, of an experience occurs. (Bloch, 1998: 201–202)

Bloch's reworking of the term effectively leads towards the notion of creative nos-talgia; the déjà vu is a shocked reawakening, a recognition of disrupted hopes from the past, littered with aborted beginnings and stalled possibilities. The déjà vu event is shocking because it opens up a moment and precipitates a fall into *that* which has been broken off, interrupted, or *overlooked*, and didn't turn out as intended (Ibid.: 205). As a utopianly loaded experience, the creative nostal-gia of the déjà vu produces a feeling that something's missing, infused with the fleeting ache for revelation and fulfilment. Bloch creates a further distinction between mere recollection, which he terms *anamnesis*, and the more active, crea-tive or future-potent form of memory, which he terms *anagnorisis*. The notion of anamnesis is taken from the Platonic doctrine that all knowledge arises from the recollection of ideas seen in the transcendental world before birth (Hudson, 1982: 78); it suggests that we have knowledge only because we formerly knew, and unfolds as though everything has been already and previously *Formed* (Landman, 1975: 178). For Bloch, Platonic anamnetic recollections are indicative of the resurfacing of fragments, events and things that have been and seen before.[6] Alternatively, anagnorisis, as a quite distinct and separate understanding of memory and knowledge, refers, instead, to the process and notion of *recognition*. Bloch repurposes the Aristotelian notion of anagnorisis to articulate and represent the momentary shock and recognition of absence within the moment, the recognition that something in the immediacy of the lived moment is missing and, as such, needs to be creatively pursued. Unlike Platonic anamnesis, anagnoretic trace recollections are unfinished, and so contain *Not-Yet-established* subjectivities of possibility. Therefore, momentary recognitions of missing aspects are never only mere reactivations but future-oriented transformatory actions (Roberts, 1990: 54).[7] Vince Geoghegan (1997) explains it thus:

> The term 'remembering the future' becomes immediately appropriate. My past memories will have a constitutive role in the forging of my present and future perceptions . . . I enter the future with a body of assumptions and preoccupations located in memory. The infinite range of possible futures is winnowed down to my possible futures through this interactive process. In this sense I can be said to be 'remembering the future'. (Geoghegan, 1997: 17–18)

Anagnorisis therefore takes account of and recognizes that the future is loaded with unmade potential; anagnoretic futures signal the possibility of re-direction towards the unfinished processes of *Being* and identity and, with it, the ability to move towards overcoming the past and transforming the future (Luz, 1993: 364).

Complex manifestations of everyday . . . utopia?

The intricacy associated with Lefebvrean complexity articulates new theoretical and praxial possibilities. Within the formative context of fractal complexity, personalized everyday splinters are associated with as-yet *unthought* of permutations. Within this, knowledge, discovery and learning, in conjunction with the emergence of personal trace-connections and artefacts and memories, should no longer be considered as irrational, meaninglessly chaotic or, indeed, totally random; instead they are to be resituated as non-linear shifts, personal and relative-perturbations of latent possibility. As a result, personalized journeys and studies of everyday life, through the *expressive* method of Creative Autobiography, enable learner collaborators to reveal secrets, inner lives and subjective mysteries, and in so doing, begin to reach beyond the mundanity of routine. For Lefebvre, all that is required to kick-start proliferative instances of rhythmatic praxis is for the familiarity of uncritical routine to be disrupted. In Proustian and Bachelardean fashion, a rhythmatic instance of refracted reflection could be incited by 'a creaking door which sounds like someone groaning – an unfamiliar expression which passes fleetingly across a familiar face' (Lefebvre, 1991: 118).

The deep subjectivity of Creative Autobiographical utterances is inevitably ambiguous. Lefebvre defends the necessity of individualized articulations, as personal rhythms and subjective stories never exhaust their bases of reality; as he notes, 'ambiguity is a category of everyday life, and perhaps an essential category . . . from the ambiguity of consciousnesses and situations spring forth actions, events, results, without warning' (ibid.: 18). Culturally détourned and expressed as complex, non-replicative fractals, the bespoke *turbulence* of personal experience can be transformed into catalysts of extraordinary associations and narrative possibilities. As a Lefebvrean praxis, the complex irruption of eclectic learner stories and cultural associations equate to relative human rhythms, where hidden enclaves of personal archives vibrate with peculiar and ambiguous possibilities. Cumulatively, these present a profusion of unique, unpredictable and refracted dialogues. As bespoke undulations, a plethora of learner voices converge and sync as shifting and multi-scalar fractal-sets; each rhythmical perturbation, while unique, constitutes an existential hunger or pang of nostalgia for a lost or as yet incomplete hope.

Unfinished existence

The next chapter of this book, 'Encounters, Stories, Connections', produces an array of edited snapshots of student works produced as part of the utopian pedagogical experience. As examples, they illustrate that Creative Autobiographical détournements, dérives and explications concoct multiplicitous divergences; the respective narratives and conceptual connections emphasize poignancy, playfulness and meaningfulness in an environment of interpretive freedom. Considered within the context of Lefebvrean praxis, the diversity of the relative utterances manifest a complexity of 'levels and partial totalities' (Lefebvre, 2008a: 240). The fragmented and fragmenting praxis of liberating everyday voices is therefore unavoidably splintered and to an extent inchoate in one sense, but within Lefebvrean parameters they are also *already* total in another sense, as every act of thought or social effectiveness 'refers to the totality via other levels' (ibid.: 237). In revealing and conjoining relations between human beings in ways that facilitate co-discoveries of disappointments, hopes and potentialities, the utopian pedagogy and the supporting Lefebvrean praxis 'reveals an extreme complexity on very varied levels' (ibid.: 236).[8] As such, within the context of Lefebvrean complexity, the accumulated fractality of each piece of learner collaborator work hints, in a kaleidoscopic fashion, towards the possibility and potential of *objective* patterns and social tendencies. Lefebvre notes on this point that 'the absolute is in the relative as we receive it historically: every piece of knowledge (every concept, every proposition, every statement) contains a grain of truth, which can only become clear in the context of an ongoing evolutionary process' (Lefebvre, 1991: 67). Within the Lefebvrean framework, the rhythmanalytical praxis of Creative Autobiography reveals, or incrementally uncovers, pathways towards *utopian* possibilities. The ambiguity of fractal and singular utterances, while relatively obscure, also reveals assumptions about the unhelpful schism between the *individual* and (the assumed, separate structural entity of) the social. Any practice which maintains and perpetuates cultural, political and educational barriers between an isolated and incoherent individual and the wider inevitable extremities of the 'system' is absurd and politically obstructive; as Lefebvre notes, the rhythmanalyst, as utopian *detective*,

> knows that the truth of praxis consists in a conscious oneness: the everyday/the whole, the individual/society, or even the individual/human race. However he sees this truth as a pure ideal outside the real, something to be created . . . in an incomplete way, mutilated, alienated, mainly because it lacks conscious expression. (Lefebvre, 2008a: 266–267)

By following the chaotic personal *rhythms* of nostalgic trace paths, small collectives of learner collaborators fractally glimpse and manifest co-possibilities of renewal and redemption. In a rhythmanalytical sense, the intersecting patterns which emerge, contain or suggest personal codes of bespoke beauty, whether arrhythmic, eurhythmic, or polyrhythmic (which would have remained hidden amid more traditional educational environments and expectations), are explicated and spoken. The 'in-between' fractal spaces of Not-Yet defined thoughts all emerge within the context of creative complexity. Each individual puzzle of revealed mystery equates to a constituent shred of *utopia-within*: non-linear gazes beyond the demarcated terrain of knowledge and strategic ideology which, in micro-turbulent ways, establish incremental nudges against the structures and authorities of regulating institutions. Armed with Proustian, Lefebvrean and Blochian tactics, loaded with dérived and culture-détourned traces, evocative *creative nostalgias* set out to redeem thwarted material from the troves of the past; in a utopian sense, the echoes and traces revive and awaken beautiful rhythms of possibility and latency.

When we follow Lefebvre and ask: 'what about urban life, the life of the people, the life on industrial housing estates? Where, how and in what experiences can its essence be discovered?' (Lefebvre, 1991: 239–240). The emerging praxis of everyday traces is the formative response, and, as part of the utopian pedagogy, its rhythmic techniques for the explication of creative relativities 'make the subject into an object for itself (and therefore more real) and the social and biological object into a subject (*of* consciousness, freedom, active power)' (ibid.: 248). Fractal connections re-establish paths between past memories and the unfulfilled or incomplete aspirations embedded within them. As such, with Lefebvre and Bloch, rhythmanalytic-utopian crowds set out to decipher deeply coded sources of everyday hope and variations of the Not-Yet. In doing so, learner collaborators amid varying sizes of groups and collaborators can grow in their awareness of latent tendencies, of the possibility and potential of subjective and collective synchronizations. The pursuit of contemporary recognitions, of hope-clues from the past, render visible everyday *empty-spaces* of routine and institutional regulation. The task is to creatively incorporate the re-enchantment of utopian *rustles* into new visions of hope, and through relative experiences of the punctum, the trace, the 3rd meaning, and reverie, encourage the navigation of possible routes towards alternative futures and new destinations. Transcending the constriction of strategic routines and institutional disciplinary structures, learner collaborators can become Proustian detectives, and through Lefebvrean notions of everyday space and time, they can re-learn how to invoke the democracy of subjective tactics and embrace the astonishment of culture-riven daydreams. As their strange and relative irruptions sputter and emerge amid a context of human complexity, they manifest similar, though ultimately unique, patterns of creative possibility.

Notes

1 It may be useful here to clarify (as much as is feasible in such short a space) the wider principles being invoked here in relation to 'complexity'. Strogatz notes that *complexity* is 'a natural outgrowth of chaos, in some ways its flip side – instead

of focusing on the erratic behaviour of small systems, complexity theorists [are] fascinated by the organised behaviour of large ones' (Strogatz, 2003: 209). Furthermore, Cohen and Stewart note that 'Complexity at any given level is a consequence of the operation of relatively simple rules . . . Simplicity breeds complexity through sheer multiplication of possibilities' (Cohen and Stewart, 2000: 219). With complexity, an organisational mystery emerges associated with the manifestation of unpredictable, though identifiable, patterns; with complexity, fractured fragments gravitate and synchronise into 'obscure though loosely associative shapes'. The development of intriguing and emergent patterns of complexity effectively collapses the ultimate meaninglessness of chaos. Following from this, Strogatz notes, where chaos, complexity and synchronisation or 'sync' is concerned, 'Chaos theory revealed that simple non-linear systems could behave in extremely complicated ways, and showed us how to understand them with pictures instead of equations. Complexity theory taught us that many simple units interacting according to simple rules could generate unexpected order . . . For reasons I wish I understood, the spectacle of sync strikes a chord in us, somewhere deep in our souls. It's a wonderful and terrifying thing. Unlike many other phenomena, the witnessing of it touches people at a primal level. Maybe we instinctively realise that if we ever find the source of spontaneous order, we will have discovered the secret of the universe' (Strogatz, 2003: 286–289). Similarly, Strogatz also asks, 'What is it about music that stirs us so? Or, the spectacle of sync in nature, the graceful movements of flocks of birds and schools of fish? What is it about dancing together that gives us such pleasure? Why do we delight in coincidences?' (ibid: 262). Strogatz goes on to further note that complexity and pattern synchronisation ('sync') can also be seen as being part of 'the most beautiful forms of human expression, in ballet, in music, even in the love shared by people whose hearts are in sync. The difference is that these are more supple forms of sync, not mindless, not rigid, not brutally monotonous. They embody the qualities that we like to think of as uniquely human – intelligence, sensitivity, and the togetherness that comes only through the highest kind of sympathy' (ibid: 274). As such, inner-rhythms of subjective experiences, perceptions, memories and dreams are 'fractal'; Benoit Mandelbrot coined and developed the neologistic term fractal from the Latin adjective *fractus*, which refers to irregularity and fragmentation; Mandelbrot also points out that fractus can be appropriately linked to the Latin verb *frangere*, which means 'to break' (Mandelbrot, 1983, p. 4). Thus, the geometry of fractals, for Mandelbrot, is capable of articulating and representing non-uniform shapes, which tend to be '*grainy, hydralike, in between, pimply, pocky, ramified, seaweedy, strange, tangled, tortuous, wiggly, wispy, wrinkled,* and the like' (Mandelbrot, 1983: 5). The uniqueness of fractal contents and shifting spaces, extending as part of tendrilous landscapes (for example, type 'Mandelbrot Set' into an internet search engine and watch the complex and intricate shapes unfold), means that they fracture from person to person. Leading on from this, 'Eve, Horsfall and Lee' (1997) make a formative move to begin to ascertain the potential relevance and paradigmatic impact of fractality and complexity within the realm of sociology. They suggest that the liberation of agency and 'free-will' via complexity illustrates the *Proto-spiritual bent for creativity*; continuing from this, they remark that the 'the fractal form embedded in any nonlinear feedback process, is the graphic and undeniable evidence of the life and freedom embodied in physical reality' (Eve, Horsfall and Lee, 1997: xxiv). They note that the wider and necessary impact of the principles of chaos and complexity theory marks the end of a major class of dichotomies within scientific and theoretical terminology and, by implication, the social sciences and sociology generally. In place of previous and entrenched theoretical systems structured around dichotomies and dualisms, with overly defined concepts and rigid vocabularies, we must confront and meet with the new paradigm, with our own sets of non-Euclidean theoretical 'shapes' and conceptual forms and practices (Eve, Horsfall and Lee, 1997: xxi).

2   It is useful to point out here the connections and close affinity of Lefebvre's work on rhythms, space and time to the epistemological and scientific works of Bachelard, along with the more relativistic *Poetics of space* and *Dialectic of duration*. Elden points out here that 'Lefebvre regularly cites the former, particularly in his *The Production of Space*, where Bachelard, is one of those he draws upon for an understanding of space' (Bloch, 1998: 13).

3   We can further define and usefully clarify Lefebvre's critical approach to the pseudo-scientific abstraction of human space and time via the following quote: 'The relations between groups and individuals in everyday life interact in a manner which . . . escapes the specialised sciences . . . It seems that once the relations identified by history, political economy or biology have been extracted from human reality, a kind of enormous, shapeless, ill-defined mass remains. This is the murky background from which known relations and superior activities (scientific, political, aesthetic) are picked out. It is this 'human raw material' that the study of everyday life takes as its proper object. It studies it both in itself and in its relation with the differentiated, superior forms that it underpins. In this way it will help to grasp the 'total content' of consciousness; this will be its contribution towards the attempt to achieve unity, totality' (Lefebvre, 1991: 252).

4   Elden in the introduction to *Rhythmanalysis* notes that Lefebvre's understanding of time was very much shaped by his reading of Proust, 'with the issues of loss and memory, recollection and repetition becoming particularly important. By the time Lefebvre became a Marxist, in the late 1920s, he therefore had a fairly worked-through understanding of questions of temporality. In his analysis of the difference between linear and cyclical time, and the contrast between clock time

and lived time, there is a difference between his understanding and that of Marxism'
(Lefebvre, 2010).

5   It is useful to point out the influence of Proustian principles on Roland Barthes and
Gaston Bachelard here; Barthes notes in *Camera Lucida* that 'photography gave me
a sentiment as certain as remembrance, just as Proust experienced it one day when,
leaning over to take off his boots, there suddenly came to him his grandmother's
true face, 'whose living reality I was experiencing for the first time, in an involuntary
and complete memory" (Barthes, 2000: 70). And Bachelard, in *Poetics of Space*, notes
that his creative take on poeticised memory 'is well this side of Proust. The liberties
that the mind takes with nature do not really designate the nature of the mind'
(Bachelard, 1994: viii).

6   Bloch, E. (1986) *The Principle of Hope*, Vol 1. p: 140. Plato's *Phaedrus* provides
us with a clear example of the anamnetic 'in action', as the soul falls to Earth, we
observe the beauty of the scene, and once born, we struggle to recall the beauty – but
the memory is still, and always 'embedded'.

7   For further elaborations of the Blochian notion of anamnesis and anagnorisis,
see Macfarlane (2000); for a useful definition of Aristotle's notion of anagnorisis,
see especially page 373. See also Landman (1975), page 178 for Bloch's 'utopian'
incorporation and interpretation of this concept within the context of his
framework. See Peter Thompson (2013: 86) for discussion of Bloch's use of
anamnesis; and Frances Daly (2013: 178) for discussion of Bloch's utopian
application of anagnorisis.

8   To cite this idea in a little more detail, Lefebvre notes that the ideas of the *level*
encompasses the idea of *differences between levels*. We could even say that the actual
or possible difference between levels is the criterion by which levels are determined.
Wherever there is a level there are several levels, and consequently gaps (relatively),
sudden transitions, and imbalances or potential imbalances between those levels.
Therefore this idea excludes the idea of the *continuous field*, although it is not
incompatible with the ideas of general context, globality or sets. Levels cannot be
completely dissociated one from the other. Analysis may determine levels, but it
does not produce them; they remain as units within a larger whole . . . Realities
rise to the surface, emerge, and take on substance momentarily at a certain level.
At the same time, the concept implies an internal determination, a relatively stable
situation overall . . . Multiple 'realities' coexist on each individual level, implying and
(mutually) implied, enveloping and enveloped, encompassing and encompassed,
unmediated and mediated (Lefebvre, 2008a: 119–120).

9

Encounters, Stories, Connections

Jane: BA (Hons) Education Studies 2014–2015

The utopian pedagogy

From my childhood days, I have always played at being a teacher and have always loved the innate creativity of children. The one important thing I wanted to achieve in life was to be a mother. I brought my children up, only working part-time, and not at all when they were young. I then helped out in my children's local school and realized at that moment that I had found my way. I realized that working with children was the path I wanted to follow. I gained my teaching assistant qualifications up to level 4. At this point I realized that I wanted to pursue my dream of being a teacher and enrolled for a degree at Blackburn. My experience of the utopian pedagogy gave me the inspiration to continue and finish my degree and become a teacher. Two weeks after finishing my degree, I secured a school placement and was lucky enough to apply for and secure a teaching post! Education has helped me to achieve part of my utopia and a better life for my family. I am extremely proud and now look towards incorporating material from the utopian pedagogy in my own teaching. I would like to think that aspects of this pedagogy can be introduced into the primary school setting. I hope that in the next five to ten years we will be using these new and interesting concepts and practices and passing them on to generation after generation.

A Dérive in Berlin

It has been a very difficult final year working full time and completing a full time degree course and running a family, but sheer determination, hope and dreams of a better life kept me on track. Working all week, studying, then studying all weekend all seemed too much by Christmas. The dark nights and endless word counts seemed daunting. Then we were introduced to a *utopian pedagogy*. I was intrigued. Little did I know that this journey would be so exciting and interesting; it inspired the whole class and allowed us to look at our own life, hopes and dreams and delve deeper into our own autobiographical lives. Looking at times that we have experienced *punctumic* moments, not realizing there was a term for such powerful moments, has been liberating. We realized that learning can be taken in infinite directions by being *situationists* and absorbing our surroundings and taking this new information in new directions. I realized that working in education doesn't mean that we have to follow a traditional pedagogy. Instead we can take experiences and encounters from *dérives*, and *détourne* them into something new and inspiring. We can be creative and pass on knowledge in new and exciting ways.

On a recent trip to East Berlin, I was mesmerized by the fascinating wall art and graffiti. The artistic political statements started to capture my interest, in particular a distinctive set of colourful and strange faces. But what were they trying to say? I drifted and absorbed all of the images and attractions around me, moving away from the established touristic locations. I wondered what hidden messages these intriguing images contained. I was very much reminded of Guy Debord's *Theory of the Dérive*, whose tactic suggests that people should '[l]et themselves be drawn by the attractions of the terrain and the encounters they find there' (Debord: 1958). I was so mesmerized by the iconic pictures that I made a note on my phone. I was amazed at the information I found about the artist Thierry Noir:

> For five years he painted the Berlin Wall illegally every day with bold, cartoon-like images of animals and human faces. With little money and no stable employment, he scavenged emulsion from building sites to paint the wall in an act of protest to 'transform it, make it ridiculous, and help destroy it'. His aim was to paint the Berlin Wall to make it stand out like a mutation in the city, not to make it a beautiful piece of public art . . . 'I could not make the wall beautiful because in fact it would have been absolutely impossible to do so'. (Wyatt, 2014)

This developed a greater understanding of the unusual, almost grotesque child-like images that I was so curious to unfold. I was so moved by what I had discovered that I wanted to pass on this information to others. I became an Edupunk, learning and applying what I had encountered in various contexts.

In December I was asked to run a club in the junior school where I work. In the true spirit of détournement, I knew straight away what I wanted to develop – an *Art* club. I produced a PowerPoint of my pictorial findings of Thierry Noir images from my Berlin trip. The year six pupils (age 10 years) were intrigued, many did not even know what the Berlin Wall was. We then decided to emulate the photos and create our own Berlin Wall, to explore and learn about separation, art and the possibility of human unity.

Rosemary: BA (Hons) Social Science 2014–2015

My early years were spent in the 1950s in a small hamlet nestled outside the town of Sangre Grande, Northeast of Trinidad; I spent my early years and late teens living with my family on a few acres of land that my parents had bought. My father was a keen gardener and he loved the land, toiling early in the morning, resting in the midday and then returning to his labour of love in the cool of the late afternoon and evening. He planted a citrus grove of orange trees and my brothers, sister and I enjoyed it as a haven for picnics. During my time there, I attended an infant school and then an elementary school, graduating with a school leaving certificate. My parents could not afford to send me to secondary school because of the fees. There was an opportunity to sit for an 11+ exam and secure a scholarship, but I failed the exams. Instead, I eventually attended a commercial school, which taught shorthand, typing and bookkeeping. My first job was as a typist at an agricultural firm; my dream was to become a nurse, but I couldn't afford to study for the necessary qualifications. I always intended to study in higher education but encountered many barriers and prejudices. Dissatisfied with my jobs and limited opportunities, I spent some time in Antigua – where I got married, then went on to live in the Bronx in the United States, where we started a family. After a number of wonderful years, my mother-in-law in England became ill, so we made a final move to be with her and support her, which brought me to Blackburn, Lancashire. Finally, many decades later, I decided to go back to education and eventually embarked on my degree in Blackburn. My experience of the utopian pedagogy has enabled me to reconnect with lost hopes, memories and people from my past, especially with my father.

Reflections of my father

I rediscovered some of my father's award certificates which had been stored in an envelope and eventually hidden in a drawer. He had won several prizes in gardening competitions. As I saw, touched and smelled the age-worn paper,

I immediately recollected my early years as a girl walking through my father's garden, the grass, the fields and different types of fresh green, yellow and red vegetables. The certificates took me on an adventure back through those fields with my father. The encounter with those certificates reminded me of Proust and the Blochian theory of *'Traces'*, the invisible marks that people make and leave. The Brooklyn years were times of innocence and naivety, where I used the papaw leaf as an umbrella to shade the bright midday sun from my eyes. I think now that the papaw leaf symbolized the shade over my life, with the veins of the leaf signifying all of the intersecting intricacies and complexities that I have faced. The certificates pull back the curtains of those years, through them I can recollect the times my father worked in the fields, tenderly cultivating his crops, anticipating the April showers, which watered the seedlings and allowed them to grow into tender plants, before reaping the harvest.

My father's early life, of growing up on the British colony of Montserrat in the Caribbean, was a sort of mystery to us. He told us stories which seemed so mystical because we didn't know the island. After WWII he visited Trinidad, met my mother, and settled there, and after a few years he started a family; he remained there until his death in 1974. As I focused on the certificates, an onrush of memories flooded my thoughts, liberated from the past. Summertime would often find us having picnics under the orange trees, and again the papaw leaf shaded me from the sun. The September rains fell with a vengeance casting a dark shadow over the fields, nothing could shelter the crops from the furious heavy drops and wild winds. My teenage years crept up on me, one minute I was a child, carefree like the wind rustling through the trees, extroverted and unin-habited, then suddenly, or so it felt, I was in the turmoil of my mid-teens. It was then that my father was taken ill; he became sad, lonely and intolerable because he could not work the land anymore. Sadly, he died two-and-a-half years after his illness. During these years I experienced under-achievement, lack of confidence and low self-esteem; my late father's counsels revealed to me the need to relax and contemplate, taking one day at a time. His certificates were with me during those times, latent. Annette Kuhn (2002), in her book *Family Secrets*, notes that 'memories . . . do not simply spring out of the image itself, but are generated in a network, an inter-text of discourses that shift between past and present' (Kuhn, 2002: 14). I can look at the certificates now and they bring out meanings beyond the sum of the printed words: a mirage of oranges which signify and reflect my father's warmth and happiness combined with his physical energy.

My Antigua years were full of independence, I was really on my own and making decisions which have impacted my life since in a positive way. Along all of these roads, the certificates were with me, accompanying my every move from airport to airport. I met my husband there. For me, Antigua was a new lease of life and I became eager to travel again, this time to the Bronx in the United States of America, my brothers and uncles were all living there and I knew that there would be a great network of relatives around me. The certificates have followed me all the way to my Blackburn years, like echoes; and now, they have granted me the opportunity to reflect on my father whose steely attitudes enhanced my hopes and dreams. I have trodden paths of anticipation, pregnant with hope, mixed with enthusiasm, sadness and joy. I think that my father's utopian dreams were at least germinated among the fields of green which brought about great satisfaction for him, but I believe he did not live to fully enjoy its fruition. My father's admonitions and counsels that one's hopes and dreams can be fully realized have stayed with me. The punctum moment which I owe to those certificates has helped me to contemplate and revive my own utopian yearnings. The traces of possibility, bestowed to me from my father's field of dreams, will flourish and grow in this chapter of my life.

Esmie: BA (Hons) Social Science 2012–2013

A journey

I loved primary school, I definitely had loads of confidence and there was a real emphasis on creative pursuits. Secondary school was unsettling, it completely challenged who I thought I was and I quickly lost my voice. The lessons were boring because they became technical and unimaginative. After college I went on to work as a qualified nursery nurse for about eight years; I enjoyed the creative side of the job, but I got tired of being treated (by others) like I didn't have a brain. I left childcare and got a job in a local card Shop. During this time my Mum was undergoing treatment for cancer, which eventually took her life; I then applied to study an Access to Higher Education Diploma Healthcare course at Blackburn College. In my grief I considered becoming a nurse, but my interest switched during the Access programme, and I ended up enrolling on to the BA (Hons) Social Science at Blackburn University Centre. The course challenged me and I felt a level of achievement that I had never experienced before. During my final year I secured some temporary paid work at my local MP's constituency office. I was subsequently offered (and accepted) a permanent position.

Wish you were here

Twelve years later, in September 2007, in the stifling heat of an evening while on holiday in Cyprus, I gazed up into the midnight blue beyond with its wildly scattered stars, as if someone had thrown a thousand diamonds upon the upper limits; quite suddenly and quite unexpectedly a shooting star blazed a glittering trail across the sky. The sighting reignited a dare to hope and, remembering the little girl who once believed, I closed my eyes and made a wish. Nearly four months later and into the New Year, my wish had been rescinded; I stayed by her hospital bedside and she called me her little angel, like she always did, but she slipped away to a place that I couldn't follow, leaving an empty space in my heart. Although time removed the numbness, it replaced it with a painful yearning; and then when I least expect it, the empty space is temporarily filled with a myriad of memories. My favourite and earliest memory, resting my head on her chest, listening to her heartbeat as she read fairytales to me, she gave me my love of fairytales; and so I continue to dream. Disengagement from the present can cause us to cease living and hoping for the future, as we become afraid at what else may be lost to us 'when the beloved who granted this happiness is far away, lost, or dead' (Bloch, 2006: 88). It is as if the heart has been placed in a chest and buried to protect it from breaking again, yet in hiding, we only become less human and detached from any hope for the future. At the most unexpected times there is the whisper of a trace, coaxed from slumber by a familiar smell of perfume or piece of music, and beneath a Kaleidoscopic rainbow of evocative images, scenes play out in the projector of my mind, a reminder that my heart continues to beat. This secret collection of memories compels me to return, time and time again, to the past, recalling the dreams and wishes of a youth who 'is powerfully and personally there, [even though] the Now grows empty in a different way' (ibid.: 88).

The world of faerie is always far more opulent in detail, the skies are bluer and the grass is greener. 'Once upon a time: this means in fairy-tale manner not only the past but a more colourful or easier somewhere else' (Bloch, 1993: 168). There are clear-cut distinctions between good and evil; evil is often found shrouded in darkness, beneath dense storm clouds, surrounded by a dark and gloomy, impenetrable forest. Good is represented through light and radiance, with courageous heroes embarking upon dangerous quests, sacrificing their life for a greater purpose. Fairytales are eternal and transcendent and continue to give comfort. Often during childhood we revel in a magical world quite separate from the adult world, our inquisitive minds prompt us to ask endless questions with eyes full of wonder and astonishment. As young adults, we are told to 'get our heads out of the clouds', we cease to ask questions and become focused on material dreams of wealth, though we may be required to work soul-destroying jobs to achieve these so-called 'dreams'. But in the adult world, fairytales and daydreams are considered something to be embarrassed about; for adults, dreams tend to take on the nature of material possessions or sexual fantasies. So much 'other' potential is locked inside a forgotten part of the mind, where childhood wishes and fairytale dreams are shelved away. Such dreams and wishes contain powerful hopes for the future; we should increasingly learn to build on nostalgic memories, figure out what it is that makes the 'then' so much better than the 'now'.

Nostalgic memory sets itself against any relationship to the present and serves us better as a 'critical utopianism' comparing the past with the present in an attempt to envisage a better future. Hiding our hearts away to prevent them from hurting only serves to make us cold and detached from the hopes and dreams that warmed our hearts in the first place, fearing to love for fear of the loss or rejection and not daring to hope for a dream that may not be fulfilled, 'Children are meant to grow up, and not to become Peter Pans. Not to lose innocence and wonder, but to proceed on the appointed journey: that journey upon which it is certainly not better to travel hopefully than to arrive, though we must travel hopefully if we are to arrive' (Tolkien, 2008: 15).

In contemporary education, hope appears to remain sealed tight within a Pandora's Box, yet it is vital to realize that hope is the secret to re-enchanting the mind and putting an end to fear. Even through the devastation of loss, the heart can return to the pursuit of hope, as 'like love, [it] is one of the very simple, primordial dispositions of the living person. In hope, man reaches 'with restless heart', with confidence and patient expectation, toward the 'not yet' of fulfilment' (Pieper, 1986: 27).

Dennis: BA (Hons) Social Science 2012–2013

Heritage

I remember a long steel case with his name inscribed upon it; it housed a long rifle, which my grandfather would oil and clean habitually. All of his male grandchildren would fight to pass him the lubricants, so that they could listen to him talk about his adventures as a soldier. It used to happen most times after evening meals, on cold winters; my grandmother would prepare dessert – probably exhausted by the tales that we were so eager to hear. There, he was the survivor, delivering life lessons and recollections from his ventures as a soldier. We would sit silently as if in a trance. Looking back, it might have been just that, amazed at how a man could survive through such trying times. The wisdom that I acquired from the old man is equivalent to gifts of gold; the lessons proved to be weapons specifically crafted for the challenges that lay ahead. Moving to a different city was agonizing; and then my childhood ended. I was a young alien torn away from my world of belonging and familiarity, trying to understand and find home in my new surroundings. Many of my new friends seemed to have forgotten their true heritage. They appeared lost and corrupted, severed from their identity.

I had to find my feet and take pride in my roots. A face from the past emerged, a slightly older cousin who listened to a particular type of music, the music of reggae. It was magical listening to some of his favourite songs, they made such perfect sense; it was as though he knew that one day I would listen to them. The songs spoke to me, my heritage began to be restored. I belonged again, I was sure. I was confident again without confusion. As my understanding of the music deepened, it all started making sense. It was like an echo of granddad's lessons. Within a short time, eruptions of enthusiasm flowed, and the will to progress was reborn. For me, reggae acknowledges grief, and at the same time it instils hope, which is essential for survival. Hope for a better future, hope and aspirations for better living conditions, individually and collectively; these aspirations connect to Ernst Bloch's concept of the not-yet (utopia). Ernst Bloch focused on identifying utopian urges embedded within literature, music and other forms of art. In this instance it is the utopian possibilities contained in reggae which have enabled me and others to dream for something better. The messages in the music can activate daydreams centred on self-improvement. The not-yet can be applied on two levels, both individually and collectively. The first one is on dreaming and acting on improving personal circumstances, and the latter is on the global scale. For Bloch, literature and art contains 'traces' which connect individual daydreams to future possibilities.

On the theme of daydreaming, Gaston Bachelard, in *The Poetics of Reverie*, emphasizes the importance of the past and also remembers hopes and aspirations from childhood. These recollections present opportunities for a person to improve himself '[w]hen he would dream in his solitude, the child knew an existence without bounds. His reverie was not simply a reverie of escape. It was a reverie of flight' (Bachelard, 2004: 100). For me, these ideas of reverie fit well with the utopian concepts of Ernst Bloch as, combined, they liberate a person to creatively find solutions to problems and obstacles. People can remember to fulfil their dreams, beyond the hindrance of work, school or other constraints, 'childhood remains within us a principle of deep life, of life always in harmony with the possibilities of new beginnings' (Bachelard, 2004: 124). The concept of reverie reminds people that they have dreams embedded beneath the stresses of life and adulthood. Bachelard places emphasis on revisiting these and remembering the beauty of dreaming for the something better; the process of daydreaming on our childhood wonders revives 'within us the spirit of childhood and above all to apply the spirit of childhood in our complex lives' (ibid.: 131). Visions of utopia can be triggered by encounters with cultural artefacts. The importance as outlined by Bloch and Bachelard is identifying when this occurs and learning how to act on it. As individuals find their inspiration, they can use it to guide them towards a place of transformation. Although visions of utopia would be different for each person, the common factors of dignity and harmony could potentially create a better world for us all.

Raeesa: BA (Hons) Education Studies 2014–2015

My heritage

I was born in Pakistan, Lahore, and moved to Dubai at the age of 2 with my family to join my dad who had lived there since 1960s. I went to a multicultural school and studied with students from all over the world, such as Sudani, Somali, Indian, Pakistani, Chinese, Arabs and so on. The school gave me a lot of confidence; I was very outspoken, not afraid to state my point of view even to the teachers. This did put me into their bad books, but I believe in saying what is right even if it means getting into trouble. At the age of 15 I was engaged, my fiancé was 18. I was the youngest in my family to get engaged. My mum and dad wanted me to complete my studies, which I was thankful for, it was definitely my priority. After completing FA in Commerce/Business (equivalent to 'A' levels) in 2003, I got married at age 18.

Moving from Dubai to Blackburn was a big change in terms of moving away from my family. My husband was very supportive, as was his family; but there was still the feeling that I was incomplete without my own family around me.

The new place, the new house, and the new family were all comforting, but I still felt alienated. Their values were different to those of my family, who were thousands of miles away. Even the weather was the opposite to that of Dubai. I felt like I was on a different planet. Different rules, different values, it all made me feel like I just wanted to run away, like I wanted to escape. As I got married at a young age, I never really got a chance to complete my studies. Education meant a lot for my parents, maybe because they never got the opportunity to complete theirs. My mum's parents passed away before she could complete her studies. She always said that she wanted one of her children to be a doctor, maybe because she wanted to fulfil her dreams through the next generation. My parents gave us the gift of virtue in relation to education, an investment that we had within ourselves, a weapon which we could use to remind ourselves whenever we wanted it or needed it. My parents have always been my strength; they are *'militant optimists'* (Bloch) who fought against culture, tradition, society, so that their children can fulfil their dreams. Every time I have told them about my assignments, interviews or any problems in my life, their support and faith in me was more than what I had in myself. I believe that it is because of their prayers and belief in me that I have achieved a part of my not-yet. I am still in the process of discovering an incomplete journey, happy that I am moving towards the possibility of an unknown utopia.

Before getting married, I had a vision of a future that I used to daydream about, where I would go to university, complete my education, get a good job and then settle down. However, that's not how things turned out; after my daughter started school, I felt lost again. With the support of my husband, I thought of going back into education again to fulfil my dream, to achieve my incomplete, the not-yet (Bloch). I sought advice from people who I assumed would also support me. But I was told that I couldn't study in the United Kingdom as my qualifications from Dubai didn't have any value, and that I would have to start all over again, do GCSEs and then A-levels. However, I'm currently working as a teaching assistant at a very good school, and I have just completed my degree. Looks like I was 'good' after all.

Pursuit of Happiness

After watching the film 'Pursuit of Happiness', I related to what Christopher Gardner felt during his struggle. The film is based on the life story of Christopher Gardner and how he transformed his life through grit and determination. I saw how my sister and brother struggled to achieve their dreams, and are still struggling but not giving up. Sometimes people just need a chance, one chance to prove themselves. I can watch the film over and over and still feel the same sense of emotion and hope as when I watched it for the first time. Especially when he tells his son to never let anyone tell him that he can't do something. Here I would add Barthes's 'Death of the Author', where the meaning changes for every individual; it's open to deep and personal interpretations. I connect to the film as it compares to the people who said to me that that I couldn't do something; the film has given me strength to show them that I can achieve. Their negative comments and advice has been a driver for me rather than a barrier. The more that they wanted to push me down, the more I wanted to achieve and show them that I am good enough to accomplish.

Liz: BA (Hons) English with Sociology 2013–2014

Mother

I have lived in Darwen with my mother and brother since I was born. My experience of secondary school was not a positive one. Although I achieved high grades, my overall personal experience was marred due to bullying, and I often felt that the education system was more concerned with my grade outcome rather than my well-being and experience at the school. This experience continued to influence me and I had little self-esteem and confidence. My college life was a little better as I was able to escape from the people who had made my secondary school life difficult. I became a young mum at the age of eighteen and was stigmatized as a result. I was told I would never become anyone or make anything of my life. When my youngest child was one-year-old I decided I did not want to conform to this label, and I enrolled onto my university course at Blackburn. As part of studying for my degree I was made to feel that my opinion and my view mattered. I am now pursuing a very different future (to the one previously assigned to me).

Daddy

Ernst Bloch suggests that the path of possibility towards utopia cannot be achieved by external factors alone; importantly, hope lies within us as a light that 'still burns, and we are beginning a fantastic journey towards it, a journey toward the interpretation of our waking dream' (Bloch, 2000: 3). Usefully, Bloch also identifies the utopistic *traces* left by personal experiences. With a certain sympathy, Roland Barthes's notion of the 'punctum' provides us with a conceptual mechanism, which facilitates the creative exploration of personal associations. Barthes developed this concept as a result of the intense personal experience of sorting through old photographs after the death of his mother. Barthes described the experience as being an 'element which rises from the scene, shoots out of it like an arrow, and pierces me' (Barthes, 2000: 26). I myself experienced the same feeling while listening to the poem *Daddy* by Sylvia Plath. I experienced an unexpected rush of anger and pain that, at the time, I did not understand. When a punctum is experienced, the person is largely unaware of the reason behind it. It wasn't until after the initial experience that I was able to isolate the intense feelings to a particular event from my past. The 'punctum' I experienced related to my own father and his lack of support when I fell pregnant at a young age.

I listened to a recital of the poem in a lecture at university, the aim of which was to critically analyse the poem and its meaning through Sylvia Plath's own experiences as a woman, a wife and a daughter. However, for me the poem was not about the experiences of women in the 20th century, the meaning was much more personal. The class was considering the meaning of the poem through a critical perspective, concentrating on the experiences of the author, but '[t]o give a text an Author is to impose a limit on that text' (Barthes, 1977: 147). It is these limits which critics find especially useful, for 'When the Author has been found, the text is explained' (ibid.: 147). However, the opposing argument is that 'a text's unity lies not in its origin but in its destination' (ibid.: 148); therefore, the poem was only united with this particular meaning at the time it reached me, not at the time it was composed by Sylvia Plath.

Once the lecture had come to an end and the punctum had been experienced, the initial wounding of the punctum, the feelings of anger and pain, changed to feelings of empowerment and triumph. The powerful final stanza of the poem took me to the space of the 'not-yet'; the 'not-yet' that I am striving towards. Even though I had entered into this space before, which had driven me towards reaching my 'not-yet' daydreams, I had pushed it 'below the threshold' (Bloch, 1986). Bloch highlights that the reason a person's 'not-yet' is pushed away from the immediate conscious is 'because our attention is occupied with other things, and hence distracted' (ibid.: 114). Bloch's essay *Triumphs of Misrecognition* describes a young couple who separate, and the male moves away from the town to travel. The young woman is initially described as conforming to traditional stereotypes, as the 'smell of sewing hung about her' (Bloch, 2006: 31), and the man can remember little else of her. However, upon his return the man expects to find the young *inferior* woman that he once left; to his surprise, he found she had become 'the head doctor . . . unrecognisable, confident, calm, distinguished, and smart' (ibid.: 32). The young woman had experienced daydreams of becoming someone more than she was expected to be, and through entering into the space of her not-yet-conscious and not-yet-become, she had been able to strive towards becoming someone beyond recognition. I refused to accept the negative expectations imposed on me and, although the impulse was initially repressed due to self-doubt, I am exceeding the negative expectations of my father. For Bloch, the utopian element that comes from exceeding expectations and becoming someone unrecognizable comes from the individual embracing the 'not-yet' as something necessarily personal, rejecting the 'final sign of an entry into the right fate . . . an entry beyond fate and into our space' (ibid.: 35), the space in which utopia can be found. *Daddy* by Sylvia Plath allowed me to enter into this space and revive my own utopian vision, one in which I exceed expectations and become someone beyond established expectations. Entering into the space of the 'not yet conscious', 'the inner house' and the 'not yet become' has enabled me to uncover *that* which I believe holds the key to an alternative utopian future.

Ruth: BA (Hons) Social Science 2014–2015

Me

I was the firstborn daughter of working-class parents in Blackburn in early 1971; my parents were shocked to discover I was profoundly physically disabled (or so the nurses labelled me!). Many of my life accomplishments are down to the determination of my parents who ensured that I refused to allow my disability to succeed in actually disabling me! Together we fought for the right to mainstream schooling, the right to learn to drive a car, and many other personal rights and achievements. After my A levels, I briefly worked in the civil service before marrying and starting a family. Gradually my health problems and other personal situations meant I was forced to become a stay-at-home mum, so I filled the years with voluntary work and perpetual college courses. When I turned forty I was convinced by friends and family to attempt my life-long desire, to challenge myself with a degree course, and for me, social science was the only choice. Again, my health threatened to get in the way and it took me four years rather than three, but I succeeded in the end. The next stage of my life-long journey is to specialize in sociology and complete an MA, following which I hope to achieve a teacher training qualification and share my love of people-watching and the meanings behind their behaviours with others who love to learn as much as I do.

My masks

Within my house, the walls are covered with collections of masks, art dolls, faces and figures. These faces hold a symbolic importance within everyday life and are the key in the lock to many of my memories. The masks on the walls of my house impart mystery and refract any notion of truth. No two individuals visualize a mask in quite the same way, each person divines a set of very different associations. My favourite mask is made of leather and gives the impression of a windswept desert nomad. There is an air of mystery about it; one can't even tell clearly if the face is male or female, as the only visible feature is a pair of partially closed eyes, everything else is wrapped up in some kind of cloak or hood. Despite this, my gaze perceives a male mask, possibly some kind of hero. Cloth also disguises the face, as it also covers and disguises much of the detail. Each reader needs to be a detective; Ernst Bloch suggests that subjective utopian clues are embedded within artefacts, traces, which need to be deciphered. At first glance, masks are nothing more than chunks of wood, porcelain, or leather, with simple decoration, but masks are also so much more. We all wear masks in order to survive social life. We all act in specific ways, wear different masks and mutate ourselves to *play a part* dependent on the given social situation. People redesign themselves and create new masks. A new mask could mean access to a new group, a subcultural acceptance. It can be a self-protective camouflage. Bloch notes that 'What we are, we do not know; we are still restless, and empty, and like ourselves, but kept hidden' (Bloch, 2000: 227). For me, masks are the ultimate not-yet, a hint of utopian possibility. For they are indeed perfect; while masks may be false in some regard, they are still entirely flawless, symbolizing a better future, an alternative version of oneself. They contain 'something here, something hidden, in the midst of ordinary, unobtrusive normality' (Adorno, 1980). Their past, present and future haunt us; they remind us of who we were, who we are and who we could become. Bloch reminds us that art can provide a window beyond constraint and disappointment.

For me, my collection of masks are an 'assemblage', a name coined by Delueze and Guattari. In this way they can be placed together, but also work separately in multiple and different ways to create their own patterns of assembly. The masks create their own links to thoughts that branch off in every direction in a rhizomatic, chaotic way (Deleuze and Guattari, 2005). Masks create an image of thought. They are multiplicitious, all alike yet totally different, everyone uses them, owns them, and makes them their own on every level of actuality. They can be ritualistic and can be a way to become fully entrenched in cultural memories and traces. At the same time, wearing a mask can determine the Janus-faced, it can force people to act in ways that are expected. We put on a show whenever we interact with others; we succumb to and intensify normalizing discourses, which infiltrate all aspects of everyday life. Masks entrench certain expectations while also increasing the probabilities of misinterpretation. My masks have many layers, many stories to tell, many hints of a not-yet Utopia. At the same time, they belie tangled webs and untruths. Returning to one of Bloch's short stories in *Traces*, where he discusses what is seen behind and beyond the sketch of a window on a hut, Bloch's red window gives clues about the possibility of unseen lives within imaginings and daydreams of alternative becomings. I would like to believe that my masks give me the capacity to do that for my own alternative futures.

Dawn: BA (Hons) Education Studies 2015–2015

A black and white photograph

The photograph was taken almost a quarter of a century ago, shortly after my first marriage; it has history hidden within it for me. My family and I moved house during the Christmas holidays, and in a manner reminiscent of Walter Benjamin when he says that 'I must ask you to join me in the disorder of the crates that have been wrenched open, so that you may be ready to share with me a bit of the mood' (Benjamin, 1999: 61), I began to empty a box of framed photographs which had been packed away for years. As I did so, some broken glass fell out from a photograph frame. This wasn't just another casualty of a difficult move, I had forgotten that photograph. Walter Benjamin spoke eloquently about the relationship between a book collector and his possessions, of the spring tide of memories which surge towards any collector as they contemplate their possessions. For Benjamin, it was in the confusion of his books; for me, it was in the unexpected confusion of 'that' photograph amidst the turmoil of the house move. Reading Unpacking My Library helped me to understand that, in as much as Walter Benjamin's books unlocked memories for him of the places from where he had acquired the books, as did my photograph.

Anybody happening upon the photograph by chance without knowing the story behind it might comment on it for its photographic properties, much as Roland Barthes suggests in *Camera Lucida*. The photograph shows a young woman tiptoeing through a stream, holding her dress up from the running water. The photograph was taken for a competition, it was studied and judged to be the winner. But on rediscovering the photograph, the studium element of the photograph was very much disturbed by a punctum; it induced an emotional response which was very much rooted in the dress I was wearing. It was a one-off creation, a collaborative work of art with my Granny. In the black and white photograph it is difficult to tell the colour or type of fabric or to see any detail. Much has been lost in the photograph. In his paper 'The work of art in the age of mechanical reproduction,' Benjamin discusses the loss of the 'aura' of a work of art when it is reproduced by photography, he wrote, 'The authenticity of a thing is the essence of all that is transmissible from its beginning, ranging from its substantive duration to its testimony to the history which it has experienced' (ibid.: 218). We can see more of the dress by adding colour, showing it worn in an informal snapshot of the bride in a carriage on the day it was made for, a formal portrait and a shot of the ceremony. But none of these exude the aura of the work of the actual work art. There is no substitute for the original with all of the stains and so on from the day it was worn.

So why the big emotional response? After all, it is only a dress, a formal photo of a wedding line-up. But for me, it is also about a relationship. I did not grow up with my Granny, I did not meet her until I was nineteen (I was adopted). As a very creative person, an artist and dress maker, Granny taught me to sew and to have the confidence to make clothes, curtains and anything out of fabric. She taught me what tools to use and how to use them correctly. She had a great sense of humour and we talked for hours about anything and everything. We shared a love of reading, and when it came to planning my wedding, Granny and I set about designing my wedding dress. It had to be the classic Cinderella, nipped in waist line, puff sleeves and huge skirt. We chose the fabric together and spent hours in her kitchen working away while my Grandfather sat at the other end of the table puffing away on his pipe and doing his crossword.

10

Beyond the Trace: Reflections from Past Learners

This chapter presents an array of comments and reflections from learner collaborators who have engaged with, and experienced, all facets of the Utopian Pedagogy – either via the BA (Hons) Social Science, BA (Hons) Sociology with English, or BA (Hons) Education Studies degree programmes – across the last three academic years. For further details relating to the questions/research activity and the process of recruiting past students to this reflective process, please see Appendices 1 and 2. Each of the separate responses below are grouped under each respective question and can be further identified by name (anonymized) and the following codes of each of the respective degree programmes: 'Ed-Studies', BA (Hons) Education Studies; 'Joint-Hons', BA (Hons) Sociology with English; and, 'Soc-Sci', the BA (Hons) Social Science.

Briefly summarize your overall thoughts, based upon your experience of engaging with the *utopian pedagogy*

Anne: Ed-Studies. One of the first things that comes to mind when thinking of the utopian pedagogy is Punctum! I wasn't sure what was meant by this when initially introduced to it as a concept, but within weeks I had what I interpreted to be my own punctum moment when watching and analysing the French film 'Les Choristes'[1] (which became my presentation topic – such was the depth of my emotion for this particular film). I loved the process of cultural analysis and sharing other people's interpretations of punctum moments; it was highly emotional and a great period of bonding with some group members. As I and three other students had joined the BA (Hons) Education Studies as a 3rd year 'top-up' student (coming from the Foundation Degree cohort), it wasn't always easy to integrate into a group which had already lived through two years of studies and experiences together. Although bonds were formed relatively early on with some members of the group, I believe that the utopian pedagogy was the mechanism which really brought the whole group together – particularly during the peer reviewed presentations. The idea of sitting through a few hours of peer presentations can be quite daunting, especially when you're due to go last! This was the first time that I (and I know most of the group felt the same way) was absolutely fascinated by the content of the presentations and felt privileged to share in the highly personal and emotive experiences of my peers. Some of the experiences and punctum moments presented/shared were particularly moving, and I felt that it was quite cathartic for the person presenting.

Eve: Ed-Studies. My overall memory of this pedagogy was that the content of the module clearly aligned with the mode of delivery and assessment. So, often within education courses the lecturer outlines the ills of didactic teaching and learning, from the front of the classroom, with no sense of irony. Occasionally they show some awareness of the gap between what they are saying and how they are behaving and dismiss it because of institutional and time constraints. So, when, with the utopian pedagogy, the tutor explained how they had worked within the system – not without some resistance – to validate a module that allowed for topics, themes, delivery, teaching and assessment in ways that addressed this dissonance, I was overjoyed. I was engaged in all of the material we discussed and have continued to make reference to theorists we considered ever since.

Esmie: Soc-Sci. What sticks in my mind was an open discussion that we had about music, and one of my peers shared her experience of a song that used to play in the coffee shop where she worked. She said it really moved her but she couldn't explain why; her recollection actually gave me shivers. I loved the importance that this pedagogical approach placed on the exploration of indefinable moments, peoples' experiences of these and how they shape us as individuals. I remember feeling awakened and inspired during and after these classes. I always felt certain songs, film and other cultural experiences spoke to me and sent me on a journey; this module explored and enabled me to interpret why I had these moments, and why they're so important.

Liz: Joint-Hons. Initially I was very reserved about what it would be like to learn through a utopian pedagogy, especially by analysing my own experiences. When I took part in the module it was at a time in my life when I was steering away from some negative events, and I was worried that perhaps this module would bring these events back to the surface. We were advised to be aware of our own restrictions and to not investigate memories that could be unnerving. However, I found that as the module progressed I began to look at my memories, my dreams and my experiences as positive events, as they made me who I am today. The turning point for me personally was when I presented my seminar; I had experienced a punctum during a poetry lecture, and I dedicated my seminar to my father. My father was whom my painful memories focused upon, but through this punctum, and from investigating the experience I had when listening to the poem *Daddy* by Sylvia Plath, I became overwhelmed with hope and positivity. Although I had been initially reluctant to consider my personal experiences, I found that once I became acquainted with the theorists, in particular Ernst Bloch and Roland Barthes, I found new hope about my life, my past and my future endeavours.

Louise: Soc-Sci. My experience of the utopian pedagogy was positive. The freedom was daunting at first, but once I began to understand what was required, I fully embraced the experience. It seemed at first that 'it was not enough' to relate theory to a personal experience, and that relating the concepts of hope and utopia to a piece of music, or other cultural artefact, was a bit *self-indulgent*. I realized afterwards that it enabled the creative practise of reinterpreting theories and concepts in relation to a personal experience.

Mark: Soc-Sci. This was a totally new, unique, engaging and collaborative learning approach. The ideas and theorists have stayed with me and continue to resonate in my life. Particularly surprising were the many shared responses and themes, interactions and contributions from all of the students (a group that consisted of a wide mix of ages and backgrounds).

Jasmin: Ed-Studies. To me the pedagogy spoke of *unlocking potential.* I really enjoyed engaging with this approach, because it introduced me to different philosophies such as those of Barthes, Proust and Bachelard and allowed me to realize that education means more than just acquiring knowledge, that it is also about empowering people to improve personally and become politically active. Also, not only did this pedagogy help me to think about myself in different ways, it nurtured my creativity and the capacity for independent and critical thinking.

Raeesa: Ed-Studies. At the beginning of the first session it felt like a boring module, but by the end of that session I had goose bumps. I think in all the years of my education it was this particular pedagogy and approach that made me immediately go home and personally engage, a poignant experience to remind ourselves why we learn and strive to progress.

John: Joint-Hons. I personally found it fascinating to observe the reactions of my mainly younger peers to this subject. A minority seemed to engage immediately while others seemed somewhat bewildered yet fascinated by its democratizing freedoms, perhaps akin to discovering the *Mary Celeste* and not knowing quite how to relate to it. Without doubt, the module structure and pedagogical methods within this type of learning has sown its seeds, which will continue to germinate in later years.

Marie: Soc-Sci. My thoughts initially of the module brought about statements like 'mind bending', 'complicated', 'totally weird', 'oh my god, what have I signed up for?' and even the contemplation of changing to a different area of study. However, after two weeks of interpreting what I was hearing, all of a sudden I had a bit of a moment when everything made sense, well, sort of. But I knew, with lots of listening, reading and researching, a better understanding would follow. It was truly a liberating and exciting experience. After two-and-a-half years of listening to lectures, regurgitating what we had been told in the form of an essay and a seminar, with pre-set questions (and expectations), to then have such an independent learning style thrust upon us was difficult to contend with. This said, the freedom to write about my life, in relation to utopia, was amazing. I personally feel that this type of pedagogy would allow for just about anyone to study the likes of Bloch, Barthes, Bachelard and so on.

How did you find the open and flexible approach to learning, knowledge and interpretation?

Anne: Ed-Studies. To begin with, somewhat scary! I found myself feeling panicked at the idea of tailoring the module's assignments to my personal experiences and emotions. I wrote in my lecture notes: 'no set assignment questions – we come up with it, very personal, what makes us come alive . . . music, films, emotional connections – OH NO!' Looking back, the general feeling in the group seemed quite tense as we tried to make sense of this alternative approach; the stabilizers were being removed from the bike! What would we write about? How would we know if it was 'right'? Which direction should we take? On reflection, I think these reactions may have stemmed from the fact that we had mostly grown up within an education system using a 'closed template', where we were expected to adhere to a set of guidelines and a question to answer.

Eve: Ed-Studies. I found it refreshing at the time. I have recognized its liberating potential, as it provided me with a learning experience which validated, rather than contradicted, my values about learning. It also offered a more authentic alignment with the values that were supposedly central to the programme of study itself. The experience has allowed me to lobby for similar shifts in pedagogy in the institutions that I have worked in (and currently work in). The only tension at the time, across the group, was that the approach was so different to the typical institutionalized expectations; as such, there were initial crises of confidence about whether the assessment would be fair and valid. On reflection, these discussions were a natural step. If there had been no resistance, it would not really have been a radical change.

Esmie: Soc-Sci. I'm going to be honest and say that at the very beginning I was uncomfortable with the idea of setting my own question titles for my seminar and essay, because I was worried I'd do it wrong and that it would jeopardize my marks. However, this was soon forgotten and it became the most liberating learning experience I've ever had. It definitely felt like a gamble to choose your own subject matter, though as long as it involved the theorists discussed in class, pretty much anything could work. The tutor wanted everyone to fully engage with the module, share experiences, trust their instincts and take risks; this was demonstrated by the tutor sharing his own experiences, which made me feel more comfortable with sharing mine.

Liz: Joint-Hons. When the module first began, I was terrified at the thought of being given the chance to experience such an open and flexible approach to learning. After being in education for such a substantial amount of time, with a very rigid and institutionalized process of teaching, an approach which was far more student-lead appeared almost alien. However, I found that this approach allowed me to develop my own strengths, discover more about particular areas that I was interested in and use these interests to my own advantage. For example, I found my interests to be around the works of Ernst Bloch and Roland Barthes; through the flexibility of the module, I was able to consider their works further and bring these into my assessments.

Louise: Soc-Sci. I found this approach to be refreshing, and enjoyed the freedom it provided, in comparison to other modules and types of pedagogy. I can see that this worked well for the subject being studied, but not sure that it would work with other subjects as part of the degree. It felt that we had opened doors to new ideas, which stopped as we left the classroom – at least in terms of the other subjects we were studying.

Mark: Soc-Sci. I had been discouraged in other classes from straying from the reading lists and writing/reading about issues/theorists not covered, something which I found contrary to the idea and principles of education. While with the utopian pedagogy I was allowed full creative freedom in incorporating a wide range of sources, including popular culture; this fulfilled the basic principles of what I feel education should be about: creative freedom, and the expression and enactment of personal/societal change. I recall some resistance from one or two students at the beginning of the module about the nature of the pedagogy, the learning process and the flexible and personal approach. Some complained that the module wasn't grounded in practicality nor did it 'relate to the real world'. Towards the end of the module, it was clear that such feelings had been misplaced. All who attended the final session were moved and/or inspired in a way, if not by others' presentations, by the process of discovery in creating their own final project/presentation. I suspect that such complaints/resistance are likely to be depressingly common, as education and the learning process are increasingly being *sold* as a means to career/economic aspiration rather than an end in itself or a means of societal/personal transformation.

John: Joint-Hons. This anarchic utopian pedagogy does what it says *on the tin*, and that is, guide and nurture without 'ruling' the learning environment, resulting in lecturer and student collaborating and bonding mutually. As a student, I feel that I have emerged as a fractalized essence of the whole course.

Marie: Soc-Sci. To have the professionalism and guidance of the lecturer was reassuring, but allowing us to be quite independent, most probably, produced some of the best academic work that any of us had produced. It cannot be denied that the security of set titles and knowing what is expected of us produce a comfortable setting, one of 'safe education'; but through the open, liberating form of the utopian pedagogy, we experienced new aspects to our own and others' personalities and abilities. The archaic academic systems that this country and many other countries adhere to are outdated. Children, the future students within our universities, are being constrained, confined within a closed and controlling system of instruction.

Poppy: Ed-Studies. The open approach encouraged discussion among the class and between student and teacher. These discussions helped me gain a deeper understanding of the theories and helped to develop intriguing and interactive sessions. It also allowed students to create their own interpretations of theories which again aided understanding. However, I do feel that, as there were no 'right or wrong' reinterpretations of the theories, some misunderstandings were evident. Nevertheless, I now understand that an interpretation, no matter how different, is individually meaningful. Compared to a more traditional approach, it was a difficult thing to grasp at first. Initially, it also seemed that there was no aim in what we were learning, as there was no question to get right at the end; however, with hindsight I now see this as a failure of the values and practices of the wider education system, rather than one of this module and pedagogy.

Which of the theorists did you particularly like/enjoy covering and engaging with (please explain why)?

Anne: Ed-Studies. I enjoyed discovering more about Paolo Freire's works, particularly his idea that educators are not there to shape or form minds, but more to enable them to become themselves. Now, as a teacher myself, I believe passionately in encouraging children to be at the centre of their own learning – they are not 'empty vessels' to be filled with information by a more knowledgeable adult. Making children interactive partners in their learning gives free rein to their natural impulses to explore and imagine – for a child, there are no limits; we seem to forget this as we 'grow up'.

Eve: Ed-Studies. I think the blend of the theorists was one of the most memorable things. Discussing Proust in the light of Bachelard and Barthes really captured my attention. I had heard of Proust and memory, but to have that idea related to Barthes 'punctum' concept and then to discuss Bachelard and the power of daydream was revelatory, it allowed me to articulate some of the vague ideas that I had developed, about how I learn, and become inspired, in much more detail.

Esmie: Soc-Sci. Marcel Proust and involuntary memory; as far back as I can remember I have had experiences of being transported back in time, to a powerful memory, through a certain smell or sound, and Proust had such a beautiful way of describing it; this definitely resonated with me. Ernst Bloch and his utopian vision of the future also struck a chord with me; the not-yet, and the ache, or longing for what could-have-been (or could still be), related, for me, to that indefinable *something*. Bloch is timeless, there's always a place for hope and a desire for something beautiful, and unmarred, by a society blighted with hatred, violence and poverty; Bloch encourages people to embrace hope and move towards a better world.

Louise: Soc-Sci. I mostly enjoyed the work of Guy Debord, in particular the concept of the dérive, and aspects of the wider work of the Situationists, and in my own research time, psychogeography. I still allow myself a little dérive from time to time, and understand that there can be value to 'day dreams' and that to wallow and experience them can be creative as well as joyful. I often prompt myself to change my route through the city and experience a new space, just for a moment, as a break from the routine and humdrum of everyday life.

Mark: Soc-Sci. Barthes's distinction of punctum and studium provided an academic understanding of why certain media and culture resonated with me, and a clearer and more meaningful understanding of the different ways that

I appreciate art/culture. This not only increased my appreciation but also being creative afforded me a better understanding of how art can provide different experiences for the audience. Connected to this, I was also drawn to the Blochian approach to popular culture; a refreshing way of appreciating, critiquing and understanding popular culture. This dispelled some of my prejudices about popular culture; it also gave me a feeling of greater connection with humanity.

John: Joint-Hons. Reading Bloch engaged me directly with the enigmas facing modern quantum physics and the concepts of infinity and zero. The notion of non-linear time has always been at loggerheads with orthodox social structures, including education. Blochian philosophy challenges these concepts head on, and is refreshing, enlivening and very inspirational.

Marie: Soc-Sci. Of all the theorists covered during the module, the one that engaged me most was Ernst Bloch; his outlook was one of positivity and hope, two elements in life that had escaped me for many years. What we find astonishing or what we may find strange, through Bloch, should all be looked at and contemplated in different and redemptive ways. I now look at the term 'utopia' in a totally different way, with a renewed sense of hope. Bloch philosophized on many areas, but his writings on music had a particular effect on me; it contextualized the way that I used (and still use) music to enable me to get through difficult, emotional times. Music is not just there as a pastime, but with Bloch, it exists to interpret and change both emotional and physical situations.

How did you find the Peer Assessment (PA) event/process?

Anne: Ed-Studies. Initially, I remember feeling uneasy about the idea that half of a grade of such an important module would be created through peer marking. As we moved through the module and discussed our ideas and projects, it became clear that we were all having similar misgivings, and that this in itself created a certain sense of solidarity. During the presentations themselves, the emotive nature of the content being discussed fostered high levels of empathy, encouragement and further solidarity. I don't remember worrying about the peer marking process once the presentations were underway – I do remember 'rooting' for every single person who stood up in front of us to present, and that the marking seemed to become a secondary consideration. There are undoubtedly many benefits to using peer assessment within education and I think that many schools could use it well. There is so much that learners can learn from each other (in some ways, perhaps as much as from trained educators). Evaluating each other's work in a positive, constructive way from an early age can encourage children to think for themselves and work collaboratively to achieve a common goal. However, from my professional experience, I think that peer assessment, particularly with children, would have some limitations.

Eve: Ed-Studies. Prior to the PA I thought it was a great idea but was a bit dragged down by other people worrying and discussing it. During the event I remember being concerned about giving an appropriate mark to my peers. I didn't want to be overly generous or unduly critical. I had done peer observing of teaching before and found it hard to be critical even when there were clear issues. I think this happened as part of the PA process, and so I may have been generous in mark, but critical with the comment, occasionally. Afterwards, it felt similar to a tutor assessed piece of work, in that I was keen to see my mark and comments, but it was great to hear what my peers thought of my presentation. I think there is huge scope to shift assessment practices. It should certainly be done in at least one module for every year of an Education Studies degree, because so much of the content on such a course is critical of didactic teaching and strongly calls for constructive alignment. The only limitation is supporting students' ability to offer robust critical feedback to their peers and to really engage with the task at hand. This could well get easier if they were exposed to the approach more frequently and earlier in their studies.

Esmie: Soc-Sci. It enabled me to speak freely and passionately about my chosen areas for both my seminar and essay. I found the essay writing to be a very cathartic experience once I let myself go, as I had reservations about sharing something that had affected me so deeply. I also applied what I learnt in this module to the writing of my dissertation and I took a risk in putting more of my personality and creative side into it, which, thankfully, paid off! Some students may struggle with the personal side of things, although I would say it took things to a whole other level. I think it helped me, as I rarely spoke in a number of my other lectures for fear of saying the wrong thing or being shouted down by my peers, that wasn't something I ever experienced on this module.

Liz: Joint-Hons. I feel as though it pushed me to make more of a connection with my audience as I conducted my seminar for the purpose of wanting them to engage with what I was presenting. It also encouraged me to try something more risky. I definitely think that when you are being assessed by your peers you are more likely to want to engage them with the presentation rather than focusing purely on the tutor's reaction. The only issue I would pinpoint in regard to this style of assessment is that I still found myself gravitating towards wanting to know the comments the tutor had made and the mark they had given me, rather than what my peers had commented.

Louise: Soc-Sci. I wouldn't say that this approach encouraged me to be more creative, I wasn't trying to impress or wow the group into giving me high marks. For my peer assessed seminar presentation, I used props to provide an experience for the people marking it, to bring the presentation to life a bit; however, I wonder if I would have done that if they weren't marking me. I was not concerned that my mark would be low if I was not liked within the group, I felt assured that the tutor would regulate the assessments and notice if there were any irregularities. I wouldn't always feel comfortable using this method for other modules, as I like feedback from the tutor. I think peer assessment as a 'practise' is good, but would not really like it as part of a formal degree mark.

Mark: Soc-Sci. I felt that as a younger male I was slightly hamstrung by the fact that I was not overly confident. On reflection, I feel I may have contributed more (of myself) had I been able to overcome this at the time. I did enjoy the freedom and with this felt that I could draw upon sources that ordinarily wouldn't be considered academic. I enjoyed the PA process as, unlike my other learning experiences, it was truly about positive engagement.

Jasmin: Ed-Studies. It inspired me to go the extra mile and to be creative, as I knew the work was not just going to be marked by the lecturer but by my peers as well. Overall, I would recommend it to be used/adopted more widely, as it does remove the single 'teacher power' and share the responsibility with the students themselves. Sometimes it can be viewed (particularly by students/peers themselves) as less credible, especially when it involves the peer group giving grades, as they may feel that a qualified lecturer's marking is more appropriate.

John: Joint-Hons. I engaged immediately with this pedagogical technique, gone were the shackles of normal assignment and seminar procedures. I was able to engage with the subject matter straight away. This was of course aided by my willingness to engage, challenge and express while being tutored in an innovative style. Some concerns were expressed verbally by my peers. Some just did not want to engage, not because of the fear of the subject matter, but more out of their fear of 'letting-go', of engaging with new learning territories.

Marie: Soc-Sci. Daunting is a word that definitely came to mind when it was made clear we would be peer assessed. What or who was to say that a fellow student knew if I were right or wrong? Their own interpretation of the theorists may not be the same as my own; this thought then planted the seed of self-doubt.

What if I am wrong? Am I going to look like a fool? However, when it was made clear as to what we would be presenting, some of the doubt and worry disappeared. Delivering a presentation, about me, instilled confidence in me, how could I possibly go wrong? After all, only I know myself, how could anyone possibly say that my memories, hopes and fears, my life journey so far were wrong? Overall, the freedom to choose just about anything to present on was liberating; at first it seemed difficult. But then the excitement of it all took hold, I realized that I could focus on one major life event and incorporate photographs, music, documents and many of the people that contributed to that one event. It was an exciting, yet sometimes emotional piece to put together; the end result enabled me to explain why and how I was here in Blackburn. I believe the scope to use this approach more widely in other subjects is just there for the taking. Of course, more factual subjects have to be precise, but to be shown different routes to an answer, or find these routes independently, will allow for the less confident student to also contribute.

Poppy: Ed-Studies. Before we started the peer assessment process, I felt that it created a more relaxed atmosphere, as we knew the people that were judging us. However, when presenting, the room became slightly less relaxed, as I remembered that the whole room was judging me. I would have preferred for a lecturer to mark my work, as I know from experience it is hard for a student to mark another's work. Marking other students' work was particularly hard in this module.

Ruth: Soc-Sci. Personally I found it more difficult to pitch a seminar topic to peers than to lecturers. I am aware that some members of the cohort found it more difficult to understand the theories. This caused worry if my language and delivery style aimed above general understanding. I suspect that was in fact the case, as marks appeared to show wide swings in grades given. I also worried about giving grades to others, as I didn't feel that I was qualified to analyse the quality of work. However, having said that, the actual assignment approach did encourage a much deeper level of creativity, and overall did develop a deeper understanding of the theorists involved. There was no regurgitation of stock quotes and descriptives from each theory, but instead there was the ability to frame them within everyday life. I do also believe that the PA approach could hold one of the keys to increasing student participation and engagement. I myself am hoping to train to teach later, and I look forward to the idea of being able to develop a similar system during my practical training and beyond.

Has the module (and the work that you produced) made you feel/think differently about the future?

Anne: Ed-Studies. As a teacher, I am conscious that children (and teachers) are under incredible pressures to succeed according to precise 'gatekeeper' set criteria. This leaves little or no time to simply ponder, or indeed daydream. Yet, surely the process of simply thinking allows us to explore new possibilities/ avenues, make new and exciting connections, create new knowledge. I do try to allow this into my professional practice when I can. In my Year 5 class, I have developed a peer assessment process of presentations produced as part of our ICT work (PowerPoint, PhotoStory, and Moviemaker). Although some children have scored certain peers either very high or very low, for the most part the 'accumulated wisdom of the crowd' has shone through. More than the mark awarded, it's the discussion that we have as a class as to the particular merits or elements for improvement in the work as a whole. I think the value attached to this is less about the particular ICT skills they may be evaluating and more about the critical thinking skills they are developing and their feeling of involvement in the process.

Eve: Ed-Studies. My experience of the utopian pedagogy has made me more confident in raising the issue of assessment in HE (being too rigid, and lacking constructive alignment to the learning material) with my department at the university, where I now work. The work of Bloch has also been helpful, as I often write about Friere and have been critical myself about idealistic models of education. By studying Bloch, I now have a powerful argument which is rooted in a critical realism about the benefits of democratic hope. I now teach on a BA (Hons) Working with Children and Families programme and a BA (Hons) Education and Professional Studies programme at UK universities. In my Research Methods modules I discuss Bachelard, Barthes and Bloch at a number of points, particularly in sessions about research proposals and getting inspiration to form research questions.

Esmie: Soc-Sci. I have spoken to a lot of friends, family and work colleagues about my experience on this module, not only because I enjoyed and engaged with it so much but because it has made me more confident and willing to challenge certain things. I've grown more confident and willing to speak my opinion on matters which is hard when working in a political and male dominated environment.

Liz: Joint-Hons. The theories of both Bloch and Barthes, and the notion that each individual can have their view of utopia, continue to influence both my personal and professional life. I am now working within the substance misuse service, and the people who I meet on a daily basis have different views of how they would like their lives to be. I believe this about myself, my children and my family; we all have different yet potent visions of our own possible utopian futures, which we should pursue.

Louise: Soc-Sci. It has given me the freedom to allow myself to think, to know that those thoughts can have value and are not as random as I had previously considered them to be. This module and pedagogy have led me to my own further research, and hopefully in the future I will pursue further study within sociology.

Mark: Soc-Sci. The theorists and ideas discussed during the module have stayed with me for a number of years now, especially shaping the way I view popular culture. I feel that it has influenced the ways in which I am creative today, often using nostalgia, longing, and utopian ideals as elements in my writing. With a number of friends, I currently run an online and print journal. The name of which is influenced by childhood nostalgia. *Pear Drop* relies heavily on the theme of nostalgia. The very first piece I contributed was a short story 'Kasia', where the protagonist goes to a partially abandoned warehouse filled with his memories – a story infused with the theories and values considered in the module.

Jasmin: Ed-Studies. Totally. Before the module, I would just do things (particularly in relation to education and studying) without knowing why. I think, through engaging with this pedagogy and all of the theories that it introduced to me, I am more able to identify my goals and know what I really want to achieve. I went on to complete a PGCE programme after finishing my degree course; the concepts covered on this module inspired me tremendously. I already apply some aspects of the utopian pedagogy in my own teaching practice. For example, the peer assessment approach was something that I have implemented, as it allows students to take responsibility for their own learning.

Ruth: Soc-Sci. As Bloch stated, utopia is the 'not yet', it is many things to many people at every different time, and as we accomplish one dream, another will be reborn. I believe that the pedagogy and the module may help me on a professional level in my journey towards becoming a lecturer, and it will give me alternative methods in the battle to develop understanding and engagement with my future students.

Marie: Soc-Sci. Engaging with this utopian pedagogy has impacted my life far more than I ever anticipated. I am applying for jobs that may be out of my league, but I am no longer put off or daunted by them. I know from reading Bloch, and incorporating a little bit of Sylvia Plath, a hint of Bachelard and Barthes, that I am ready to go for a career that has been a long time coming. None of my course readers have been sold; I feel for the future, they will always be a source of reference. However, since finishing university, I find myself adding to the collection of academic works; although a huge fan of Bloch, I have acquired the first two volumes of Proust's epic 'In Search of Lost Time'. I cannot wait to make them my 'summer read'. These books, had they been presented to me in the past, would have filled me with dread and a notion that I am not educated enough to possibly understand them, let alone relate them to my own life. Now, it is a different story, I know I have the capability to read, understand and apply what I have understood from these writings. I may not go on to teach people about these treasures, but for now they are accompanying me on a continuing journey of transformation.

Note

1   *Les Choristes* (The Chorus) 2004; directed by Christophe Barratier (Pathe).

11

Conclusion Elpis/Eidos – Elpeidetics: Hopeful Visions?

Harvey Cox, in the foreword to Bloch's *Man on His Own*, recounts a conversation between Adolph Lowe and Ernst Bloch; the unfolding dialogue is recorded as follows:

> A few years back at a late afternoon tea in the home of a friend, someone challenged the old man to sum up his philosophy in one sentence. 'All great philosophers have been able to reduce their thought to one sentence,' the friend said. 'What would your sentence be?' Bloch puffed on his pipe for a moment and then said, 'That's a hard trap to get out of. If I answer, then I'm making myself out to be a great philosopher. But if I'm silent, then it will appear as though I have a great deal in mind but not much I can say. But I'll play the brash one instead of the silent one and give you this sentence: S is not yet P'. (Bloch, 1970: 9)

Here, with this beautifully succinct and philosophically loaded formula, Bloch invokes the Aristotelian category of 'Subject is Predicate' (or '*S* is *P*'), which, if I might briefly summarize – in an admittedly *crude* sense – means that 'subject', or *Being*, is ultimately predicated, established, or completed. With the addition of his category of the Not-Yet, Bloch reformulates and challenges the assumptions inherent in this postulate. In order to appreciate the wider implications of Bloch's re-working of the '*S* is *P*' formula, we must also consider Bloch's repurposed notion of Aristotle's related concept of entelechy or 'creative matter'. A little excursive meander into this territory will shed some explanatory light on the context of these Blochian challenges.

In *The Metaphysics* Aristotle proposes the following postulate, 'it is impossible for the same thing at the same time both to be-in and not to be-in the same respect' (Aristotle, 2004: 88); and he continues from this to state that '[h]ere, indeed, we have our securest of all principles, which entirely fits the standards that we have set for it. No one can believe that the same thing both is and is-not . . . It is, then, not possible for opposites to be-in the same subject at the same time' (Aristotle, 2004: 88). Later, in section *Delta*, Aristotle suggests that '[t]he upshot is that . . . [in] giving an account of substance, as the ultimate subject, [it] is never predicated of something else' (ibid.: 127). The subject-predicate logic of Aristotle dictates that *subject as substance* in its fundamental constitution must be predicate or ultimately established. However, considered in conjunction with his notion of creative matter, or entelechy, Aristotle goes on to suggest that the subject (as matter-in-potential) must also recognize and accommodate change and alteration. So, while *Subject-is-Predicate*, as it is also matter-in-potential, and so engages with and manifests aspects of change. In support of this, Aristotle notes that 'if there is something that is both the one and being, then it is necessary that its substance be the one and being, for it will not be some other thing predicated of it . . . indeed if unity itself and being itself exist, then there is a great puzzle how there will be anything apart from them' (ibid.: 71). While proposing the *predicateness* of 'subject', clearly, Aristotle recognises the need to account for change and transformation. In a philosophi-cal move to resolve this anomaly, in *Physics*, Aristotle suggests that the indi-visible 'one' also has a substratum of potential 'contraries', which cause – or allow – certain non-fundamental changes to take place, as he states, 'subject is one numerically, though it is two in form' (Aristotle, 2002: 18). Leclerc (1958) identifies that for Aristotle *subject-as-substance* must be changeless in its *essen-tial* nature, and this must be the case in order for it to remain *one and the same*, and to retain its *individuality* or self-identity. For *subject* and change to be accommodated within the Aristotelian schema, alterations can and do occur, but these ultimately are a result of transitions associated with non-essential fea-tures. Change is therefore a manifestation of superficial flux; this in turn leaves the fundamental constitution of 'subject' unaffected. As Leclerc suggests:

> [With] 'changelessness' difficulties enter. It gives rise to one of the crucial meta-physical problems, for 'changelessness' has somehow to be adjusted to the fac-tor of 'change' . . . Aristotle in his statement that the most distinctive mark of substance appears to be that, while remaining numerically one and the same, it is capable of admitting contrary qualities. That is to say . . . [it] is conceived as remaining changeless in its essential nature, whilst undergoing changes of quality and relation . . . It was this line of thought which led Aristotle to his conclusion that the most distinctive mark of substance appears to be that while

remaining numerically one and the same, it is capable of admitting contrary qualities. This unchanging 'something' is readily conceived as a 'stuff', 'matter', 'material'. (Leclerc, 1958: 59–62)

For Aristotle, the *stuff, substance* or *matter* of the subject is ultimately completed, but, through its entelechtic qualities, it still has the potential for change and adaptation. It is this Aristotelian aspect that Bloch's 'S is Not-Yet P' formula fundamentally challenges. For Bloch, the entirety of matter (whether subjective substance or otherwise) is still open to fundamental adaptations and changes. Hudson points out that for Bloch the 'entelechy of matter itself is dialectically developing . . . The entelechy of matter is 'not yet', in the sense that what the final state of matter can be is undetermined' (Hudson, 1982: 137).[1] Continuing wth this point, Hudson clarifies that for Bloch and the Blochian *Subject-is-Not-Yet-Predicate* logic, the form and matter of subject, being and identity is Not-Yet fully established or completed; as such, it

> is not mechanical solidity, but, according to the implied meaning of the Aristotelian definition of matter, both 'being-according-to-possibility' *(kata to dynaton)* and 'being-in-possibility' *dynamei on)*; both what has come to be . . . and what is not yet fully possible: futuristic real possibility which constitutes the open and developing active substratum of the process. (Ibid.: 136)[2]

The Blochian 'S is Not-Yet P' challenge to the Aristotelian 'S is P' logic fundamentally inverts the proposition. For Bloch, contradictory states can indeed co-habit the same subjective life world; for the alternative Blochian postulate, the foundation and matter of 'subject' both *is* and is *Not-Yet*. This means that the immediacy of the *Now* of the present, draped in the apparel of the past, is existent within and dialectically coupled with the perpetual immanence of the future Not-Yet; a perpetually impending and unwritten sequence of hieroglyphic possibilities. With Bloch, matter, subject and the future are a latent and mysterious puzzle, within which lies an end-game that has everything to play for (related to this is Bloch's philosophical reworking of *eschatology* – see the following endnote for a definition and brief exposition of this concept).[3] Blochian entelechy and his anticipatory ontology of hope suggest that the promise of human *treasure* at the end of history is something that must be passionately, creatively and expressionistically fought for. Subjective and wider collective futures are far from written and settled; in order to arrive at new destinations, we have to embark on journey towards new possible ideas (or *ideals*). With this ontological twist from Bloch, the *potential* of the substance of creative matter, located as part of subjective and multiplicitous *hosts*, experiences the flashing and incremental nudges of potential; through what we might term the *Eidetic* Hope-Form, the mystery of future matter and creative, anticipatory possibility dwells on the subjective and collective horizons of the future.

Eidos and Elpis

Rather than develop the notion of *Eidos* (and the Eidetic) – which equates to intuitive seeing, or human revelation – through the parameters of Aristotelian philosophy, I will invoke Edmund Husserl's treatment of *Eidos*. His particular definition and application of this term, along with his wider phenomenological framework, contain many similarities and sympathies which usefully align with the ontological creativity, theoretical contexts and subjective ruptures contained in the chapters and utopian pedagogy of this work. For Husserl the phenomenological experience of Eidos, or seeing, equates to the subjective and fluctuant human realm of thought and imagination; in a fashion quite sympathetic to many of the Blochian points teased out above, Husserl clarifies that *seeing* in an *Eidetic* sense consists of the waxed and morphing creative process of intuition. Eidetic events, moments or revelations are comparable to the analogy of *pregnant* seeing; as such, it is 'an intuition of an essentially *peculiar* and *novel sort* in contrast to the sorts of intuition which correlatively belong to objectivities of other categories' (Husserl, 1983: 10). The 'other' categories or objectives hinted to here relate to the very different sphere of *matters of fact*; for Husserl, the physical sciences, with their emphases upon spatiotemporal facts and the generation of concrete propositions, are important and essential for the furtherance of certain types of knowledge. But, in contrast, the phenomenological nature of Eidetic knowledge is something fundamentally different; the subjective intuition of hazy and *possible* knowledge consists 'not of phenomena that are real, but of phenomena that are transcendentally reduced' (ibid.: xx). The apparitional notion of subjectively refracted creative revelation equates to an experience of intuition that

> *something* can become transmuted into *eidetic seeing (ideation)* – a possibility which is itself to be understood not as empirical, but as eidetic. What is seen when that occurs is the corresponding *pure* essence or Eidos . . . Eidos as a pure essence is a transcendent impulse, which operates to draw out an infinity of thoughts and formative thinking experiences, so that, every experiential

multiplicity, no matter how extensive, still leaves open more precise and novel determinations. (Ibid.: 8–9)

Through the mortal, human experience of a *transcendent* Form (or essence), Eidetic connections lead us to 'the eidos, the general features' (Follesdall, 2006: 112) of otherwise hidden revelatory possibilities. Eidetic particularizations and singularizations of intuitive and revelatory essences can be encountered and articulated by many subjects in transformed and unique ways. When we experience an intuitive instance, we perform what Husserl refers to as an Eidetic reduction, an intuitive seizing upon an essence, which '*implies not the slightest positioning of any individual factual existence; pure eidetic truths contain not the slightest assertion about maters of fact*. And thus not even the most insignificant matter-of-fact truth can be deduced from pure eidetic truths *alone*' (Husserl, 1983: 11). Human experience and context is essential in order to make sense of – or start to make sense of – Eidetic reductions. With that in mind, it is important that the unfolding exposition of this final chapter, especially at the tail end of the preceding chapters, be aligned and fused with a Blochian-influenced context of hope and utopia. Here then, Eidos, or the notion of revelatory, intuitive and pregnant *seeing*, is conjoined with the Greek term *Elpis* – or hope – and, in so doing, will come to define and operationalize the subjective experience of visions containing threads of transformed possibility.

As recounted by Hesiod in *Works and Days*, *Elpis* or hope was one of the elements contained inside *Pandora's jar*. Pandora (which means All-Gifts) was a beautiful woman co-created by the gods and offered as a gift to dwell among humans. Endowed with her array of gifts, she was offered to Epimetheus (whose name translates as After-Thought), who was the *hasty* brother of Prometheus (or Fore-Thought). Prometheus had previously warned Epimetheus to never accept gifts from Zeus; and yet, despite the warnings, Epimetheus accepted Pandora as a gift. Once accepted, she opened her sealed jar, and in doing so unleashed a host of evils and misfortunes sent to punish and plague the mortal humans. As Pandora moves to reseal the jar, one thing remains inside: *Elpis* (or Hope). One suggestion is that the Pandora myth presents Hope as something detained or delayed in the jar, and serves as a symbol of potential for better times. However, other, more pessimistic, interpretations suggest that *Elpis* is something that should be seen as the worst of all of the evils; a cruel human facet, which perpetuates suffering and serves only to prolong unrealistic dreams and aspirations (Post, 2006).

Ivan Illich in *Deschooling Society* (2002) suggests that to interpret the intriguing incarceration of Elpis, we must uncover and appreciate the distinction between hope and expectation. Hope in itself means maintaining optimism and, along with this, trust and faith in the overriding possibility of human goodness and endeavour. In isolation, hope can therefore be equated with anticipation; however, Illich – invoking sentiments sympathetic to Blochian hope – suggests that hope's anticipation can be infused with the more constructive and proactive notion of expectation. Expectant hope brings with it a renewed zeal which can crack open the horizon and invoke creative and collaborative ideals aimed at transforming obstacles and overcoming constraints. Illich warns that the guarded and distantiated cage of human reticence – the overly cautious and guarded characteristics of Prometheus – means that the 'Promethean ethos has now eclipsed hope' (Illich, 2002: 105–106), and so the revival of expectant hope (and its creative, transformative tendencies) needs to be rediscovered as a potent and dynamic social force. The Promethean mind-set, and associated risk-averse practices, has resulted in humans engineering institutions which practice socio-orthopaedic compulsions for rule-following and conformity

> through which they planned to cope with the rampant ills. They became conscious of their power to fashion the world and make it produce services they also learned to expect. They wanted their own needs and the future demands of their children to be shaped by their artifacts. They became lawgivers, architects, and authors, the makers of constitutions, cities, and works of art to serve as examples for their offspring. (Ibid.: 106)

For Illich – as has been argued by Roland Barthes and Guy Debord in earlier chapters of the book – the chains of organizational stability, routine and legislation have ensnared the Epimethean characteristics of impulse and liberation. Educational institutions, along with all other bureaucratically militarized social institutions, have lost touch with the uninitiated radicality of expectant hope. Illich, on this point, notes that humanity is now 'trapped in the boxes [made] to contain the ills Pandora allowed to escape. The blackout of reality in the smog produced by our tools has enveloped us. Quite suddenly we find ourselves in the darkness of our own trap' (Illich, 2002: 109). Eidetic images and daydreams of intuitive and inspirational visions of transgressing our constraints are homeless and without value in the midst of legalized, sanitized and stagnant futures. Illich suggests that if we can adopt the position of the *Man in the Moon*, we can maybe once again gaze in inspired awe, and anticipatory wonder, at Gaia's blue and beautiful aura. With a renewed nostalgia, we can reawaken the Eidetic intuitions of humanity, rediscover the expressive impulse of Epimetheus and resuscitate Pandora to bestow the last and most powerful of her gifts to humanity. For Illich, the Pandora myth of incarceration can be transformed into a hopeful prophecy, as 'it tells us that the son of Prometheus was Deucalion, the Helmsman of the Ark who like Noah outrode the Flood to become the father of a new mankind which he made from the earth with Pyrrha, the daughter of Epimetheus and Pandora' (ibid.: 115). As such, we need to rename the drive and the hunger 'for those who value hope above expectations. We need a name for those who love people more than products . . . We need a name for those who love the earth' (ibid.: 115).

With Aristotle, Bloch and Husserl (along with Barthes, Bachelard, Debord and Lefebvre), there is a recognition, albeit in different ways, of the dynamic incompleteness of subjectivity and of wider human existence; with the tactics and counter-strategies inherent to each of the theorists and approaches, we should be reminded that we have the potential to be active and expectant participants in a process of creative hope and *becoming*. Herein lies the crux of the wider and nagging problem for HE: its auspices and practices are entrenched and increasingly built upon assumptions that knowledge is a solidified matter, something that can be packaged and epistemologized into *matter-of-fact* states, tamed and encapsulated into cages of measured scrutiny. This appears to be the impending fate of knowledge and knowledge acquisition across the Academy. But as Bloch and Husserl, and indeed all of the theorists addressed as part of this work, have illustrated, this is only one limited facet of knowledge; its burgeoning and unwieldy *potential* is littered with many more options and opportunities. The *ante rem* and the *future-unknown* of knowledge can be liberated and redeemed, so that its Eidetic and utopian beauty can take creative flight once again, with the revival and release of Elpis. With Elpis and Eidos – generically and retrospectively referred to as *Elpeidetic encounters across the framework of the utopian pedagogy* – a chaos of creative minds can glance towards the refracted haze of future's potential and connect to the puzzle of redemptive hope.

The potent mystery emitted by (what we might term) the Elpeidetic 'hopeform' is open to transformational and creative encounters; and as an essence, it remains fuzzy enough to infuse cultural-anthelia with traces of its possibility, explicated through multicultural dérives and détourned translations.[4] Learner collaborators kaleidoscopically splinter as utopian particles of incomplete possibility, and through creative and bespoke everyday encounters with culture-works, they engage with the hieroglyphic cipher-symbols of Elpeidetic encounters. For Bloch and Illich, Elpeidetic whispers, pregnant with a complexity of possibilities, pose a challenge and a call (to any/all future-concerned educational practitioners), a call to recover the dreams and visions of the potential for a new *heaven* (on earth). Previously thwarted and misdirected at the ideological hands of state-sanctioned wastrels, the challenge, through an archaeological recovery of Elpeidetic traces, is to revive and refocus multi-rhythms of expressive and expectant hope, and to re-align the now-time of the *everyday* with re-enthused narratives and stories for better and transformed tomorrows.

This audacious fusion of Bloch, Husserl and Illich suggests that beyond the chaotic quanta of subjective worlds, an over-arching utopian plan can indeed be divined. For Bloch, the future is Not-Yet made or guaranteed and, as such, contains an openness which can be influenced and shaped in new and transformed ways. Therefore hope, the hunger for hope, and each successive irruption that emanates from within the traces of a self-encounter contain an undisclosed code of potential transformation; meanders and daydreams of reaching-out towards the possibility of progressive and creative newness become politically loaded (Bloch, 1986). This is indeed the stuff of hope, and, in some respects, a *militant optimism* or 'faith' in the redemptive unmadeness of possible futures. However much *off-kilter* with contemporary constraints and academic objectives this maybe, I for one believe in taking this step, because without the creative audacities and chaos of Elpeidetic serendipities, the only other road seems to be a rather drab journey towards a perdition of apathetic inaction and uncritical conformity.

Notes

1   Although Kolakowski suggests that 'Bloch does not seem to be aware that his use of the concepts of energy, potentiality, and entelechy differs from Aristotle's in one major respect . . . Aristotle used them, in fact, to describe the empirical process of development in the organic world and in purposive human activity' (Kolakowski, 1978: 433). However, Leclerc challenges this perspective assertion and points out that 'the subject-predicate logic, whose relevance is primarily to the things of everyday living, has been taken to be equally relevant to metaphysical thought' (Leclerc, 1958: 62).

2   In relation to this, Bloch notes that 'Aristotle brought out the crucial idea . . . of real, objective possibility, according to which matter, apart from being the mechanical condition for phenomenon to arise *Kata to dynaton* ('according to possibility'), was also, above all, the *dynamei on*, the 'being-in-possibility' itself. Unfortunately, this was still thought of in passive terms: matter was as undefined as a lump of wax, and the 'active, formative idea' impressed the particular form into it like a seal' (Bloch, 2009: 215). Similarly, Kolakowski suggests that for Bloch, matter is 'not a

mere mechanical lump but – in accordance with the implicit sense of Aristotle's definition – it is both being-according-to-possibility (*kata to dynaton*, i.e. that which determines every historical phenomenon in accordance with the conditions and with historical materialism) and also being-in-possibility (*dynamei on*, i.e. the correlative of that which is objectively and really possible or, ontically speaking, the possibility-substrate of the dialectical process' (Kolakowski, 1978: 439). This is further supported by Thompson, who notes that 'It is the merging of Aristotle's *dynamei on* – or what might be possible in the future – with *kata to dynaton* – or what is possible at the moment – in which all things, including both the human species and matter itself, will be changed in to something which cannot yet be determined' (Thompson, 2009: xviii).

3 Also related to this (which requires a slightly lengthy patchwork of references and clarifications) is Bloch's notion of *eschatology*. With Bloch, the speculative fluidity and unfolding futurity of his framework identifies 'open human history, 'pioneer history', [filled] with *creator spiritus*: with pre-semblances, arduous and difficult breakthroughs and extensions beyond what has already developed . . . It goes forward as the experiment of that which is not yet really successful . . . and does so with the only real eschatology of the present, which is known as creative expectation' (Bloch, 1970: 89). Peter Thompson further supports this and notes that, importantly, 'Bloch's treatment of Christ as Son of Man rather than Son of God and Kyrios emphasizes the revolutionary nature of Christian eschatology, which he sees as existing underneath and behind all mystification. The creation of the world, according to this reading of the Bible, does not involve Christ at all in any of his forms. Christ is merely one of the figures, one of the particles, which are key to the recreation of a 'just world'. In a way Christ is kept in reserve as 'becoming-son' for a point at which he is to be the active principle at the end of time' (Thompson, 2009: xxiii–xxiv). The implications of Bloch's entelechtic take on the present, and his eschatological utopianization of the future, is succinctly summarized by Moltmann, who notes that the manipulation of what has come to be viewed as the traditional notion of Christian eschatology implies the already *madeness* of not only the *beginning* but also of the *end* of times, the Alpha and the Omega of the existing and new kingdom on earth; but these should be seen as events that 'will one day break upon man, history and the world at the end of time . . . The more Christianity became an organisation for discipleship under the auspices of the Roman state religion and persistently upheld the claims of that religion, the more eschatology and its mobilising, revolutionising, and critical effects upon history as it has now to be lived were left to fanatical sects and revolutionary groups' (Moltmann, 2002: 1). Bloch supports this and suggests that during later developments associated with Hellenistic Christianity, a divine and cultic status was to be granted and foisted onto what he refers to as the figure of Jesus as Kyrios-Christos; the reification of a God-Created Imperial figure, who

usurped the apocalyptic potency associated with Jesus the Son of Man. For Bloch, the ideological ransacking of the Son of Man at the hands of the legalistic and hierarchical development of the Church meant that the eschatological seeds of revolution passed over to those who 'kick against the realm of the On-high'. As Bloch notes, the 'Kyrios-Christos God admirably suited the purposes of those who would reduce the Christian community to a sort of military . . . allegiance to worldly rulers . . . The other future, the dawning of the 'better age', belonged to the early community and to its Son of Man' (Bloch, 2009: 149).

4   'Anthelion' is a term taken from the study of atmospheric optics; loosely translated from its Greek 'root' meaning, the term refers to ant-helios (or, opposite the sun). The anthelion (or anthelic effect) is produced when climatic conditions – temperature and ice-crystals – elicit a crossing arc of the sun's rays. Where the reflected arc crosses (opposite to the sun), this produces a bright 'false sun', (for more details see Talman, 1913; Tape, 1994; and Tape and Moilanen, 2006). I intend for this term to refer to the secondary 'trace' apparition of *something* that is imperceptible in its 'pure' form. I am proposing the embryonic and draft term of 'cultural-anthelia', within the context of this study, be refunctioned to articulate a – cultural – event, where the mirage of an otherwise invisible source, an Elpeidetic refraction of the utopian hope-form, becomes secondarily and fractally 'visible'. In a Blochian and wider *utopian pedagogical* sense, popular and mass cultural sources elicit distantiated traces of incomplete possibility. For Bloch, the trans-subjective gravity of the Not-Yet, glimpsed through the cultural-anthelia of the Elpeidetic Hope-Form, contains eschatological traces of utopia's mysterious essence; as *matter-in-potential*, a cultural-anthelion hope puzzle is latently embedded within the legacies of subjective history, and active with the potential unfolding of Not-Yet articulated futures (Bloch, 1987). As a fundamental source of human hunger for transformation, the Elpeidetic Hope-Form prompts the catalytic inducement of possibilities, aimed at establishing concrete instances of dignity and the *Upright Gait* (Bloch, 1971).

Appendix 1

Student Contact Emails

Message 1 (Invitation)

On 15 Jun 2015 12:27, 'Craig Hammond' <craig.hammond@blackburn.ac.uk>
wrote:

Hi –

A quick message and request (it's Craig Hammond, your – lecturer here). I've
secured a book contract with Bloomsbury Academic Press. The title of the book
is 'Hope, Utopia and Creativity in Higher Education: Pedagogical Tactics for
Alternative Futures'. The structure of the book will consist of three sections: the
first section develops the key theorists (Bloch, Barthes and Bachelard); the second section then sets out creative pedagogical counter-strategies; and the third
section creates space for the voices of current and past students to emerge, and
to talk about their thoughts and experiences of engaging with this 'utopian
pedagogy'. The book is really a vehicle to bring together the developments and
experiences generated through the development of the module that you studied.

The reason for my contacting you is to ask if you would consider maybe contributing a little to one of the chapters in the third section of the book. If you
are interested in doing this, I will send to you (by email) a document that will
contain further details and a set of open questions for you to consider and crea-
tively/reflectively comment upon. As part of this, you will be free to mention
(and provide honest opinions on) your own creative journey, your own ven-
tures/engagement with the theories, and any impact of the theories/pedagogical
tactics that we've covered and any of your current or future developments.

If you are willing and able to contribute to this exciting project, let me know (by responding to this email), and I will send you more detailed and reflective documents and consent form.

Hope to hear from you soon; many thanks, Craig

Message 2 (follow up and consent)

Hello –,

Many thanks for agreeing to participate in the reflective process and discussion of your work, it is very much appreciated. Please find attached a document that sets out all the details of the proposed book; the final section of the attached document also contains the reflective questions that I'd like you to consider and respond to.

I'm not sure what kind of workload you have at the moment, but if it's possible for you to return your completed consent, reflections and comments to me within the next four weeks, that would be fantastic. If you can't make that deadline, just let me know by email, and we can discuss.

In order for me to include any of your work and/or anonymized comments and reflections, it is essential that you respond to all the questions in the *personal details and consent* section (section 4 of the document) and, importantly, sign it (electronic signatures are also acceptable). Also, it would be helpful if you could indicate (where appropriate) your permission for the use of excerpts from the creative work that you produced as part of the module. Please let me know, via email, if you are also prepared to be interviewed/recorded as part of this project (to discuss some of the themes, contained in the questions below, in a little more detail).

I'm really looking forward to working with you in this.

Many thanks again. Craig

Appendix 2

Student Information, Questionnaire and Permissions

Book Information

Hope, Utopia and Creativity in Higher Education: *Pedagogical Tactics for Alternative Futures*

Summary

This book will develop a theoretical and practical framework for a *mainstream* Higher Education 'utopian pedagogy'.

Short description of the proposed book

No work has yet been developed which systematically applies the works of Ernst Bloch, Roland Barthes and Gaston Bachelard to the areas of hope, utopia, creativity and education. Reappraising ideas associated with Bloch, Barthes and Bachelard, within the context of a utopian pedagogy, reframes the transformative, creative and collaborative potential of education, which becomes endowed with new concepts, tactics and pedagogical possibilities. Through these theorists and subsequent strategies, an array of alternative ways of analysing and democratizing not only pedagogical conception, knowledge and delivery but also the learning experience and processes of negotiation and peer-assessment are developed and offered as part of this work.

Proposed structure and chapters

The current draft of proposed chapters for the book are as follows (your thoughts, work and/or ideas may contribute towards Chapters 9 and 10 of the book).

Introduction: Critical Pedagogies – Horizons of Possibility

Part I Tactics: Conceptualizing Hope, Utopia and Creativity

Chapter 1   Ernst Bloch, Hope and Utopia: The Stuff of Possibility
Chapter 2   Roland Barthes: Punctum! The Death of the Author
Chapter 3   Gaston Bachelard: Poetics, Space and Daydreaming

Part II Pedagogical Strategies for Creative Possibilities

Chapter 4   Dérive and Détournement: Pedagogical Strategies for Creative Engagement
Chapter 5   Bye Bye Badman: The Redemption of Hope through Popular Culture
Chapter 6   The Wisdom of the Crowd: Liberating Creativity

Part III Learner Stories, Reflections and Projections

Chapter 7   A Garland of Rhythms
Chapter 8   Encounters, Stories, Connections
Chapter 9   Beyond the Trace: Reflections from Past Learners
Conclusion   Elpis/Eidos – Elpeidetics: Hopeful Visions?

Student: Questions/Questionnaire

Personal details, contact information and consent

Name:

Degree Course/Module (please tick the appropriate box)

BA (Hons) Social Science ☐ BA Joint Honours ☐	Utopian Visions and Everyday Culture
BA (Hons) Education Studies ☐	Alternative Education

Contact number:

Mobile Number (if different):

Preferred email address contact:

Would you be prepared to take part in a brief recorded interview to discuss the areas/questions (given below) in a little more detail?

Yes ☐	If yes, I will contact you to arrange a date/time	No ☐

In order to include any references to your work, comments and/or information, I will need to anonymize you (i.e. change your name). Do you have a preferred alternative name for use in my published material?

Yes ☐	If yes, please state:	No ☐

Do you consent to the author re-arranging aspects of any work, and/or comments that you have produced for inclusion as part of this publication (e.g. title, cultural references – in case of any 'permissions' issues) in order to establish a consistency of style/writing for the book?

Yes ☐	No ☐

I recognize, acknowledge and agree that my anonymized work and contributions (as part of this project) may be included/edited for the purposes of wider research, publication and dissemination by Dr Craig A. Hammond.

Yes ☐	No ☐

I recognize, acknowledge and agree that if my anonymized work and contributions are included as part of any publication(s) by Dr Craig A. Hammond, I will have no copyright or contractual claim over the work.

Yes ☐	No ☐

Student/research participant signature (electronically typing name also acceptable):	**Date:**

Questions: Student comments, thoughts and reflections

As part of your possible contribution to this work, I would like you to consider and respond to the following questions. Please do take some time to think about and reflect on the questions.

Please also feel free to write as much as you like. My intention is to find out how you 'personally' felt/feel about your journey on the module (so feel free to include any positive as well as critical reflections), the impact of the module and this type of learning (on you), and whether there are any aspects of the module/learning that have remained with you and any areas that you have continued to practice or develop.

Please feel free to contact me to discuss or further explore any of the questions (or thoughts / themes that emerge from the questions).

1. Please provide a brief description of your schooling experience: life after school (college/employment); your journey to UCBC; and finally, your journey after UCBC.
2. Please summarize, in a paragraph, your overall memories/recollections (and experiences, if any) of the module.
3. How did you find the open and flexible approach to learning, knowledge and interpretation across the module?
4. Which of the theorists do you still particularly remember (which did you like/enjoy covering and engaging with), and why (Ernst Bloch, Gaston Bachelard, Roland Barthes, Guy Debord)?
5. How did you find the Peer-Assessment (PA) event/process (if applicable to you)?
   Prior to the PA event, during and then after the PA event.
   To what extent did this approach to producing and delivering an assignment enable you to be creative?
   To what extent do you think there is scope to use this approach more widely (e.g. on other modules, and other educational/schooling contexts)?
   Any particular limitations to this approach?
6. Did the module (and the work that you produced) make you feel/think differently about the future; please explain?
7. In what ways (if any) have you incorporated materials, concepts, experiences and connections (and so on) from this module to your own personal and/or professional life?
8. Any other comments, reflections that you wish to include.

Bibliography

Adorno, T. (1980). Bloch's Traces: The Philosophy of Kitsche. *New Left Review*, *1/121*, 49–62.

Adorno, T. (1991). *Notes to Literature* (Vol. One). (S. W. Nicholsen, Trans.) New York: Columbia University Press.

Adorno, T. (2001). *The Culture Industry* (2nd ed.). (J. M. Bernstein, Ed.) London: Routledge.

Aristotle. (2003). *Poetics*. (M. Heath, Trans.) London: Penguin Classics.

Aristotle. (2004). *The Metaphysics*. (H. Lawson-Tancred, Trans.) London: Penguin.

Baccolini, R. and Moylan, T. (Eds). (2003). *Dark Horizons*. New York: Routledge.

Bachelard, G. (1964). *The Psychoanalysis of Fire*. (A. C. Ross, Trans.) London: Routledge & Kegan Paul.

Bachelard, G. (1994). *The Poetics of Space*. (M. Jolas, Trans.) Boston: Beacon Press.

Bachelard, G. (2000). *Dialectic of Duration*. (M. M. Jones, Trans.) Manchester: Clinamen.

Bachelard, G. (2002). *Formation of the Scientific Mind*. (M. M. Jones, Trans.) Manchester: Clinamen.

Bachelard, G. (2004). *The Poetics of Reverie: Childhood, Language and the Cosmos*. (D. Russell, Trans.) Boston: Beacon Press.

Bachelard, G. (2011). *Air & Dreams: An Essay on the Imagination of Movement*. (E. R. Farrell and F. C. Farrell, Trans.) Dallas: Dallas Institute Publications.

Bachelard, G. (2013). *Intuition of the Instant*. (E. Rizo-Patron, Trans.) Illinois: Northwest University Press.

Barratier, C. (Director). (2004). *Les Choristes (The Chorus)* [Motion Picture]. Pathe.

Barry, J. M. (2015). *Peter Pan*. London: William Collins.

Barthes, R. (1970). *Writing Degree Zero*. (A. Lavers and C. Smith, Trans.) London: Beacon Press.

Barthes, R. (1972). *Critical Essays*. (R. Howard, Trans.) Evanston: Northwestern University Press.

Barthes, R. (1975). *The Pleasure of the Text*. HarperCollinsCanada.

Barthes, R. (1977). *Image, Music, Text*. (S. Heath, Trans.) London: Fontana Press.

Barthes, R. (1978). *A Lovers Discourse*. HarperCollinsCanada.

Barthes, R. (1989a). Writers, Intellectuals, Teachers. In R. Barthes, *The Rustle of Language* (R. Howard, Trans., pp. 309–343). Los Angeles: University of California Press.

Barthes, R. (1989b). On Reading. In *The Rustle of Language* (R. Howard, Trans.,
    pp. 33–43). Los Angeles: University of California Press.

Barthes, R. (1989c). Freedom to Write. In *The Rustle of Language* (R. Howard, Trans.,
    pp. 44–46). Los Angeles: University of California Press.

Barthes, R. (1989d). The Death of the Author. In *The Rustle of Language* (R. Howard,
    Trans., pp. 49–55). Los Angeles: University of California Press.

Barthes, R. (1989e). Research: The Young. In *The Rule of Language* (R. Howard, Trans.,
    pp. 69–79). Los Angeles: University of California Press.

Barthes, R. (1989f). The Rustle of Language. In *The Rustle of Language* (R. Howard,
    Trans., pp. 76–79). Los Angeles: University of California Press.

Barthes, R. (1989g). Writing the Event. In *The Rustle of Language* (R. Howard, Trans.,
    pp. 149–154). Los Angeles: University of California Press.

Barthes, R. (1989h). The Return of the Poetician. In *The Rustle of Language* (R. Howard,
    Trans., pp. 172–175). Los Angeles: University of California Press.

Barthes, R. (1991). *Mythologies*. (A. Lavers, Trans.) New York: The Noonday Press.

Barthes, R. (1997). *The Eiffel Tower and Other Mythologies*. (R. Howard, Trans.)
    Berkeley: University of California Press.

Barthes, R. (2000). *Camera Lucida*. London: Vintage Press.

Barthes, R. (2015a). *A Very Fine Gift: And Other Writings on Theory* (Vol. 1). (C. Turner,
    Ed.) London: Seagull Books.

Barthes, R. (2015b). Am I a Marxist? In R. Barthes and C. Turner (Eds), *The "Scandal"
    of Marxism* (Vol. 2, pp. 46–48). London: Seagull Books.

Benjamin, W. (1999). *Illuminations*. (H. Zorn, Trans.) London: Pimlico.

Berghahn, K. L. (1997). A View Through the Red Window: Ernst Bloch's Spuren. In
    J. O. Daniel, and T. Moylan, *Not-Yet: Reconsidering Ernst Bloch*. London: Verso.

Bloch, E. (1970). *A Philosophy of the Future: An Azimuth Book*. (J. Cummings, Trans.)
    London: Herder & Herder.

Bloch, E. (1971). *On Karl Marx*. (J. Maxwell, Trans.) New York: Herder & Herder.

Bloch, E. (1977). Nonsynchronism and the Obligation to Its Dialectics. *New German
    Critique* (11), 22–38.

Bloch, E. (1986). *The Principle of Hope* (Vols. 1–3). (S. Knight and P. Plaice, Trans.)
    London: Blackwell.

Bloch, E. (1987). *Natural Law and Human Dignity*. (D. J. Schmidt, Trans.)
    Boston: MIT Press.

Bloch, E. (1988). Discussing Expressionism. In E. Bloch, G. Lukacs, B. Brecht,
    W. Benjamin and T. Adorno, *Aesthetics and Politics* (R. Livingstone, Trans.,
    pp. 16–27). London: Verso.

Bloch, E. (1991). *Heritage of Our Times*. (N. Plaice, and S. Plaice, Trans.)
    Cambridge: Polity Press.

Bloch, E. (1993). *The Utopian function of Art & Literature*. (F. Mecklenberg and J. Zipes,
    Trans.) Cambridge: MIT.

Bloch, E. (1998). *Literary Essays*. (A. Joron and others, Trans.) Palo Alto: Stanford University Press.

Bloch, E. (2000). *The Spirit of Utopia*. (A. A. Nassar, Trans.) Palo Alto: Stanford University Press.

Bloch, E. (2006). *Traces*. (A. A. Nassar, Trans.) Palo Alto: Stanford University Press.

Bloch, E. (2009). *Atheism in Christianity: The Religion of the Exodus and the Kingdom*. (J. T. Swann, Trans.) London: Verso.

Boscagli, M. (2014). *Stuff Theory: Everyday Objects Radical Materialism*. New York: Bloomsbury.

Burgin, V. (2006). *The Remembered Film*. London: Reaktion Books.

Chimisso, C. (2001). *Gaston Bachelard: Critic of Science & the Imagination*. Abingdon: Routledge.

Cohen, J. and Stewart, I. (2000). *The Collapse of Chaos: Discovering Simplicity in a Complex World*. London: Penguin.

Coverley, M. (2010). *Psychogeography*. Harpenden: Pocket Essentials. www. pocketessentials.com

Crowther, G. (2016). *The Haunted Reader and Sylvia Plath*. Stroud: Fonthill Media.

Culler, J. (2002). *Barthes: A Very Short Introduction*. Oxford: Open University Press.

Daly, F. (2013). The Zero-Point: Encountering the Dark Emptiness of Nothingness. In S. Zizek and P. Thompson (Eds), *The Privatisation of Hope: Ernst Bloch and the Future of Utopia* (pp. 164–202). Durham: Duke University Press.

Dayton, T. (1997). The Mystery of Pre-history: Ernst Bloch and Crime Fiction. In T. Moylan and J. D. Owen, *Not Yet: Reconsidering Ernst Bloch* (pp. 186–201). Verso.

de Certeau, M. (1984). *The Practice of Everyday Life*. (S. Randall, Trans.) Berkeley: University of California Press.

Debord, G. (1957). *Report on the Construction of Situations*. (K. Knabb, Ed.) Retrieved 12 November 2015, from Bureau of Public Secrets: www.bopsecrets.org/SI/report.htm

Debord, G. (1958). *Theory of the Dérive (Internationale Situationniste #2)*. Retrieved 30 June 2012, from www.nothingness.org: http://library.nothingness.org/articles/SI/en/display_printable/314

Debord, G. (1961, May 17). *Perspectives for Conscious Alterations in Everyday Life (Internationale Situationniste #6)*. Retrieved 30 June 2012, from www.nothingness. org: http://library.nothingness.org/articles/SI/en/display/89

Debord, G. (1970). *Society of the Spectacle*. Detroit: Black & Red.

Debord, G. (2004a). One Step Back. In T. McDonough (Ed.), *Guy Debord & the Situationist International: Texts & Documents* (T. McDonough, Trans., pp. 25–27). Cambridge: MIT.

Debord, G. (2004b). Report on the Construction of Situations and on the Terms of Organization and Action of the International Situationist Tendency. In T. McDonough (Ed.), *Guy Debord & the Situationist International: Texts & Documents* (T. McDonough, Trans., pp. 29–50). Cambridge: MIT.

Debord, G. (2004c). One More Try If You Want to Be Situationists (The SI in and against Decomposition). In T. McDonough (Ed.), *Guy Debord & the Situationist Internationale: Texts & Documents* (J. Shepley, Trans., pp. 52–59). Cambridge: MIT.

Debord, G. (2004d). Theses on Cultural Revolution. In T. McDonough (Ed.), *Guy Debord & the Situationist International* (J. Shepley, Trans., pp. 61–65). Cambridge: MIT.

Deleuze, G. and Guattari, F. (2005). *A Thousand Plataeus: Capitalism & Schizophrenia*. (B. Massumi, Trans.) Minneapolis: University of Minnesota Press.

Ehrmann, J. (1966). Introduction to Gaston Bachelard. *MLN, 81*(5), 572–578.

Eve, R. A., Horsfall, S. and Lee, M. E. (Eds). (1997). *Chaos, Complexity and Sociology: Myths, Models and Theories*. London: Sage.

Freire, P. (2000). *Pedagogy of the Heart*. (D. Macedo and A. Oliveira, Trans.) New York: Continuum.

Freire, P. (2005). *Pedagogy of the Oppressed*. (B. Ramos, Trans.) New York: Continuum.

Game, A. (1995). Time, Space, Memory, with Reference to Bachelard. In M. Featherstone, S. Lash and R. Robertson (Eds), *Global Modernities* (pp. 192–209). London: Sage.

Geoghegan, V. (1996). *Ernst Bloch*. London and New York: Routledge.

Geoghegan, V. (1997). Remembering the Future. In T. Moylan and J. Owen, *Not-Yet: Reconsidering Ernst Bloch*. London: Verso.

Gillam, K. and Wooden, S. R. (2008). Post-Princess Models of Gender: The New Man in Disney/Pixar. *Journal of Film & Popular Culture, 36*(1), 2–8.

Giroux, H. (1995). Memory and Pedagogy in the "Wonderful World of Disney": Beyond the Politics of Innocence. In E. Bell, L. Haas and L. Sells, *From Mouse to Mermaid: The Politics of Film, Gender & Culture*. Indianapolis: Indiana University Press.

Giroux, H. (2001). *The Mouse That Roared: Disney and the End of Innocence*. Lanham: Rowman & Littlefield.

Giroux, H. A. (2011). Rethinking Education as the Practice of Freedom: Paul Freire and the Promise of Critical Pedagogy. In H. A. Giroux, *On Critical Pedagogy* (pp. 129–139). New York: Continuum.

Giroux, H. and McLaren, P. (1997). Paulo Friere, Postmodernism, and the Utopian Imagination: A Blochian Reading. In J. O. Daniel and T. Moylan (Eds), *Not Yet: Reconsidering Ernst Bloch* (pp. 138–162). London: Verso.

Goodson, I. and Gill, S. (2013). *Critical Narrative as Pedagogy*. London: Bloomsbury Academic.

Griffin, S. (2000). *Tinker Belles & Evil Queens*. New York: New York University Press.

Habermas, J. (1983). Ernst Bloch: A Marxist Schelling (1980). In J. Habermas, *Philosophical-Political Profiles* (F. G. Lawrence, Trans., pp. 61–77). London: Heinemann.

Hammond, C. A. (2012). *Towards a Neo-Blochian Theory of Complexity, Hope and Cinematic Utopia*. Lancaster: Lancaster University (PhD Thesis).

Hammond, C. A. (2015). Monstrosity and the Not-Yet: Edward Scissorhands via Ernst
Bloch and Georg Simmel. *Film-Philosophy*, *19*, pp. 221–248. Retrieved from
http://www.film-philosophy.com/index.php/f-p/article/view/992

Heisenberg, W. (2000). *Physics and Philosophy*. London: Penguin.

Hetherington, K. (2007). *Capitalisms Eye: Cultural Spaces and the Commodity*.
New York: Routledge.

hooks, b. (1994). Teaching to Transgress. In *Teaching to Transgress: Education as the
Practice of Freedom* (pp. 1–22). New York: Routledge.

hooks, b. (2003). Heart to Heart: Teaching with Love. In b. hooks, *Teaching
Community: A Pedagogy of Hope* (pp. 127–137). New York: Routledge.

Horkheimer, M. and Adorno, T. (1969). *Dialectic of Enlightenment*. (J. Cumming,
Trans.) New York: Continuum.

Hudson, W. (1982). *The Marxist Philosophy of Ernst Bloch*. London: Macmillan.

Hunt, C. (2013). *Transformative Learning through Creative Life Writing: Exploring the
self in the learning process*. Abingdon: Routledge.

Husserl, E. (1983). *Ideas Pertaining to a Pure Phenomenology and to a Phenomenological
Philosophy: First Book*. (F. Kirsten, Trans.) Martinus Nijhoff.

Illich, I. (2002). *Deschooling Society*. London: Marion Boyars.

Jameson, F. (1971). A Marxist Hermeneutic III: Ernst Bloch and the Future. In
F. Jameson, *Marxism and Form: Twentieth-Century Dialectical Theories of Literature*
(pp. 116–156). Princeton, NJ: Princeton University Press.

Kelley, D. and Kelley, T. (2013). *Creative Confidence: Unleashing the Creative Potential
Within Us All*. London: Willam Collins.

Kellner, D. and O'Hara, H. (1976). Utopia and Marxism in Ernst Bloch. *New German
Critique*, *9*, 11–34.

Kelly, M. (2000). Demystification: A Dialogue between Barthes & Lefebvre. *Yale French
Studies*, *98*, 79–97.

Kibbey, A. (2005). *Theory of the Image: Capitalism, Contemporary Film & Women*.
Bloomington: Indiana University Press.

Knabb, K. (2006). *Situationist International Anthology* (Revised and Expanded ed.).
Bureau of Public Secrets.

Kofman, E. and Lebas, E. (2000). Recovery and Reappropriation in Lefebvre
& Constant. In J. Hughes and S. Sadler (Eds), *Non-Plan: Essays on
Freedom, Participation & Change in Modern Architecture & Urbanism*.
London: Architectural Press.

Kolakowski, L. (1978). Ernst Bloch: Marxism as a Future Gnosis. In L. Kolakowski,
Main Currents of Marxism: Its Origin, Growth & Dissolution (P. S. Falla, Trans.,
Vol. III The Breakdown, pp. 421–449). Oxford: Clarendon Press.

Korstvedt, B. M. (2010). *Listening for Utopia in Ernst Bloch's Musical Philosophy*.
Cambridge: Cambridge University Press.

Kuhn, A. (2002). *Family Secrets: Acts of Memory and Imagination*. London: Verso.

Landmann, M. (1975). Talking with Ernst Bloch: Korcula 1968. *Telos*, *25*.

Leclerc, I. (1958). *Whitehead's Metaphysics: An Introductory Exposition*. London: Unwin Brothers.

Lefebvre, H. (1991). *Critique of Everyday Life Volume 1*. (M. Trebitsch, Trans.) London: Verso.

Lefebvre, H. (2008a). *Critique of Everyday Life Volume 2*. London: Verso.

Lefebvre, H. (2008b). *Critique of everyday life volume 3*. London: Verso.

Lefebvre, H. (2010). *Rhythmanalysis: Space, Time and Everyday Life*. (S. Elden and G. Moore, Trans.) London: Continuum.

Levitas, R. (2011). *The Concept of Utopia*. Oxford: Peter Lang.

Levitas, R. and Sargisson, L. (2003). Utopia in Dark Times. In R. Baccolini and T. Moylan, *Dark Horizons: Science Fiction and the Dystopian Imagination*. London: Routledge.

Luz, E. (1993). Utopia and Return: On the Structure of Utopian Thinking and its Relation to Jewish-Christian Tradition. *The Journal of Religion, 73*(3).

Macfarlane, J. (2000). Aristotles Definition of Anagnorisis. *American Journal of Philology, 121,* 367–383.

McDonough, T. (2004). Situationist Space. In T. McDonough (Ed.), *Guy Debord & the Situationist International: Texts & Documents* (pp. 241–265). Cambridge: MIT.

McLaren, P. (2015). *Pedagogy of Insurrection: From Resurrection to Revolution*. New York: Peter Lang.

McManus, S. (2003). Fabricating the Future: Becoming Bloch's Utopians. *Utopian Studies, 14.*

Mandelbrot, B. (1983). *The Fractal Geometry of Nature*. New York: W. H. Freeman.

Meek, A. (2010). *Trauma and the Media: Theories, Histories & Images*. New York: Routledge.

Moltmann, J. (2002). *Theology of Hope*. (J. W. Leitch, Trans.) London: SCM Press.

Moylan, T. (2000). *Scraps of the Untainted Sky*. Virginia: University of Virginia Press.

Neary, M. and Amsler, S. (2012). Occupy: A New Pedagogy of Space and Time? *Journal for Critical Education Policy Studies, 10*(2).

Nice, J. (2011). *Shadowplayers: The Rise and Fall of Factory Records*. London: Aurum Press.

Pieper, J. (1986). *On Hope*. (M. F. McCarthy, Trans.) San Francisco: Ignatious Press.

Post, D. (2006). A Hope for Hope: The Role of Hope in Education. *Philosophy of Education.*

Poster, M. (1977). *Existential Marxism in Postwar France: From Sartre to Althusser*. New Jersey: Princeton University Press.

Proust, M. (2003). *In Search of Lost Time* (Slp ed.). (R. Howard, ed. and C. S. Moncrieff, Trans.) London: Modern Library.

Rabinbach, A. (1977). Unclaimed Heritage: Ernst Bloch's Heritage of Our Times and the Theory of Fascism. *New German Critique, 11.*

Roberts, R. H. (1990). The Prolegomena to Hope: Thinking Means Venturing Beyond. In R. H. Roberts, and L. S. Cunningham (Eds), *Hope and its Hieroglyph: A Critical*

Decipherment of Ernst Bloch's Principle of Hope (Vol. American Academy of Religion: Studies in Religion No. 57, pp. 27–48). Atlanta, GA: Scholars Press.

Robinson, K. (2011). *Out of Our Minds: Learning to be Creative* (2 ed.). Chichester: Capstone.

Roger, L. (2014). The Pedagogical Philosophy of Bachelard. *Antistasis, 4*(2), 34–37.

Ross, K. (2004). Lefebvre on the Situationists: An Interview. In T. McDonough (Ed.), *Guy Debord & the Situationist International: Texts & Documents* (pp. 267–284). Cambridge: MIT.

San Juan, E. (2015). Foreword. In P. McLaren, *Pedagogy of Insurrection: From Resurrection to Revolution* (pp. xv–xix). New York: Peter Lang.

SI. (1959). *Détournement as Negation and Prelude (Internationale Situationniste #3).* Retrieved 30 June 2012, from www.nothingness.org: http://library.nothingness.org/articles/SI/en/display/315

SI. (1960a). *Instructions for an Insurrection (Internationale Situationniste #6).* Retrieved 30 June 2012, from www.nothingness.org: http://library.nothingness.org/articles/SI/en/display/321 http://library.nothingness.org/articles/SI/en/display/321

SI. (1960b). *The Use of Free Time (Internationale Situationniste #4).* Retrieved 30 June 2012, from www.nothingness.org: http://library.nothingness.org/articles/SI/en/display/317

SI. (2004). Editorial Notes: The Meaning of Decay in Art. In T. McDonough (Ed.), *Guy Debord & the Situationist International: Texts & Documents* (J. Shepley, Trans., pp. 85–93). Cambridge: MIT.

Skwarek, M. (2014). Augmented Reality Activism. In V. Geroimenko (Ed.), *Augmented Reality Art: From an Emerging Technology to a Novel Creative Medium* (pp. 3–29). New York: Springer.

Smith, R. C. (1982). *Gaston Bachelard.* Boston: Twayne Publishers.

Stanley, J. (1998). *Writing Out Your Life: A Guide to Writing Creative Autobiography.* London: Scarlet Press.

Strogatz, S. (2003). *Sync: The Emerging Science of Spontaneous Order.* London: Penguin.

Surowiecki, J. (2005). *The Wisdom of Crowds: Why the Many are Smarter than the Few* (New ed.). London: Abacus.

Talman, C. F. (1913, March). The Language of Meteorology. (J. M. Cattell, Ed.) *The Popular Science Monthly, LXXXII*, pp. 272–279.

Tape, W. (1994). *Atmospheric Halos* (Vol. 64 Antarctic Research Series). Washington: American Geophysical Union.

Tape, W. and Moilanen, J. (2006). *Atmospheric Halos and the Search for Angle X.* Washington: American Geophysical Union.

Thompson, P. (2009). Ernst Bloch and the Quantum Mechanics of Hope. In E. Bloch, *Atheism in Christianity: The Religion of the Exodus and the Kingdom* (J. T. Swann, Trans., pp. xi–xxx). London: Verso.

Thompson, P. (2013). Religion, Utopia, and the Metaphysics of Contingency. In S. Zizek and P. Thompson (Eds), *The Privatisation of Hope: Ernst Bloch and the Future of Utopia* (pp. 82–105). Durham: Duke University Press.

Tiles, M. (1984). *Bachelard: Science & Objectivity*. Cambridge: Cambridge University Press.

Tolkien, J. R. (2008). *On Fairy Stories*. (V. Flieger and D. A. Anderson, Eds) London: Harper Collins.

Vaneigem, R. (1963). *Basic Banalities (Internationale Situationniste #7)*. Retrieved 30 June 2012, from www.nothingness.org: http://library.nothingness.org/articles/SI/en/display/10

Vaneigem, R. (2004). Comments against Urbanism. In T. McDonough (Ed.), *Guy Debord & the Situationist International* (J. Shepley, Trans., pp. 120–128). Cambridge: MIT.

Vaneigem, R. (2006). *The Revolution of Everyday Life*. Rebel Press.

Wark, M. (2015). *The Beach beneath The Street: The Everyday Life and Glorious Times of The Situationist International*. London: Verso.

Weissberg, L. (1992). Philosophy and the Fairy Tale: Ernst Bloch as Narrator. *New German Critique, 55*.

West, T. H. (1991). *Ultimate Hope Without God: The Atheistic Eschatology of Ernst Bloch* (Vol. 97: Theology and Religion). American University Studies.

Wyatt, D. (2014, May 2). Meet Thierry Noir: The street artist who 'mutated' the Berlin Wall in protest. *The Independent*. Independent Print Ltd.

Zimmermann, R. E. (2009). *The Klymene Principle: A Unified Approach to Emergent Consciousness*. Universität-Gesamthochschule Kassel. Philosophy Preprints (PP981201).

Zipes, J. (1993). Introduction: Toward a Realization of Anticipatory Illumination. In E. Bloch, *The Utopian Function of Art and Literature* (pp. xi–xliii). (F. Mecklenberg and J. Zipes, Trans.) Cambridge: MIT.

Zipes, J. (2002). *Breaking the Magic Spell: Radical Theories of Folk and Fairy Tales* (Revised and Expanded Edition ed.). The University Press of Kentucky.

Zipes, J. (2006). *Fairy Tales and the Art of Subversion*. London: Routledge.

Index